The
Hyperactive
Child

Series on . . .

CHILD BEHAVIOR AND DEVELOPMENT,
edited by Dennis P. Cantwell, M.D.

Volume 1:
The Hyperactive Child: Diagnosis, Management, Current Research
D.P. Cantwell, M.D., editor

The Hyperactive Child

Diagnosis, Management, Current Research

Editor,
Dennis P. Cantwell, M.D.
Neuropsychiatric Institute
University of California, Los Angeles

S P Books Division of
SPECTRUM PUBLICATIONS, INC.
New York

Distributed by Halsted Press
A Division of John Wiley & Sons

New York   Toronto   London   Sydney

SPECTRUM PUBLICATIONS, INC.
86–19 Sancho Street, Holliswood, N.Y. 11423

Distributed solely by the Halsted Press division of John Wiley & Sons, Inc., New York

Library of Congress Cataloging in Publication Data

Cantwell, Dennis P
  The hyperactive child.

  1. Hyperactive children. I. Title [DNLM:
1. Hyperkinesis—In infancy and childhood. WS350 C234h]
RJ506.H9C36   618.9′28′5   74–34352
ISBN 0–470–13441–0

Printed in the United States
1 2 3 4 5 6 7 8 9

To Susan,
  Suzi, Denny, Coleen, and Erin

Contributors

Dennis P. Cantwell, M.D.
Assistant Professor of Psychiatry
Mental Retardation and Child Psychiatry Program
University of California, Los Angeles

Anne Feighner, M.S.W.
Psychiatric Center at Alvarado
San Diego, California

Barbara Fish, M.D.
Professor of Psychiatry
Mental Retardation and Child Psychiatry Program
University of California, Los Angeles

Steven Forness, Ed.D.
Associate Professor of Psychiatry in Residence
Mental Retardation and Child Psychiatry Program
University of California, Los Angeles

Edward R. Ritvo, M.D.
Associate Professor of Psychiatry in Residence
Mental Retardation and Child Psychiatry Program
University of California, Los Angeles

James H. Satterfield, M.D.
Director of Research, Gateways Hospital
Los Angeles, California

James Q. Simmons III, M.D.
Chief, Child Psychiatry
Associate Program Director,
Mental Retardation and Child Psychiatry Program
University of California, Los Angeles

Preface

„Ob der Philipp heute still
Wohl bei Tische sitzen will?"
Also sprach in ernstem Ton
Der Papa zu seinem Sohn,
Und die Mutter blickte stumm
Auf dem ganzen Tisch herum.
Doch der Philipp hörte nicht,
Was zu ihm der Vater spricht
Er gaukelt
Und shaukelt,
Er trappelt
Und zappelt
Auf dem Stuhle hin und her,
„Philipp, das missfällt mir sehr!"
Hoffmann, 1854

In these words of doggeral verse, a German physician named Heinrich Hoffmann told the tale of the humorous activities of "fidgety Phil who couldn't sit still". Written in 1854, this poem is the first recorded description of the hyperactive child syndrome. Focusing on clinical, research, and management aspects of the syndrome, this present monograph attempts to review what we know about hyperactive children today, one hundred and twenty years since Hoffmann first wrote about fidgety Phil.

The first section details the clinical picture of the children, describes what seems to happen to them as they grow up, and outlines a scheme for evaluating a child who is referred for hyperactivity. The second section consists of reviews of three areas of current research into the etiology of the syndrome: neurophysiological, biochemical and genetic. In the third section, four clinicians present their views on a specific form of therapeutic intervention. These are followed by a critical review of the evidence for the efficacy of the major forms of treatment that have been used with hyperactive children.

ix

Unfortunately, the picture that emerges of these children in 1974 is not as humorous as the one that was described in 1854. The hyperactive child is truly "Wednesday's child, full of woe". Although the data presented in this monograph indicate that we do know a lot about the syndrome, we need to learn much more about etiology, treatment and prevention. It is hoped that this monograph will serve not only as a source book of current knowledge but also as a stimulus to further research in our areas of ignorance.

Thanks are due to all of the contributors for taking time from their busy schedules to prepare their chapters, to Ms. Tobi Hernandez for typing the manuscript, to Mss. Lois Will, Sue Marsh, Sue Dodd and Lisa Levie for their work in proofing the manuscript and to Maurice Ancharoff of Spectrum Publications for his encouragement and assistance. Acknowledgement is due to several individuals. The interview with the parents and the interview with the child described in Chapter 2 are modified from those in use at the Maudsley Hospital in London where they were developed by Michael Rutter, Professor of Child Psychiatry who taught them to the author during his tenure as an NIMH special research fellow.

The rating scale for the interview with the child is slightly modified from one originally devised by Michael Rutter and Philip Graham and originally published in the *British Journal of Psychiatry*. The six-stage model for clinical and research work with hyperactive children described in Chapter 12 is modified from a 5-stage model developed by Samuel B. Guze and Eli Robins of the Washington University Department of Psychiatry for work with psychiatric disorders of adults. In addition, the preparation of this monograph was supported in part by Grant NIMH MH 17039–0452; Easter Seal Research Foundation; Maternal and Child Health Grant #927; SRS 59–P–45192; and Child Psychiatry Training Grant MC 08467.

January, 1975   Dennis P. Cantwell, M.D.
                                                  Los Angeles, California

CONTENTS

PART I.

The Hyperactive Child Syndrome: Clinical Aspects

Epidemiology, Clinical Picture and Classification of the Hyperactive Child Syndrome

DENNIS P. CANTWELL, M.D.

The hyperactive child syndrome was first described by the German physician Heinrich Hoffmann over one hundred years ago (Hoffmann, 1845). Since then, several authors have outlined a syndrome which begins early in life, is more common in boys and is manifested by a symptom pattern of hyperactivity, impulsivity, distractibility and excitability (Anderson, 1963; Bakwin, 1949; Bradley, 1955; Burks, 1960; Laufer and Denhoff, 1957; Stewart et al., 1966; Werry, 1968). Aggressive and antisocial behavior, specific learning problems and emotional lability are often considered part of the syndrome (O'Malley and Eisenberg, 1973).

TERMINOLOGY

Terms such as "brain damage syndrome" (Strauss and Lehtinen, 1947), "minimal brain damage" (Gessel and Amatruda, 1947) and "minimal brain dysfunction" (Clements, 1966) are often used synonymously with the term "hyperactive child syndrome." This has had a number of unfortunate consequences. Since the above designations have been used in widely divergent ways by different investigators, the same children have been described by different terms and different children by the same terms. Thus research findings cannot be readily compared.

Moreover, these designations imply "brain damage" or "brain dysfunction" as being present (and presumably etiologic) in the hyperactive child syndrome. However, if "brain damage" is used in its literal sense to mean structural abnormality of the brain, then "brain damage syndrome" is an inaccurate and misleading term. While *some* hyperactive children may suffer from frank brain damage, it is clear that the majority do not (Werry, 1972). Likewise, *most* brain damaged children do *not* present with the hyperactive child syndrome (Rutter et al., 1969).

"Brain dysfunction" may be a more accurate term than "brain damage" to describe those children who present with less well-defined disorders manifested by more subtle neurological signs. These more subtle defects in coordination, perception or language may only occasionally be associated with actual damage to the brain (Rutter, 1968). However, many hyperactive children do not demonstrate even these subtle neurologic signs. Thus "brain dysfunction syndrome" is inappropriate in describing the large percentage of hyperactive children who present primarily with behavioral abnormalities. Finally, techniques for the reliable and accurate quantification of "brain dysfunction" in children are not available, yet prefixing the word "minimal" to "brain dysfunction" implies just such a determination.

In this book, therefore, the term "hyperactive child syndrome" will be used to denote a behavioral syndrome only, with no implications as to etiology.

EPIDEMIOLOGY

The prevalence of the syndrome will vary greatly with the diagnostic criteria employed, methods of investigation and population studied. Studies using rating scales tend to give higher prevalence rates than those using direct observation and those, like most British studies, requiring the child to demonstrate hyperactivity in an interview setting. Only two hyperactive children were found in a total population study of 2,199 children aged ten and eleven on the Isle of Wight (Rutter et al., 1969). This compares with figures of from 5 percent to 20 percent in school-age populations in the Netherlands (Prechtl and Stemmer, 1962), Vermont (Huessy, 1967), St. Louis, Missouri (Stewart et al., 1966) and Montgomery County, Maryland (Wender, 1971). Teachers' reports formed the data base in most of the latter studies.

The boy/girl ratio varied from 4:1 to 9:1, but factors likely to affect prevalence rates such as socioeconomic status and racial and ethnic composition were not mentioned (Omenn, 1973). The prevalence in children referred to a psychiatric clinic is considerably higher (Wender, 1971). More studies on a total population with a wider age range of children, using precise diagnostic criteria and with attention to ethnic and socioeconomic factors, are sorely needed (Omenn, 1973).

CLINICAL PICTURE

The typical child with the hyperactive child syndrome is generally brought to professional attention early in his elementary school years. However, careful questioning usually reveals symptoms present from early childhood. The clinical picture varies from the little boy who is silly, immature and not performing academically up to expected standards to the markedly active, aggressive and antisocial child who is unable to be managed in a regular classroom setting.

Hyperactivity

Symptoms of hyperactivity are usually present from an early age. Parents report that the child has always seemed to have an unusual amount of energy, with less need for sleep than his sibs, and that he wore out shoes, clothes, bicycles, etc., faster than other children. Parents and teachers note: fidgetiness, inability to sit still for any length of time, talking a great deal and inability to keep his hands to himself. Objective quantification of the activity level would be a help in the diagnosis and evaluation of treatment of hyperactive children. A number of methods have been tried, including the use of ballistographic, mechanical, photoelectric and ultrasonic devices (Foshee, 1958; Sprague and Toppe, 1966; Schulman and Reisman, 1959; Bell, 1968; Ellis and Pryer, 1959; McFarland et al., 1966), telemetry and motion pictures (Davis et al., 1969; Herron and Ramsden, 1967; Lee and Hutt, 1964) and direct observation and ratings by observers (Doubros and Daniels, 1966; Hutt et al., 1966; Ounsted, 1955; Patterson et al., 1965). Unfortunately, results have been inconclusive and there is serious question whether hyperactive children actually have a clearly *greater amount* of daily motor activity or a *different type* of motor activity than non-hyperactive children.

Distractibility

Distractibility is more noticeable in the school but is usually reported by parents also. The typical child is unable to persevere with class-work and homework, frequently daydreams, is easily distracted from projects by extraneous stimuli and is unable to listen to a story or take part in table games for any length of time.

Impulsivity

Impulsivity is shown by such behaviors as jumping into the deep end of a swimming pool without knowing how to swim, running into the street in front of cars, climbing out on too high rooftops and ledges, and blurting out tactless statements.

Excitability

The excitability of the hyperactive child is manifested by temper tantrums and fights over trivial matters, low frustration tolerance and a tendency to become overexcited and more active in stimulating situations, especially in large groups of other children.

These symptoms of hyperactivity, distractibility, impulsivity and excitability show remarkable consistency in the clinical descriptions of hyperactive children by many authors (Werry, 1968b; Stewart et al., 1966; O'Malley and Eisenberg, 1973) and it may be concluded that these are the cardinal symptoms of the syndrome. Other symptoms that are often—but not necessarily—associated with the hyper-active child syndrome are: aggressive and antisocial behavior, cognitive and learning disabilities, and emotional symptoms such as depression and low self-esteem.

Antisocial Behavior

It was originally thought by many investigators that aggressive, antisocial behaviors were a necessary component of the hyperactive child syndrome (Strauss and Lehtinen, 1947; Bradley, 1955; Laufer and Denhoff, 1957; Stewart et al., 1966) and some feel that there is no evidence that the hyperactive child syndrome is a distinct clinical entity separate from other "conduct disorders" (Quay, 1972; Werry, 1972).

Careful clinical studies reveal that only a small—but significant—minority of hyperactive children present with antisocial behavior when initially seen (Weiss et al., 1971; Stewart et al., 1966; Satterfield and Cantwell, 1970). Since the percentage of hyperactive children who develop significant antisocial symptomatology increases with age, it could be hypothesized that the antisocial behavior develops as a reaction to the primary symptoms which define the syndrome. Children who are unable to succeed in an academic setting, who are unable to develop satisfactory peer relationships, who find rejection at home and at school, are likely prospects to act out and rebel against the values of society.

A likely hypothesis remains, however, that "antisocial hyperactive" children form an etiologically distinct subgroup of the hyperactive child syndrome. There are several lines of evidence which tend to support such a hypothesis. Family studies suggest a familial—and probably genetic—relationship between antisocial personality in adults and the hyperactive child syndrome (Cantwell, 1972, 1973; Morrison and Stewart, 1971, 1973). Recent research on waking autonomic functions and EEG patterns in hyperactive children and in antisocial adults suggests that the majority of both groups may have the same underlying neurophysiological abnormality: lower levels of basal resting physiological activation than age-matched normals (De La Pena, 1973). Finally, there is a suggestion that among hyperactive children antisocial, aggressive behaviors may be mediated by dopamine while the symptoms of hyperactivity may be mediated by norepinephrine (Arnold et al., 1973). This would tend to indicate a biochemical difference between "antisocial hyperactive" children and those without antisocial behavior. (See Chapters Five and Twelve.)

Cognitive and Learning Disabilities
Virtually all clinical studies of hyperactive children have emphasized learning difficulties as being of major importance in the syndrome (Chess, 1960; Cruickshank et al., 1961; Knobel, 1959; Menkes et al., 1967; Stewart et al., 1966; Werry, 1968b). However, the prevalence, the nature and the educational expression of these difficulties are unclear and need more investigation.

Most authors have emphasized that overall academic achievement is low for hyperactive children (Keogh, 1971), but some attribute this solely to low intellectual potential. Palkes and Stewart (1972) found that the mean WISC Full-Scale, Verbal and Performance IQ's were significantly lower for hyperactive children than for a matched group of normal children. When the group means of the Reading, Spelling and Arithmetic scores on the Wide Range Achievement Test were adjusted for WISC Full-Scale IQ, there were no significant differences between those of the hyperactive and normal children. Their conclusion was that hyperactive children learned at a rate normal for their measured intellectual performance. The exact opposite conclusion was reached by Minde et al. (1971). The hyperactive children in their study were significantly poorer than the control group in almost all academic subjects. And while the hyperactive children did more poorly on a group IQ test than the controls, intelligence alone was ruled out as the main contributor to their academic failure. Cantwell, in studying a group of hyperactive children and a matched group of normal public school children, used a multiple regression equation technique (Thorndike, 1963; Yule, 1967) to determine whether each normal and each hyperactive child was functioning above or below grade level in Reading, Spelling and Math predicted on the basis of chronological age and full-scale IQ. More than three-quarters of the hyperactive group were educationally retarded to some degree in each of the three academic subjects—a significantly greater number than the control group. Moreover, the more severe degrees of educational retardation were found almost solely in the hyperactive group. Approximately half of the hyperactive group were behind more than one grade level in one subject, about one-third in two subjects and nearly 10 percent in all three academic subjects.

Three hypothetical mechanisms have been proposed to explain the learning problems of hyperactive children (Keogh, 1971). The first hypothesis states that some type of neurologic impairment causes both the behavioral syndrome and cognitive disabilities. The second states that the motor activity of the hyperactive child interferes with his ability to attend to a task, thus disrupting acquisition of information. The last hypothesis implicates the decision process in learning and assumes that hyperactive children make decisions too quickly. All of these hypotheses have some empirical data to support them, but none are definitively established (Keogh, 1971; Douglas, 1972).

The Montreal group has been the most active in investigating the nature of the cognitive disabilities of hyperactive children (Douglas, 1972). They have shown that hyperactive children show more variability from subtest to subtest of the WISC than normals but they were able to find no consistent subtest pattern. Their hyperactive children also had unusual difficulties on visual motor tasks, tasks requiring fine and gross motor coordination, and tasks designed to measure attentional variables (Sykes et al., 1971, 1972). They had most difficulty with a continuous performance vigilance task and, compared with normals, their reaction times were slower. Campbell (1969; Campbell et al., 1971), in an investigation of cognitive styles found hyperactive children to be more impulsive, more field-dependent and more constricted in their ability to control attention than normal children. This impulsivity and field-dependence seemed to persist into early adolescence. The Montreal group failed to find any evidence of impairment in language abilities, comprehension or conceptual thinking. Somewhat surprisingly, the hyperactive children appeared to be less distracted by extraneous stimuli than clinical reports would suggest (Douglas, 1972). This area requires careful research if effective remedial educational approaches are to be directed to the mechanisms underlying the cognitive and learning disabilities manifested by hyperactive children. (See Chapter Nine.)

Other Emotional Symptoms

A wide variety of emotional and behavioral symptoms are seen in hyperactive children in addition to the "core" symptoms noted above. Aside from antisocial behavior, the most significant symptoms are depression and low self-esteem. Weiss et al. (1971), in their five-year follow-up study, noted significant depression, markedly low self-esteem and lack of ambition in a majority of the children. They felt that this was a reaction to continuing failures. Other authors have also voiced the same opinion (Werkman, 1970). However, some authors consider the hyperactive child syndrome to be a "depressive equivalent" (Malmquist, 1971). According to this view, the same etiologic factors that lead to a classical affective picture in adults lead to the picture of hyperactivity in childhood, presumably due to developmental differences in the expression of symptoms. It could be argued that since some hyperactive children respond to antidepressants (Huessey, 1967), this is evidence for a "depressive core." If it could be shown that the hyperactive children who respond to antidepressants also have an increased prevalence rate for affective disorder in their close relatives, and go on to develop affective disorder in later life, then one could make a strong argument that in this group the hyperactive child syndrome may be a manifestation of a primary affective disturbance. To date this has not been done.

Maturational Changes in Symptom Pattern

Although implicit in the above discussion, it is worth emphasizing that one of the characteristics of the clinical picture of the hyperactive syndrome is that it changes with the age of the child (Wender, 1971; Denhoff, 1973). The diagnosis is most difficult to make in infancy and the early preschool years. Mothers often report the baby seemed to be unusually active, hyperalert and difficult to soothe. General irregularity of physiological functions manifested by colic, sleep and eating disturbances, and frequent crying also are commonly reported. But none of these disturbances are characteristic of hyperactive children alone (Thomas et al., 1968).

Once the child begins to walk, other symptoms begin to emerge. It is at this point that the activity level and attentional difficulties become more noticeable. The typical child seems to have a distinct lack of a sense of danger, moves from one activity to another very quickly, and is relatively impervious to disciplinary measures that the parents found effective with their other children.

It is when the hyperactive child reaches the school system that the diagnosis is most often and most easily made. Behaviors which were disturbing but tolerable in the home setting are not so easily tolerated in a classroom setting. Academic problems increase with passage of time and antisocial behaviors become more prevalent.

In adolescence educational retardation, antisocial behavior, depression and low self-esteem are the most common presenting problems. Combined with a diminution in the classic symptoms of hyperactivity, distractibility, impulsivity and excitability, the primacy of these "secondary" problems during adolescence often obscures the diagnosis. A careful developmental history will usually reveal the earlier symptoms of the hyperactive child syndrome.

The clinical picture of the hyperactive child as an adult remains unclear. There are no published anterospective studies of the hyperactive child syndrome that have followed the children past adolescence. However, indications are that the hyperactive child is at risk for the development of significant psychopathology in adulthood. (See Chapter Three.)

ETIOLOGY AND CLASSIFICATION

The WHO Seminars on Classification in Child Psychiatry proposed a multiaxial classification scheme (Rutter et al., 1969; Tarjan and

Eisenberg, 1972). Axis I specifies the clinical psychiatric syndrome. Axis II describes the child's level of intellectual functioning (regardless of etiology). Axis III notes any associated or etiological biological factors. And Axis IV describes any associated or etiological psychosocial factors. In this classification scheme, the term "hyperactive child syndrome" is used on Axis I to describe a "developmental disorder" with the chief characteristics of poorly regulated, extreme overactivity, distractibility, short attention span and impulsiveness. In order for the term to be used, the child's disorder must clearly not be secondary to any other psychiatric syndrome.

This behavioral syndrome frequently occurs in children who would have no abnormalities listed on Axes II, III and IV. The term "developmental hyperactivity" has been frequently used to describe such children (Werry, 1968a; Feighner and Feighner, 1973). However, the hyperactive child syndrome is also known to be common in children with low IQ (Pond, 1961), with frank brain damage (Ingram, 1956) and with epilepsy (Ounsted, 1955). These factors would be classified in the appropriate way on Axes II and III. Clinical studies of the parents of children with the hyperactive child syndrome indicate that a significant percentage were themselves hyperactive as children and are psychiatrically disturbed as adults (Morrison and Stewart, 1971; Cantwell, 1972). In these cases an appropriate notation would be made on Axis IV. The question whether the hyperactive child syndrome occurring in children with a low IQ, or with evidence of frank brain damage or with psychiatrically disturbed parents is a different condition than the hyperactive child syndrome occurring in children with no evidence of abnormalities on Axes II, III and IV is unanswered at the moment. Present evidence suggests that the term "hyperactive child syndrome" describes a heterogeneous group of children with different etiologies. In some cases the disorder may be due to a structural abnormality of the brain (Werry, 1972); in others there may be an abnormality of physiological arousal of the nervous system (Satterfield et al., in press); in others there may be a genetic basis for the disorder (Cantwell, 1973; Morrison, 1973); in still others there may be still undiscovered important etiologic factors. The clear elucidation of specific etiologic factors for different groups of children presenting clinically with the hyperactive child syndrome is a task for future research and will allow a subclassification of the syndrome based on etiology.

SUMMARY

(1) The term "hyperactive child syndrome" should be used to denote a behavioral syndrome only, with no implications as to etiology.

(2) The syndrome is more common in boys, begins early in life and is characterized by four cardinal symptoms: hyperactivity, impulsivity, distractibility and excitability.

(3) Antisocial behavior, specific learning disabilities and depressive symptoms occur in many but not all children with the syndrome.

(4) The children with this syndrome form a heterogeneous group. It is likely that many different etiologic factors, either alone or in combination, can lead to the syndrome.

(5) Epidemiological studies indicate that the syndrome is relatively common in the general population and a leading cause of referral to child guidance clinics.

REFERENCES

Anderson, W. (1963). The hyperkinetic child: a neurological appraisal. *Neurology* 13:968–73.

Arnold, L., Kirilcuk, V., Corson, S., and Corson, E. (1973). Levoamphetamine dextroamphetamine: differential effect on aggression and hyperkinesis in children and dogs. *American Journal of Psychiatry* 130:165–71.

Bakwin, H. (1949). Cerebral damage and behavior disorders in children. *Pediatrics* 6:271–382.

Bell, R. (1968). Adaptation of small wrist watches for mechanical recording of activity in infants and children. *Journal of Experimental Child Psychology* 6:302–05.

Bradley, C. (1955). Organic factors in the psychopathology of childhood. In Hoch and J. Zubin, eds., *Psychopathology of Childhood.* New York: Grune & Stratton.

Burks, H. (1960). The hyperkinetic child. *Exceptional Children* 27:18–26.

Campbell, S. (1969). Cognitive styles in normal and hyperkinetic children. Unpublished doctoral dissertation, McGill University.

―――, Douglas, V., and Morgenstern, G. (1971). Cognitive styles in hyperactive children and the effect of methylphenidate. *Journal of Child Psychology and Psychiatry* 12:55–67.

Cantwell, D. P. (1972). Psychiatric illness in the families of hyperactive children. *Archives of General Psychiatry* 27:414–17.

―――（in press). Genetic studies of hyperactive children. *American Psychopathology Association Annual Report.*

Chess, S. (1960). Diagnosis and treatment of the hyperactive child. *New York State Journal of Medicine* 60:2379–85.

Clements, S. (1966). Minimal brain dysfunction in children. NINDB Monograph #3. Washington, D.C.: U.S. Public Health Service.

Cruickshank, W., Bentzen, F., Katzeburg, F., and Tannhauser, M. (1961). A teaching method for brain-injured and hyperactive children: a demonstration pilot study. Syracuse, New York: Syracuse University Press.

Davis, K., Sprague, R., and Werry, J. (1969). Stereotyped behavior and activity level in severe retardates: the effect of drugs. *American Journal of Mental Deficiency* 72:721–27.

De La Pena, A. (1973). The habitually aggressive individual. Progress report to the National Institute of Mental Health.

Denhoff, E. (1973). The natural life history of children with minimal brain dysfunction. In *Minimal Brain Dysfunction*, Annals of the New York Academy of Sciences 205:188–206.

Doubros, S., and Daniels, G. (1966). An experimental approach to the reduction of overactive behavior. *Behavior Research and Therapy* 4:251–58.

Douglas, V. (1972). Stop, look and listen: the problem of sustained attention and impulse control in hyperactive and normal children. *Canadian Journal of Behavioral Science* 4:249–82.

Ellis, N., and Pryer, R. (1959). Quantification of gross bodily activity in children with severe neuropathology. *American Journal of Mental Deficiency* 63:1034–37.

Feighner, A., and Feighner, J. (1973). Multi-modality treatment of the hyperkinetic child. Presented at the 126th Annual Meeting of the American Psychiatric Association.

Foshee, J. (1958). Studies in activity level: I. simple and complex task performance in defectives. *American Journal of Mental Deficiency* 62:882–86.

Gessel, A., and Amatruda, C. (1947). *Developmental Diagnosis,* 2nd ed. New York: Noeber, p. 248.

Herron, R., and Ramsden, R. (1967). Continuous monitoring of overt human body movement by radio telemetry: a brief review. *Perceptual Motor Skills* 24:1303–08.

Hoffmann, H. (1845). *Der Struwwelpeter: oder lustige Geschichten und drollige Bilder.* Leipzig: Insel-Verlag.

Huessey, H. (1967). Study of the prevalence and therapy of the choreatiform syndrome of hyperkinesis in rural Vermont. *Acta Paedopsychiatrica* 34:130–35.

Hutt, D., Jackson, P., and Level, M. (1966). Behavioral parameters and drug effects: a study of a hyperkinetic epileptic child. *Epilepsia* (Amst.) 7:250–59.

Ingram, R. (1956). A characteristic form of overactive behavior in brain damaged children. *Journal of Mental Science* 102:550–58.

Keogh, B.(1971). Hyperactivity and learning disorders: review and speculation. *Exceptional Child* 38:101–09.

Knobel, M. (1959). Diagnosis and treatment of psychiatric problems in children. *Archives of General Psychiatry* 1:310–21.

———— (1962). Psychopharmacology for the hyperkinetic child—dramatic considerations. *Archives of General Psychiatry* 6:198–202.

Laufer, M., and Denhoff, E. (1957). Hyperkinetic behavior syndrome in children. *Journal of Pediatrics* 50:463–74.

Lee, D., and Hutt, C. (1964). A play-room designed for filming children: a note. *Journal of Child Psychology and Psychiatry* 5:263–65.

McFarland, J., Peacock, L., and Watson, J. (1966). Mental retardation and activity level in rats and children. *American Journal of Mental Deficiency* 71:381–86.

Malmquist, C. (1971). Depressions in childhood and adolescence, II. *New England Journal of Medicine* 284:955–61.

Menkes, M., Rowe, J., and Menkes, J. (1967). A twenty-five year follow-up study on the hyperkinetic child with minimal brain dysfunction. *Pediatrics* 39:392–99.

Minde, K., Lewin, D., Weiss, G., Lavigueur, H., Douglas, V., and Sykes, E. (1971). The hyperactive child in elementary school: a five-year, controlled follow-up. *Exceptional Child* 38:215–21.

Morrison, J. (in press). Polygenic inheritance in hyperactive children. *Diseases of the Nervous System.*

—— and Stewart, M. (1971). A family study of the hyperactive child syndrome. *Biological Psychiatry* 3:189–95.

—— and Stewart, M. (1973). The psychiatric status of the legal families of adopted hyperactive children. *Archives of General Psychiatry* 28:888–91.

O'Malley, J., and Eisenberg, L. (1973). The hyperkinetic syndrome. *Seminars in Psychiatry* 5:95–103.

Omenn, G. (1973). Genetic issues in the syndrome of minimal brain dysfunction. *Seminars in Psychiatry* 5:5–19.

Ounsted, C. (1955). The hyperkinetic syndrome in epileptic children. *Lancet* 269: 303–11.

Palkes, H., and Stewart, M. (1972). Intellectual ability and performance of hyperactive children. *American Journal of Orthopsychiatry* 42:35–39.

Patterson, G., James, R., Whittier, J., and Wright, M. (1965). A behavior modification technique for the hyperactive child. *Behavior Research and Therapy* 2:217–26.

Pond, D. (1961). Psychiatric aspects of epileptic and brain-damaged children. *British Medical Journal.* Lectures I & II, 1377–82, 1454–57.

Prechtl, H. F. R., and Stemmer, C. (1962). The choreiform syndrome in children. *Developmental Medicine and Child Neurology* 4:119–27.

Quay, H. (1972). Patterns of aggression, withdrawal, and immaturity. In Quay and Werry, eds., *Psychopathological Disorders of Childhood.* New York: John S. Wiley & Sons, pp. 1–30.

Rutter, M. (1968). Lésion cérébrale organique, hyperkinesie et retard mental. *Psychiat Enfant* 11:475.

——, Lebovici, S., Eisenberg, L., Sneznevskij, A., Sadoun, R., Brooke, D., and Lin, T. (1969). A tri-axial classification of mental disorders in childhood. *Journal of Child Psychology and Psychiatry* 10:41–61.

Satterfield, J., and Cantwell, D. Unpublished data.

——, Saul, R., Cantwell, D., Lesser, L., and Podosin, R. (in press). CNS arousal level and response to stimulant drug treatment in hyperactive children. In Siva Sankar, D.V., ed., *Studies on Childhood Psychiatric and Psychological Problems.* PJD Publications, Ltd.

Schulman, J., and Reisman, J. (1959). An objective measure of hyperactivity. *American Journal of Mental Deficiency* 64:455–56.

Sprague, R., and Toppe, L. (1966). Relationship between activity level and delay of reinforcement in the retarded. *Journal of Experimental Child Psychology* 3:390–97.

Stewart, M., Pitts, F., Craig, A., and Dieruf, A. (1966). The hyperactive child syndrome. *American Journal of Orthopsychiatry* 36:861–67.

Strauss, A., and Lehtinen, L. (1947). *Psychopathology and Education of the Brain-Injured Child.* New York: Grune & Stratton.

Sykes, D., Douglas, V., and Morgenstern, G. (1972). The effect of methylphenidate

(Ritalin) on sustained attention in hyperactive children. *Psychopharmacologia* 25:262–74.

———, Douglas, V., Weiss, G., and Minde, K. (1971). Attention in hyperactive children and the effect of methylphenidate (Ritalin). *Journal of Child Psychology and Psychiatry* 12:129–39.

Tarjan, G., and Eisenberg, L. (1972). Some thoughts on the classification of mental retardation in the United States of America. Supplement to *American Journal of Psychiatry* 128:11, 14–18.

Thomas, A., Chess, S., and Birch, H. (1968). *Temperament and behavior disorders in children.* University of London Press.

Thorndike, R. (1963). *The concepts of over- and under-achievement.* New York: Bureau of Publications, Teachers College, Columbia University.

Weiss, G., Minde, K., Werry, J., Douglas, V., and Nemeth, E. (1971). Studies on the hyperactive child. VIII. Five-year follow-up. *Archives of General Psychiatry* 24:409–14.

Wender, P. (1971). *Minimal brain dysfunction in children.* New York: Wiley-Interscience.

———, Epstein, R., Kopin, I., and Gorson, E. (1971). Urinary monoamine metabolites in children with minimal brain dysfunction. *American Journal of Psychiatry* 127:141–45.

Werkman, S. (1970). Brain dysfunction in adolescence. IV. Implications of the research. *American Journal of Orthopsychiatry* 40:336–37.

Werry, J. (1968a) Developmental hyperactivity. *Pediatric Clinics of North America* 15:3, 581–99.

——— (1968b). Studies on the hyperactive child. IV. An empirical analysis of the minimal brain dysfunction syndrome. *Archives of General Psychiatry* 19:9–16.

——— (1972). Organic factors in childhood psychopathology. In Quay and Werry, eds., *Psychopathological Disorders of Childhood.* New York: John S. Wiley & Sons, pp. 83–121.

Yule, W. (1967). Predicting reading ages on Neale's analysis of reading ability. *British Journal of Educational Psychology* 37:252–55.

Chapter Two

Diagnostic Evaluation of the Hyperactive Child

DENNIS P. CANTWELL, M.D.

When a child is referred for evaluation of "hyperactivity" it is mandatory that a thorough, comprehensive work-up be undertaken prior to instituting any form of therapy. This chapter will outline a suggested format for evaluating hyperactive children which can also be applied to the evaluation of children with other types of psychiatric disorders. There are six aspects to the evaluation each of which yields a somewhat different type of information:

Interview with the Parents
Interview with the Child
Behavior Rating Scales
Physical Examination
Neurologic Examination
Laboratory Studies

The first two parts of the evaluation will be spelled out in some detail, as they are not generally so described in other sources.

INTERVIEW WITH THE PARENTS
Whether the clinician sees the child first or the parents first is a matter of personal preference. The author prefers to see the parents first and obtain a detailed history. This also allows the doctor to explain to the parents what he would like them to tell the child about his upcoming interview.

General Points About the Parental Interview

In evaluating a child referred for hyperactivity it is important, even at the first diagnostic interview, to begin to evaluate the child's family as well. Knowledge of the family may aid in understanding how the child has developed, and in certain cases important etiologic factors may lie within the family unit. In all cases, an appreciation of the strengths and weaknesses of the family unit will be important in planning the child's treatment. It is also necessary to know what impact the child's behavior has had on the family's life and how the parents and sibs have reacted to the situation caused by the index child's problem. As a practical point, it is always desirable to see both the mother and the father at the time of the first interview. It is unacceptable to rely only on a secondhand account of the father as he is perceived by the mother. An interview with the two parents together also provides a good opportunity for observing parental interaction and relationships.

There are two different aspects to the interview with the parents: (1) the obtaining of specific factual information about events, happenings and behaviors, and (2) the observation of feelings, emotions or attitudes concerning these events and the individuals participating in them. It is quite important that this basic distinction be made between events and happenings in the family on the one hand, and feelings, emotions or attitudes about these events on the other. The interviewer needs to know both *what people do* in their family and also *how they feel about what they do,* but different approaches are needed to elicit these two types of information (Rutter, 1972). Direct questions are only of limited value in assessing feelings and emotions. For this purpose the interview must be used as a standard situation to elicit emotions and attitudes. Attention should be paid to the *way* things are said by the parents as well as to *what* is said in order to assess their attitudes and emotions. Differences in the tone of voice as shown in the speed, pitch and intensity of speech can be helpful in the recognition of emotions, as can the observation of facial expressions, gestures and posture. Where the parents' feelings are in doubt, direct questions such as "Does this kind of thing ever cause tension in the home?" or "Does that ever make you feel on edge?" can be useful but should only be used sparingly.

A different approach from that described above, however, is required for the obtaining of factual information about specific events and items of behavior. In order to find out *what* happens in the family, systematic and detailed questioning about actual happenings in the recent past is required. Regardless of whether the chief complaint of the parents is "hyperactivity," "school problems" or something else, it is always necessary to question systematically about *all* the major aspects of the child's behavior, since parents are often quite inconsistent in the spontaneous complaints they make about their children's behavior.

While the importance of the family unit cannot be minimized in the child's life, it is also common for all children to have important relationships outside their nuclear family, and it is necessary to inquire systematically about these. The parents should be asked whether there are relatives, friends, neighbors, teachers or other adults to whom the child seems particularly attached. Within the nuclear family, of course, the child's relations with his siblings are very important and those should be inquired about in the same systematic way. The child's relationships with other children, both at school and in the neighborhood, are quite significant. Peer relationships are probably the best single indicator of overall adjustment in the school-age child (Sundby and Kreyberg, 1969). The parents should always be asked about the child's friendships and how he gets along with other children. The names of his best friends that he spends a good deal of time with should be taken for later use with the child. It is important, however, for the interviewer to recognize that parents may be poorly informed on this aspect of their child's life. Their account must be supplemented by a report from school and by an interview with the child himself.

Finally, the child's own temperament and personality characteristics always influence the parents' reaction and attitudes toward him (Bell, 1971). The temperamental and personality characteristics of the child will sometimes have played a principal role in the development of the emotional or behavioral difficulties which the child is showing (Graham et al., 1973). When a child is referred for a problem like hyperactivity, it is not easy—and at times impossible—to disentangle the child's premorbid personality characteristics from the present problems which have led to the referral. But an attempt should always be made to do so. The child's own personality characteristics are frequently best shown in his response to new situations, new events and new people, but attention should be paid to his general mode of functioning in routine situations.

Suggested Outline for Interview with Parents

The interview can be conveniently divided into six areas which cover the main features that should be explored in any diagnostic interview with parents:

Referral Source
Chief Complaint
Symptom Inventory and Recent Behavior
Temperament and Personality Characteristics
Past History and Developmental History
Family History

However, this outline is provided for guidance in interviewing only. It is not meant to be used as a questionnaire that is followed rigidly with each patient. Care must be taken to ensure that questions are put in a way which are appropriate to the particular child being seen.

Referral Source. The interviewer should inquire about what led the parents to seek help with regard to the child's problem *at this particular point in time.* It is important to make clear who initiated the referral, how it was initiated and for what reason. If the referral originated from someone other than the parents, they should be asked about how they feel about the necessity for the referral and whether they would have come themselves if the problem had not been brought to their attention by someone else.

Chief Complaint. The parental interview usually begins with an inquiry about the problems or difficulties which are the chief cause of concern to the parents and which necessitated the referral. The complaints that are spontaneously offered about the child are important in their reflection of the parents' attitudes. Thus, it is important to let the parents tell their story in their own words and, as far as possible, obtain a verbatim account of the history. When the parents finish their account of the difficulty, they should then be asked an open-ended question such as "Do you think there are any other difficulties?" This part of the interview gives the examiner an opportunity to assess parental feelings and attitudes and these should be carefully noted and described. Only when the parents offer no more problems spontaneously should the interviewer proceed with more systematic questioning.

In the case of a child referred for hyperactivity, the spontaneous comments of the parents will generally be around several major complaints such as activity, excitability, impulsivity and distractibility. If all of these areas are not covered spontaneously by the parents, specific questions should be asked. Some suggested questions in these areas are listed below:

Activity level—Is he more active than his siblings? Is he more active than his peers? Is he, for example, unable to sit through: a meal? a school period? a TV program? a movie? a haircut? Is he unable to stay in a doctor's or dentist's office waiting for an exam? Does he wear out things like shoes, clothes, his bike, etc.? Does he run over desks, furniture, bookshelves, etc.? Is he a fidgety child (wiggles his hands, rocks his legs, etc.)? Is he into things that don't concern him (breaking dishes, tools, appliances, etc.)? Is he overtalkative? Does he monopolize a conversation?

Excitability—Is he easily upset by rather trivial things? Does he have a low frustration tolerance? Is he irritable or quick-tempered? Does he get wound up and overexcited around groups of children? Does he get wound up and overexcited in stimulating new situations? Does he have trouble taking "no" for an answer? Does he have trouble taking corrections?

Impulsivity—Is his behavior unpredictable or variable (like Jekyll and Hyde)? Does he tend to do reckless or dangerous things like: climbing out onto the roof and out of upper windows? running out into the street? riding his bike in front of cars?

Distractibility—Does he have trouble completing projects? Does he daydream? Is he unable to listen to a story or attend to a TV program for any length of time? Is he easily distracted from projects by stray outside stimuli? Is he unable to follow through a set of directions or instructions?

The parents should then be asked for a more detailed description of the symptoms that have been mentioned spontaneously as well as those that are elicited by more specific questions around the cardinal symptoms of hyperactivity. *Recent examples* of the behavior in question should always be obtained, as well as the *frequency* of the behavior, the *severity* and the context of its *occurrence*. What is "hyperactive" behavior to a parent with one child may be considered quite normal by a parent who has three or four children who are equally as active. Also, "aggressive behavior" to one parent may mean that the child hits his sister once a week while to another parent it may mean the child chases people with an ax. The importance of obtaining *specific examples* of behavior cannot be overemphasized. The circumstances which appear to precipitate certain aspects of behavior and those which ameliorate difficulties should always be noted. The interviewer should attempt to find out what methods have been used to deal with the problem by the parents. A frequent answer of a frustrated parent to such questions is "We've tried everything," but it is important for the interviewer to obtain specific examples of methods they have tried, in what context and what success (or lack of it) has been obtained. This is often the easiest point in the interview—to ascertain what effect the child's symptoms have had on the rest of the family.

In the case of suspected hyperactivity, it is most important to determine the time of onset of the disruptive behavior. The account should go back to the point in the child's development when his behavior first caused concern to the parents, the teacher or whoever suggested that there was something wrong. In general, children with the hyperactive child syndrome have evidence of disturbed behavior dating back to toddler years and earlier. It is highly unusual for a classic hyperactive child to go unnoticed by anyone until the age of six, seven or eight years old. Although his behavior may be more intolerable in the school setting, hence leading to referral at that age, when careful questioning is done the parents usually report that the child exhibited deviant behavior at a much earlier age. Possible stresses that may have occurred at the time when the behavior first became noticed should be inquired into.

After completion of a detailed description of the main complaint, as outlined above, it is then useful to proceed with more systematic questioning on other recent behavior and other aspects of the emotional state of the child. Some of these, such as antisocial behavior and school difficulties, will be very common in hyperactive children. Others will be less common, but they should be inquired into nonetheless.

Symptom Inventory and Recent Behavior.

School adjustment—How many schools has he attended? Type of school and class now attending? Repeated or failed grades? Suspended/expelled? Felt to be a behavior problem, poor learner or underachiever? Ever reluctant to go to school? Played hooky or been truant? Has he had any remedial educational help?

Aggressive and antisocial behavior—Does he get into frequent fights?

Ever hurt someone badly? Worried he might do so? Cruel to animals? Fire setter? Destructive? Does he steal? Run away? Problem with drugs or alcohol? Any contact with police or juvenile authorities? When in trouble—usually alone or with a group? When caught—any remorse or concern—if so, only about being caught?

Affective state—What is his mood *generally* like? Ever depressed or elated for more than a week for no apparent reason? Crying spells? Sleeping difficulties? Appetite change? Suicidal thoughts, acts? Poor self-image?

"Neurotic" symptoms—Anything he is particularly afraid of? How does he show it? What do you do when he is frightened? Is the child a "worrier"? Is he particular about things? Does he like things just so? Does he get ideas in his mind that he can't get rid of, even if they don't make sense? Is he upset by changes in routine? Does he have to do some things the same way or get upset about it? Any silly habits or rituals?

"Psychotic" symptoms—Any suggestion of hallucinations or delusions? Do people talk about him? Spy on him? Try to do him harm? Any strange or unusual feelings about his body? Can people read his mind? Place thoughts in his mind? Has he ever appeared to be hearing voices or seeing things? Heard his thoughts broadcast out loud? Held to strange beliefs? Acted or talked as if he had some strange power other people don't have?

Sexual behavior—Any interest in opposite sex? How shown? Masturbation? Development of body hair? Has he had any instruction in sexual matters at home or at school? (Menstrual history if female.)

Neurologic symptoms—Preferred hand and foot? Head banging? Rocking? Any mannerisms or tic? Blinking spells? Fainting or dizzy spells? Ever passed out or been knocked out? Spells of amnesia or blank spells? Headaches?

Peer relations—How does he get along with other children? Number of close friends? Trouble *making* or *keeping* friends? Reasons? Does he belong to any organized groups or play any organized sports? Is he a loner? A bully? Or does he get picked on by other kids? Reasons?

Relationships with adults—How does he get along with his mother and father? Is he an easy child to get along with? Compared to his sibs, how has he been to raise? In what ways does he annoy or irritate the parents? How would they like him different? How does he get along with other adults? Relatives? Teachers? Is he particularly attached to any of them? How does he show it? Is his behavior better with certain adults than it is with others?

General physical health—A general medical review of systems should conclude this part of the interview.

Temperament and Personality Characteristics. Much information about the child's personality will be obtained from other parts of the interview. An inquiry into the following six areas will give the interviewer a chance to find out what the child was like prior to the onset of his deviant behavior and also how the child acts now in situations which don't directly involve his presenting problems.

Meeting strange people—How does he react when he meets children he hasn't met before (new children in neighborhood, at parties, at the park, etc.) or when he meets new grownups (friends of family, baby-sitting, workmen coming to home, etc.)? Does he go up to speak to someone new? Is he friendly with people he doesn't know? Does he tend to be at all shy? Or cling to mother? How quickly does he adapt to someone new?

Strange situations—How is he when going to new places (starting at school, going away on vacation, visiting relatives, etc.)? Does he like to explore? Does he tend to hang back? Is he anxious to try out new things, e.g., household gadgets, foods, etc.? How quickly does he adapt to something new?

Emotional expression—How vigorously does he express the way he's feeling? When upset does he tend to whimper and whine or does he shout and scream? When happy does he just smile or does he more often get very excited and laugh and run around? Before the present condition began, was he usually a happy or a miserable child? How does he react when he is frustrated or can't get what he wants, or when he is mad or punished?

Affections and relationships—Is he a child who shows his feelings easily or is he more reserved? How does he show them? Is he an affectionate child? How? Making friends? Shy at all? How long do his friendships last?

Regularity of bodily functions—How regular is he in his sleeping habits—in the time he goes to sleep and wakes up? Does he wake up at night? How regular is he in the amount he eats? How regular are his bowel habits?

Sensitivity—How does he respond if he sees another child hurt—or an animal hurt (such as on TV)? How does he react if he's done something wrong? Does he get upset and tell you or try to hide it (e.g., if he's accidentally broken something)? Do you think he is a "sensitive child"? If "Yes"—in what way? Can you give me an example?

Past Personal History and Developmental History.

Pre- and perinatal history—Number of previous pregnancies? Any miscarriages? Any problems with mother's physical or mental health during pregnancy? Premature or postmature? Birth weight? Any complications at the delivery?

Neonatal and infancy—Breast- or bottle-fed? Any feeding problems, spitting or colic? Sleeping problems? Active or placid baby? How responsive as an infant?

Milestones—Age when the child first: sat without support on a flat surface? walked without help or holding on? first used single words *with meaning?* first put three words together with meaning? gained consistent bowel control? gained consistent bladder control by day? by night? At the time was he considered slow in any of these things? Was he slower, faster or about the same as his sibs in any of these milestones?

Medical history—List all hospitalizations, operations, emergency-room visits and significant illnesses. Child's reaction to these? Pay careful attention to: head injuries, convulsions, allergies, frequent ear infections, suspected speech, hearing or visual problems.

Early experiences—Has child lost a parent, close relative or close friend through death? Age of child and reaction? Any prolonged separations from parents? Details of each: age of child, length of time, reason, surrogate care, child's reaction to separation and reunion.

Family History. A detailed family history is important for several different reasons. Knowing how the parents themselves behaved and were raised as children may aid the clinician in understanding their current behavior and attitudes toward their children. A history of hyperactivity, other developmental disorders or psychiatric problems in close relatives of the index child can have significance for both genetic and environmental reasons.

For organization purposes the family history may be thought of as consisting of three aspects. Depending on time limitations, all aspects of the family history can be obtained at the first interview or certain points deferred until later interviews. Information about family interaction and relationships should always be obtained at the first interview.

Family structure and home circumstances—Does the family live in a house or apartment? How many rooms? What are the sleeping arrangements? Is there adequate play space for the children? How long has the family lived in their present home? What is the neighborhood like? Who supports the family? Total family income? Are there any pressing financial or other problems?

For each person living in the home, the full name, age, sex, religion, education, occupation and relation to index patient should be recorded. The same information should be recorded for all sibs and half-sibs not living in the home. If either natural parent is not in the home, the above information should be recorded plus the amount of contact the index child has with that parent.

The education, occupation and marital history of both parental figures? What were the grandparents' occupations? Obtain a description of the home and family life of each parent and of the child-rearing techniques of the grandparents. Are the grandparents still alive? Does the child have any contact with them and with maternal and paternal aunts and uncles? How does the child relate to them? Is he particularly attached to anyone?

Family history of illness—Has any family member ever had a history of hyperactivity, developmental disorder, neurologic disorder or emotional disorder at any time in his life? The interviewer should specifically state that by "family member" he means not only parents and sibs, but also grandparents, aunts, uncles and cousins. He should then specifically inquire about the following conditions:

Hyperactivity (illness like index child)
Learning problems in school, repeated grades
Speech problems—including slow development
Mental retardation
Epilepsy or other "spells"
Neurologic disorder (other than epilepsy)
Behavior problems in school
Trouble with "nervousness"
"Nervous breakdown"
Depression
Mania
Schizophrenia
Problem with alcohol
Problem with drugs
Antisocial behavior

Juvenile hall
Police record
Jail, prison or workhouse confinement
Multiple physical complaints (hysteria)
Sexual perversion
Suicide (completed)
Suicide (attempted)
Habitually aggressive
Homicide (completed)
Homicide (attempted)
Outpatient psychiatric care
Inpatient psychiatric care
Shock treatment
Psychotropic drug prescription

All positive answers should be explored as fully as possible to allow a diagnosis to be made.

Family interaction and relationships—This part of the interview provides the best opportunity for the interviewer to note the quality of the child's relationships with other family members and to observe positive or negative interaction between the parents. The parents should be encouraged to talk freely and spontaneously about the family, and the interviewer should carefully note not only *what* is said but *how* it is said.

How do the parents get along? What do they enjoy doing together? How do they spend their evenings and weekends? Does the father give any help around the house? Are there any specific areas of conflict or dissatisfaction?

Does the index child take after the mother or the father? Is he more likely to confide in or seem to be more attached to either parent? How much time does each parent spend with the child in a typical week? Doing what? Do the parents enjoy spending time with the child?

How does the index child get along with his siblings? What kind of things do they do together? Is he particularly attached to or particularly jealous of any of them?

How much of a role does the child play in everyday family activities? Does he help around the house? Have an outside job? Go alone to school? Go alone to the store? Does he need to be nagged to do things?

Which of the parents usually reprimands the child? What methods are used to discipline him? How effective are they? Does he have a curfew? A regular bedtime? Can he go out without his parents after dark? Travel by bus alone? Choose his own friends, clothes, hair style?

INTERVIEW WITH THE CHILD
Considering that the interview with the child is the one investigative and therapeutic procedure that most distinguishes the child psychiatrist from other medical specialists, it is surprising that so little has been written about it. It is particularly noteworthy that there has been so little work done on the skills and techniques required for an accurate and valid diagnostic interview with the child. There are several published descriptions of interviews with children (Simmons, 1969; Goodman and Sours, 1967; DHEW, 1973), and Tapia has produced a valuable thirty-eight minute teaching film containing excerpts of interviews with four children. However, only Rutter and Graham (1968) seem to have provided data on inter-rater reliability and validity for their diagnostic interview with the child. The interview outlined below is a modified version of the one they have described.

General Points About the Child's Interview
The interview with the child is only part of the diagnostic work-up. Since information from several other sources is likely to be available to the clinician at the time of the interview it should be used to clarify and confirm impressions gleaned from these other sources. And although an individual interview must be geared to each child's age, intelligence, interests and presenting problem, a systematic review of specific areas must also be conducted with each child. This not only assures that no significant areas will be overlooked in an individual case but it allows the clinician to build up his own "normative" standard for his interview with different age groups and different diagnostic problems.

The diagnostic work-up of the child seeks to answer three related questions: (a)Does the child have a psychiatric disorder? (b)What is the nature of the psychiatric disorder? (c)What are the possible etiologic factors? The interview with the child, as part of the total diagnostic evaluation, seeks to provide information relevant to each of these questions. However, most of the information obtained from the diagnostic interview with the child usually pertains to the first two of these questions. Moreover, it should also be remembered that an interview with a psychiatrist (or other professional) is an event of considerable emotional significance to a child. If the child is to be seen again for treatment, his subsequent relationship with the treating individual is likely to be profoundly influenced by the impression created at the first contact. And even if the child is only seen once for diagnostic purposes, that one contact may well in itself have considerable impact. Thus, it is important to make that contact a therapeutically beneficial one.

The setting of the interview is important. The interview room should not be cluttered with toys or other distracting objects. Any toys or games which are available should be situated so that the child can see them but not reach them without moving. Chairs and table should be arranged so that the examiner and child are not separated by the table but can sit close to each other at the side or corner of the table.

With younger children (below about age six) a relatively greater portion of the interview will consist of nonverbal communication and interaction will generally be easier if it occurs in a play situation. The older the child, the more reliance will be placed on talking with the child. And with more mature adolescents, the closer the interview will approximate a psychiatric interview as conducted with adults.

Specific Points About the Child's Interview

Regardless of the age of the child, the interview can be considered as consisting of two parts: (1) an unstructured part and (2) a relatively structured part. The interview also provides two different types of data: (1) *behavior* of the child *observed* during the interview, and (2) *information offered* by the child during the interview. The initial diagnostic interview should be about thirty to forty-five minutes in duration, with about half of the time devoted to the unstructured part and the rest of the time devoted to the more structured part.

In almost all cases the child will have been brought for evaluation not because of his concern for his problems, but because of the concern of someone else, usually the parents. The child is thus already on the defensive since he knows complaints have been made about him. For this reason the author feels it is not wise to bring up the major complaints at the beginning of the interview. It is also imperative that the doctor make clear to the child, by his behavior and actions toward him, that he respects the child as an individual, that he is interested in what he says and does, and that he is not going to judge him, "change" him, or "do things to fix him up."

The aim of the first part of the interview is to get the child relaxed and talking freely, to assess the relationship he is able to form in such a setting, the level and lability of his mood, the organization of his thinking, his conversational speech and any habitual mannerisms. The child's spontaneous preoccupations should be noted—whether he discusses these freely or with evasion and guarding, and with what accompanying affect. The child should be encouraged to talk about recent events and activities; what sort of thing he likes doing after school and on weekends; what he does with his friends and with his family; the games he plays and the things he is interested in; what he enjoys and what he does not enjoy at school, etc. He may also be asked about his hopes for the future—such as what he wants to do when he leaves school or when he is grown up.

The interviewer should react naturally with interest, concern or enthusiasm as may be appropriate. The aim is to set a relaxed and informal atmosphere, to try to elicit a range of emotions in the child, to assess the emotional responsiveness of the child and the kind of relationship he forms with the examiner. If the emotional responsiveness of the child is to be adequately assessed, it is necessary for the psychiatrist himself to show a range of emotions (being more serious or concerned when asking about feelings of distress or worry, and more lively when responding to the child's account of what interests or amuses him).

After fifteen minutes or so of this type of conversation the examiner may introduce the presenting complaints, if they have not come up spontaneously already. The child's perception of why he was brought for evaluation, whose idea it was, and what the specific complaints of parents, teachers, etc., are should be explored. The child should be asked if *he* feels he has any problems or concerns that he would like to talk about.

Certain specific problem areas need to be covered with all children, regardless of whether they come up in the initial parts of the interview. This systematic review should be conducted naturally, with the examiner showing concern for the child's feelings and problems. The interview should not be conducted in a rigid manner as if using a questionnaire. The wording of the questions should be modified to suit each child and the questions woven into a natural sequence, varying according to the particular preoccupation of each child.

The child should also be asked if he has any friends. What their names are, what he does with them, how he gets along with other children at home and at school. Does he ever feel lonely, get into fights, get teased or picked on? If he is picked on, does it happen more than with most other children? Why does he think he is picked on? Similarly, he should be asked about how he gets along with his brothers and sisters. If he gets into fights, does he like fighting? Are they "real" fights or "friendly" fights? After questioning the child about fights, it is convenient to ask the child to hit the examiner's hand—and then to tell him several times to "hit it harder." The child should be observed to see if he extends this action. He should be asked specifically about anxieties, feelings of apprehension, worries, ruminations, fears, unhappiness, bad dreams, what sort of things make him feel angry. For example, he might be asked: "Most people tend to worry about something. What kind of things do you worry about? Do you ever lie awake at night worrying about things? Do you ever get nasty thoughts on your mind that you cannot get rid of?" The possibility of hallucinations can often be explored at this point in appropriate cases by questions such as: "Do you ever see or hear scary things at bedtime? Ever have scary thoughts then?"

Further exploration can then be done if these questions are answered positively. Do you ever get fed up? Miserable? Cry? Feel really unhappy? Are there things you are particularly afraid of? What about the dark, or spiders or dogs? Do you ever dream? What about bad dreams? Or nightmares? What kind of things make you get angry and annoyed? Do you ever feel so miserable that you want to go away and hide, or that you want to run away? How often do you feel like that? What sort of things make you feel fed up? Do you feel like that at home, at school, etc.?

Each child should be asked the best and worst things about his home. What type of rules are followed? Are they fair? Why? Do you get blamed for things at home? Unfairly: Why? Are you treated differently from your brothers and sisters? Why?

Similarly he should be asked the best and worst things about his school, the hardest and the easiest things for him at school. Does he like his teacher? Does she like him? Why? He should be asked if he thinks he is as smart as most children in his class. How many are smarter? How many are not as smart? Each child should be specifically asked if he has trouble sitting still at school, if he has to get up and down a lot, if he talks out of turn, and if he has trouble keeping his mind on things.

The interviewer should reword or explain any question the child does not understand. Any positive answers should be probed for the severity, frequency and setting of the behavior and how the child feels at the time the behavior occurs.

It should be realized that children are very suggestible and will sometimes produce answers they think the doctor wants. However, the anxious or depressed child can usually be distinguished by his affective state when talking about worries, fears, feeling fed up, etc. Although it is important to ask the child systematically about these issues, it is also necessary for much of the interview to consist of neutral or cheerful topics. Note whether the child *spontaneously* mentions worries or extends his answers on these topics beyond what is required by the question.

In order to assess attention span, distractibility and persistence, the child must be given some tasks. These need to be near the limits of his ability but within them, since the intent is not to test his cognitive abilities. The child should be asked to get the paper and pencil, write his name and draw a picture of anything he'd like. He should also be asked to draw a picture of a man and a woman and then to make up a story about each of them. If desired he may be asked to copy some designs, such as the Bender-Gestalt figures. He can be asked to give the days of the week forward and backward, as well as the months of the year, and to do some simple arithmetic. Recognition of words and reading of grade level of paragraphs are other tasks which might be employed. During this period of the interview the child's response to a task, including his physical behavior, attention, persistence, fine coordination and visual motor functioning should be carefully noted. Besides noting how much the child is distracted by incidental noises, movements of the examiner, people passing by the room, etc., the interviewer should make an effort to distract the child by coughing, jingling coins in his pocket, tapping a pencil and dropping a book on the floor.

While the same issues are important and the principles identical, it is necessary to modify the form of the interview for the younger child. A play setting will usually be more appropriate for the child of six years or less, but depending on the maturity of the child it may also be desirable sometimes to use a play-interview with older children.

Games and toys should be chosen to (1)be suitable for the child's age, sex and social background, (2)provide an *interaction* with the interviewer and (3)encourage communication. Only a limited selection of toys should be on view. Paper and pencil, crayons, simple puzzles, family dolls, a toy gun, a ball, and cars provide a varied but ample selection. Imaginative games such as the squiggle game (making a drawing out of the child's squiggle and getting the child to do the same with your squiggle), playing with family figures, etc., may offer the best opportunity for eliciting a range of behavior and emotions. However, it is important to allow the child to get used to the situation before the examiner makes an approach. Initially, it may be useful just to let the child explore the room and the toys while the doctor makes a friendly remark or two and responds to the child's approaches, but to make no approach himself. The speed with which the child may be engaged in interaction and the way in which the approach is best made will vary considerably and must be judged in relation to each individual child. An attempt should be made to provide some activity known (from the parents' interview) to interest the child. Toy cars, toy animals, building bricks or a game the child brings in himself might be used.

Where possible the child should be seen without the parents, though with very young children it may often be better to allow them to come in with the child at first and then, after a short while, leave the room.

The play situation should be utilized to make the same kind of assessment as with the older child and, where appropriate, the child should be questioned in a manner suitable for his level of maturity. However, many young children cannot be expected to give good descriptions of their feelings or to answer abstract questions. Nevertheless, they can often tell you about what they do at home, whom they play with, etc.

It may be impossible in selected cases to get the child to talk at all initially. In such cases the child can be told that he is free to play with the toys. His spontaneous behavior with the toys should be observed for ten to fifteen minutes. If the child does not spontaneously accompany his play with any talk, the examiner should ask "What's happening now?" or "Tell me about that." The examiner can then proceed with the task behavior as outlined previously, all the while trying to engage the child in conversation. An attempt should be made first to review the specific problem areas as outlined above. Finally, increasingly specific questions should be asked about the presenting complaints and increasing pressure should be placed on the child to respond, as careful noting of his behavior and affect is made.

In writing up the interview, the doctor should start with a lifelike description of the child: his general appearance, manner, style of dress, whether he appears big or small for his chronological age; how he responded to the separation from parents, to entering the interview room and to the doctor's attempts to engage in interaction with him. The course of the interview should be outlined in detail, relating what was done and what was said by the doctor and by the child.

Positive *and negative* findings should be recorded under the various topics discussed with the child; the child's mental state should then be described more systematically by making the following ratings:

	None	Slight	Marked	Not Known
1. Apprehension when entering room	1	2	3	9
2. Apprehension of other things	1	2	3	9
3. Anxious expression	1	2	3	9
4. Sad, miserable or unhappy expression	1	2	3	9
5. Startle response	1	2	3	9
6. Tremulousness	1	2	3	9
7. Adequacy of peer relationships (based on child's account)	1	2	3	9

8. Preoccupation with topics of   1   2   3   9
anxiety (only spontaneous remarks
or definite extensions to
answers are relevant for this
item)

9. Preoccupation with depressive   1   2   3   9
topics (only spontaneous remarks or
definite extensions to answers are
relevant for this item)

10. Preoccupation with aggressive   1   2   3   9
topics (only spontaneous remarks or
definite extensions to answers are
relevant for this item)

11. Tearfulness   1   2   3   9

12. Muscular tension
(include only muscle tension at
rest—fidgetiness is rated
separately; check individual
tension items which are present
and make overall rating based on
severity and duration through
interview)
    clenching of jaws
    sitting stiffly on edge of chair
    gripping sides of chair, table, etc.
    gripping hands together
    other (specify_____)
    Overall rating: 1   2   3   9

13. Habitual mannerisms
(repetitive stereotyped movements
—include tics but do not
include general fidgetiness;
check individual mannerisms which
occur and make overall rating

based on duration of mannerisms
throughout interview)
  facial mannerism (frown, grimace,
    pursing of lips, etc.)
  sucking of object or part of the
    body (finger, thumb, strands of
    hair, etc.)
  biting of nails, fingers or
    objects
  rocking
  twisting of hair
  whole body movements
    (jumping up and down,
    whirling, etc.)
  picking of nose
  flapping of arms
  twisting movements of hands
    or fingers in the air
  tapping with fingers or hands
  holding or touching of genitals
  other repetitive movements
    (specify_____
  Overall rating: 1   2   3   9

14. Overactivity

  1—definitely underactive: very little spontaneous movements.

  2—normal: child sits in chair throughout interview except when
    instructed to do otherwise.

  3—tendency to increased activity: child gets up from chair spon-
    taneously at least once or moves about at least once when
    should be standing.

  4—child definitely and markedly overactive *relative* to situation;
    several times gets up from chair or moves around room when
    expected to stay still.

  5—child definitely and markedly overactive to absolute extent;
    not only gets up and moves around, but *tempo* of activity also
    increased.

  9—not known.

15. Fidgetiness (*not* including tics)
    1—no squirming, wriggling or fidgetiness.
    2—occasional fidgety movements, but not present most of the time.
    3—wriggling, squirming or fidgetiness present for most of the interview.
    9—not known.

16. Attention span and persistence
    1—persists at tasks given until completed (child may be momentarily distracted but must spontaneously return to the task).
    2—on some tasks needs occasional prompting or reminding to persist until completion.
    3—usually needs prompting or reminding to continue with tasks until completion.
    9—not known.

17. Distractibility (pay most attention in rating to the child's response to incidental usual stimuli)
    1—not distracted (or only rarely) by usual stimuli when attention engaged in any activity; not distracted or only momentarily distracted at onset of unusual stimuli (as specified in instructions) when engaged in a task.
    2—occasionally distracted by usual stimuli and/or repeatedly distracted by unusual stimuli.
    3—distracted by usual stimuli or slight unusual stimuli, so that attention frequently diverted from any activity or task.
    9—not known.

18. Irritability (overall judgment)
    1—normal level of irritation.
    2—occasionally irritated during interview (limited to task situations or affect laden areas).
    3—definitely irritated during interview (not limited to task situations or affect laden areas).
    4—definitely and markedly irritable: erupts easily, shouts angrily, screams at examiner, overtly and directly hostile.

19. Observed anxiety (overall judgement: based on apprehension, expression, autonomic disturbance, tremulousness, tension and preoccupation *at interview* with topics of anxiety or worry)
    1—no or very little anxiety.
    2—some anxiety.
    3—marked anxiety or anxiety very readily provoked.
    9—not known.

20. Emotional responsiveness (to interviewer)
    1—emotionally responsive in normal way to interviewer; shows range of emotions appropriate to interview situations (may, however, show excess of emotion, e.g., crying).
    2—limited emotional response to interviewer; definite evidence of some appropriate response, but restriction of emotional involvement.
    3—markedly lacking in emotional response to interviewer (seems difficult to "get through" to child, very little emotional involvement with interviewer).
    9—not known.

21. Relationship with examiner
    1—good rapport established and maintained.
    2—rather difficult to gain or maintain rapport (for any reason, e.g., autism, negativism, belligerence, uncooperativeness).
    3—rapport not obtained or severely limited (for any reason)
    (If rating of 2 or 3 is made, specify which of the following interfered with rapport:
        1—not applicable
        2—withdrawal
        3—negatism, uncooperative behavior
        4—suspicious affect
        5—other (specify_____)
        9—not known

22. Observed mood level (based on facial expression, tearfulness, preoccupation with depressive topics at interview, depressive apathy, etc.)
    1—not depressed; normal or elevated mood level.
    2—general mood level normal or near normal but child appears

easily cast down when emotionally loaded topics (such as wanting more friends or frequency of depressed feelings) are broached; alternatively, generally mildly depressed.

3—generally moderately depressed or markedly depressed at times (e.g., when emotionally loaded topics are discussed).

9—not known.

23. Disinhibition

1—some reserve, as normal with a strange adult.

2—treats examiner in an easy, friendly manner with little or no reserve; rather disinhibited for the interview situation.

3—treats examiner as if a longstanding friend of his own age, that is, markedly disinhibited and over-friendly for the interview situation; may be cheeky, make unprompted remarks about the room or the examiner or his clothes, ask a lot of questions, etc.

4—disregard of the interviewer or his instructions shown by proceeding with own interests with little attention to the demands of the interviewer; may ask spontaneous questions or make unprompted comments, but not cheeky or friendly. This kind of disregard is self-centered rather than outgoing and over-friendly.

9—not known.

24. Spontaneous talk (specify actual number of spontaneous comments—put 10^+ if more than 10)

1—at least four spontaneous comments during the interview.

2—one to three spontaneous remarks.

3—no spontaneous comments.

9—not known.

25. Speech and language

1—normal.

2—articulation defect only.

3—executive defect only (aphasia, echolalia, etc.; include retardation of speech).

4—articulation and executive defect.

9—not known.

26. Comprehension of speech
    1—normal.
    2—slight abnormality.
    3—marked abnormality.
    9—not known.

27. Smiling
    1—smiles appropriately.
    2—smiles only occasionally.
    3—no or very little smiling.
    9—not known.

An opinion should be expressed on whether (and how) the child's mental state departs from that expected in relation to his age, intellectual level, sex and social class background.

Finally, an overall judgment of the psychiatric state should be made using the following rating:

1—normal (questionable abnormalities are compatible with this rating).

2—mild or uncertain abnormality (i.e., uncertain because of mildness of definite abnormality or because abnormality, although marked, may be entirely situation-specific).

3—definite and clinically significant abnormality. (Specify type of abnormality and reasons for assessment of abnormality.)

In making the final evaluation of psychiatric state, the examiner should use all relevant data. However, only the behavior of the child observed during the interview and information reported by him should be used when writing up the description of the interview. The nature of the psychiatric disorder and the evidence noted in the interview for its presence should always be spelled out in detail.

BEHAVIOR RATING SCALES

A number of rating scales of children's behavior for completion by parents and by teachers are available. For a very complete discussion of this area the reader is referred to a recent review by Conners (1973), who is also the author of three scales recommended for use in evaluating hyperactive children: A Parent Symptom Questionnaire, a Teacher's Questionnaire and an Abbreviated Symptom Questionnaire.

Conners Parent Symptom Questionnaire (PSQ)

Conners has devised a rating scale for completion by one or both parents which consists of ninety-three items of behavior, grouped under twenty-five major headings. Each item represents a symptom commonly seen in behavior disorders of childhood. The parents are asked to rate their child as he is currently functioning with regard to each symptom on a four-point scale: NOT AT ALL, JUST A LITTLE, PRETTY MUCH, or VERY MUCH. They are also asked to indicate the items they are most concerned about or those they think are the most important problems their child has, and to rate the overall severity of their child's problem. Space is also provided for the parents to describe in their own words any other problems they have with their child.

Scoring is achieved by giving a numerical weighting (0, 1, 2, 3) to the parents' rating of each item. A higher score indicates greater pathology. A total symptom score can be obtained by totaling the ninety-three weighted items. In addition, Conners (1970) has carried out a factor analysis of the questionnaire on a sample of normal children and a sample of clinic outpatients between the ages of six and fourteen. Eight factor scores can be obtained by totaling the weighted ratings for forty-two of the PSQ items. The eight factors are labeled: Conduct Problems, Anxiety, Impulsive-Hyperactive, Learning Problem, Psychosomatic, Perfectionism, Antisocial, and Muscular Tension. Discriminant function analysis has shown that 70 percent of clinic outpatients, 83 percent of normal controls, 77 percent of neurotic children and 74 percent of hyperactive children can be identified from factor scores. The factor scores have also been shown to be relatively stable across ages and a wide range of social class.

Conners Teacher Questionnaire (TQ)

The questionnaire for completion by teachers consists of thirty-nine items of behavior grouped under three major headings: Classroom Behavior, Group Participation, and Attitude Toward Authority. The teacher is asked to rate the child with regard to each item of behavior on a four-point scale: NOT AT ALL, JUST A LITTLE, PRETTY MUCH, or VERY MUCH. In addition, the teacher is asked how long she has known the child, to briefly describe the child's main problem, and to globally rate the child's behavior compared to other children the same age on a five-point scale from "much worse" to "much better." The teacher is also asked if any children in the same family attend the school and present any problems. Finally, she is requested to add any information concerning the child's family relationships which might have bearing on his attitudes and behavior. The first page of the questionnaire contains areas for filling in: results of standardized intelligence tests and most recent achievement tests; the child's actual level of classroom performance in school subjects; and any special placement or help the child has received. Thus the questionnaire gives a very complete picture of the child's functioning and achievement in school.

Scoring is achieved by giving a numerical weighting (0, 1, 2, 3) to the teacher's rating of each item of behavior with a higher score indicating greater pathology. A total symptom score can be obtained by totaling the thirty-nine weighted items. Factor analysis of this questionnaire has yielded five factors: Aggressive Conduct, Day-dreaming-Inattentive, Anxious-Fearful, Hyperactivity, and Sociable-Cooperative (Conners, 1969). These five factors seem to have high test-retest reliability and to be quite sensitive to changes due to medication. This questionnaire seems to be the most widely used teacher evaluation procedure for hyperactive children. Normative data have been obtained for the questionnaire (Kupietz et al., 1972); it has been shown to clearly distinguish normal children from hyperactive children (Sprague et al., in press) and it has been shown to be quantitatively very sensitive to the behavioral effects of psychotropic drugs (Sprague and Werry, 1974).

Ten items on the PSQ and TQ are identical and have been combined to form an Abbreviated Symptom Questionnaire (ASQ) which can be used to obtain frequent follow-up assessments of the child by both parents and teachers. This abbreviated scale has been found to have almost the same sensitivity in obtaining statistically significant differences in psychotropic drug studies with hyperactive children (Sprague and Werry, 1974).

PHYSICAL EXAMINATION

The physical examination is usually completely normal in hyperactive children. However, it should always be done as part of the evaluation since in a minority of children defects of vision or hearing may be picked up (Stewart et al., 1966) as well as abnormalities of speech (DeHirsch, 1973). Base-line height and weight should be recorded in all children with frequent follow-up of those children selected for stimulant drug therapy. One group of investigators (Waldrop and Halverson, 1971) has reported a high incidence of minor physical anomalies in hyperactive children such as epicanthus, widely spaced eyes, curved fifth finger, adherent earlobes, etc. The findings were more consistent for boys than for girls. These authors have suggested that the same factors operating in the first week of pregnancy led to both the congenital anomalies and the hyperactive behavior. In a study of seventy-six hyperactive boys, not only did Rapoport (Rapoport et al., 1974) confirm the incidence of minor physical anomalies, but in this population the presence of these anomalies was associated with severity of hyperactivity, a history of hyperactivity in the father, a history of early obstetrical difficulty in the mother, and a higher than normal mean plasma dopamine β-hydroxylase activity. These findings suggest that those hyperactive children with minor physical anomalies may form a distinct subgroup of the total population and that the physical examination early in life may detect children "at risk" for the development of the hyperactive child syndrome.

NEUROLOGIC EXAMINATION

A careful pediatric neurologic examination should be part of the standard work-up of every hyperactive child, if only to rule out a treatable or progressive neurologic disease. However, since only a very small minority of hyperactive children will demonstrate "hard" evidence of neurological involvement, careful attention must be paid to the detection of minor neurologic abnormalities generally referred to as "soft signs" in the literature. Several good descriptions of developmental neurologic examinations designed to elicit these minor neurologic abnormalities exist (Rutter et al, 1970; Peters et al., 1973; Close, 1973; Werry et al., 1972) and Goodman and Sours (1967) have described a "play" neurological examination which can be done in conjunction with a psychiatric interview with the child.

There is agreement that certain of these minor neurological signs are more frequent among hyperactive children (Werry, 1972). However, most studies suffer from methodological deficiencies such as absence of proper control groups and failure to use a reliable, standardized neurological examination (Werry, 1972; Schain, 1972). Only one study has compared carefully matched hyperactive, neurotic and normal groups of children using a standardized neurological examination of demonstrated reliability (Werry et al., 1972). The hyperactive children did have an excess of minor neurologic abnormalities indicative of sensorimotor incoordination. However, the hyperactive group did not have an excess of major neurologic abnormalities or of EEG abnormalities, or histories suggestive of trauma to the brain. The source and significance of these minor neurologic abnormalities thus remains obscure (Rutter et al., 1970). Their value in the diagnosis of the hyperactive child syndrome is questionable since only about one-half (Satterfield, 1973; Millichap, 1973) of behaviorally defined hyperactive children have even "soft" neurologic signs. However, there is some evidence that those with such signs are distinguished from those with no such neurological signs by a greater likelihood of response to stimulant drug treatment (Satterfield, 1973; Millichap, 1973), suggesting that this may be a meaningful subgroup. Further investigation in this area is required.

LABORATORY STUDIES

Laboratory findings are generally more reliable, precise and reproducible than are clinical descriptions. If some measure could be found that was consistently associated with the hyperactive child syndrome, it would simplify diagnosis and permit a more refined classification and subdivision of the syndrome into meaningful subgroups. Relevant laboratory studies that might be considered in the work-up of a hyperactive child are discussed below.

Electroencephalogram Studies

Electroencephalographic studies with hyperactive children have produced variable findings. Different studies have reported 35 to 50 percent of hyperactive children to have abnormal EEG's (Satterfield, 1973; Werry et al., 1972), with an increase in slow wave activity being the most common finding. There are no EEG abnormalities specific to the syndrome. There is even some question as to whether hyperactive children have a greater number of EEG abnormalities than carefully matched normal and non-hyperactive emotionally disturbed children (Werry et al., 1972; Eeg-Olofsson, 1970; Petersen et al., 1968). In view of the expense to the family and the low return of clinically useful information, an EEG should be obtained only when the history or neurological examination suggests some definite neurological abnormality or attack disorder.

Neurophysiologic Evaluations
Chapter Four reviews current neurophysiologic research with hyperactive children. While it must be said that this appears to be a fruitful area for future research, these evaluations are currently not available to most practitioners and are generally only done in a research setting.

Chromosome Studies
The only reported chromosome study of hyperactive children failed to find evidence of sex chromosome aneuploidy or other chromosome abnormality (Warren et al., 1971). In view of the evidence for a possible genetically determined subgroup of hyperactive children (Chapter Six), chromosome studies may be indicated in families with multiple cases of the syndrome or where examination of the child suggests a possible chromosome abnormality.

Metabolic and Biochemical Studies
Disorders of monoamine metabolism in hyperactive children have been proposed by several investigators but experimental evidence to support such abnormalities is sparse (Chapter Five). Such investigations are only in the research realm at the present time.

It has been variously claimed that hyperactive children suffer from vitamin deficiencies, allergies to certain food additives and disorders of glucose metabolism. This, in turn, has led to enthusiastic reports of positive results from treatment with megavitamin therapy, allergin-free diets and hypoglycemic diets (Hoffer, 1972; Cott, 1969; Hoffer, 1971; Rimland, 1972; Feingold, 1973). None of these claims has been substantiated as yet by proper studies, and laboratory investigations in these areas cannot be justified on a routine basis. In individual cases such laboratory studies may be indicated if the history or other aspects of the examination suggest a possible metabolic abnormality.

Clinical Laboratory Studies
A complete blood count and urinalysis should be done as part of the physical examination. In those children placed on drug therapy, certain other selected clinical laboratory studies should be obtained at

base-line and at follow-up intervals. The reader is referred to a recent article by Gershon (1973) for a discussion of this area.

Psychometric Studies

A proper psychological assessment should be part of the work-up of every hyperactive child. The evaluation should include assessment of general intelligence, academic achievement, language functions, motor functions, memory and perception (Conners, 1967; Werry, 1968). Specific deficits in intellectual, sensory, perceptual or motor functions may be uncovered in an individual child which can be remediated (Conners, 1967). Moreover, psychological tests which have been shown to be reliable can also be considered to be laboratory tests in the same vein as biochemical findings (Robins and Guze, 1970) and, as such, may be helpful in the diagnosis of the hyperactive child syndrome and in subdivision of the syndrome into meaningful groups.

As a group, when compared with normal children, hyperactive children have been shown to be inferior on a wide range of intellectual, conceptual, visuo-spatial, academic, motor, and sensory-perceptual functions (Conners, 1967; Douglas, 1972). However, no battery of tests has been adequately standardized to ensure discrimination of an individual hyperactive child from a child suffering from other psychiatric or learning disorders (Conners, 1967), although the battery devised by Reitan and his associates (Reitan and Boll, 1973) shows promise. Thus, though psychological tests continue to play an important part in the clinical evaluations of hyperactive children, their exact role and utility is still debated. Knights (1973) advocates a "profile similarity approach" using patterns of scores on a neuropsychological test battery as an aid in the diagnosis of the hyperactive child syndrome. Conners (1973) recommends classifying hyperactive subjects into homogeneous subgroups on the basis of types or patterns of psychological test response. His factor analysis of a battery of test scores by hyperactive children yielded five factors: (1)General IQ, (2)Achievement, (3)Rote Learning, (4)Attentiveness and (5)Impulse Control. He next identified six separate patterns of factor scores or "cluster types." Validity of this grouping procedure was demonstrated by showing that the six groups differed significantly from each other on the Lincoln-Oseretsky test of motor development, response to drug and placebo treatment, and cortical evoked response (Conners, 1973). Thus the groups of children classified on the basis of psychological functioning seemed to be homogeneous groups sharing disabilities of certain underlying psychological and physiological processes and perhaps common etiologies.

At some point in the future behavioral, neurologic, neurophysiologic, biochemical and other data may be linked with such psychological test profiles to permit greater subdivision of the heterogeneous group of hyperactive children.

DISCUSSION

The evaluation outlined in this chapter should "ideally" be carried out with every child referred for hyperactivity. Immediate questions of the busy family practitioner or pediatrician are: "How much of this evaluation *must* be carried out with each child?" "How much *can* be carried out in an office setting?"

The clinical picture of the child is best defined in the interview with the parents and by the behavior rating scales. Mailing the scales to the parents and to the teacher for their completion prior to the first interview will often facilitate the evaluation, particularly if the child has been tested psychometrically at school and the results of these tests recorded on the teacher rating scale. Some of the parental interview can also be written up on a standardized form for completion by the parents prior to the first meeting, though this must not substitute for an in-depth initial interview with the parents.

The interview with the child is important for a number of reasons, but it is unlikely that a diagnosis will be made *solely* on the basis of this interview without evidence for the diagnosis also coming from the parents and/or the teacher (Rutter et al., 1970). It is much more likely that the child will *not* appear hyperactive in the one-to-one setting in the office while he does at home and at school.

With practice, most physicians will develop familiarity with a developmental neurological examination and will establish "norms" for their examination with different age groups. The neurological examination can be done in conjunction with the physicians usual physical examination.

It is in the area of laboratory tests and special evaluations such as psychological, language, and educational screening that many private physicians find themselves at a loss, often due to a lack of access to resources. However, there are a number of recent publications available to the practitioner which offer help in this regard. The *Physician's Handbook: Screening for MBD* (Peters et al., 1973) contains hearing and language screening examinations, an articulation screening test, educational screening tests, geometric designs for copying and a preschool screening examination. Hartlage and Lucas' *Mental Development Evaluation of the Pediatric Patient* (1973) contains a check list of verbal and nonverbal developmental milestones for children from age two to nine; check lists of school readiness for the first three grades; and age-graded human figure drawings, geometric designs for copying, and picture recognition tasks.

Most of these evaluations can be performed in a brief period of time by office personnel. They offer a very quick and reliable way of screening for significant problems in a wide variety of areas. Any child who seems to have a problem in one or more areas can then be referred for a more thorough evaluation of that area only rather than being referred for an entire battery of tests. The *Physician's Handbook* referred to above also contains a developmental neurological examination, a behavior rating scale, and a family data form to be completed by parents that covers much of the medical and social history. A special issue of the *Psychopharmacology Bulletin* (DHEW, 1973) contains a medical and social history, a neurological examination, all three of the Conner's rating scales, and the entire battery of evaluation forms recommended by the Early Clinical Drug Evaluation Unit of the NIMH for drug studies with children. The office practitioner will find both of these publications of invaluable assistance in evaluating children with all types of behavior and learning disorders.

REFERENCES

Bell, R. (1971). Stimulus control of parent or caretaker behavior by offspring. *Developmental Psychology* 4:63–72.

Close, J. (1973). Scored neurological examination. *Psychopharmacology Bulletin,* Department of Health, Education and Welfare, 142–50.

Conners, C. K. (1967). The syndrome of minimal brain dysfunction: psychological aspects. *The Pediatric Clinics of North America.* 14:749–67.

_____ (1969). A teacher rating scale for use in drug studies with children. *American Journal of Psychiatry* 126:152–56.

_____ (1970). Symptom patterns in hyperkinetic, neurotic and normal children. *Child Development* 41:667–82.

_____ (1973). Deanol and behavior disorders in children: a critical review of the literature and recommended future studies for determining efficacy. *Psychopharmacology Bulletin*, Department of Health, Education, and Welfare 188–95.

Cott, A. (1969). Treating schizophrenic children. *Schizophrenia* 1:44–60.

DeHirsch, K. (1973). Language development and minimal brain dysfunction. *Annals of the New York Academy of Science—Minimal Brain Dysfunction* 205:158–64.

Department of Health, Education and Welfare (1973). *Psychopharmacology Bulletin.*

Douglas, V. (1972). Stop, look and listen: the problem of sustained attention and impulse control in hyperactive and normal children. *Canadian Journal of Behavioral Science* 4:249–82.

Eeg-Olofsson, O. (1970). The development of the electroencephalogram in normal children and adolescents from the age of 1 through 21 years. *Acta Pediatrica Scandinavica*, Suppl. 208.

Feingold, B. (1973). Food additives and child development. *Hospital Practice* 8:11–12, 17–19.

Gershon, S. (1973). Pediatric psychopharmacology—clinical laboratory standards. *Psychopharmacology Bulletin*, Department of Health, Education and Welfare, 167–81.

Goodman, J., and Sours, J. (1967). *The Child Mental Status Examination.* New York: Basic Books, Inc.

Graham, P., Rutter, M., and George, S. (1973). Temperamental characteristics as predictors of behavior disorders in children. *American Journal of Orthopsychiatry* 43:328, 339.

Hartlage, L., and Lucas, D. (1973). *Mental Development Evaluation of the Pediatric Patient.* Springfield, Ill.: Charles C. Thomas.

Hoffer, S. (1971). Vitamin B-3 dependent child. *Schizophrenia* 3:107–13.

_____ (1972). Treatment of hyperkinetic children with nicotinamide and pyridoxine. *Canadian Medical Association Journal* 107:111–12.

Knights, R. (1973). Problems of criteria in diagnosis: a profile similarity approach. *Annals of the New York Academy of Sciences* 205:124–31.

Kupietz, S., Bialer, I., Winsberg, B. G. (1972). A behavior rating scale for assessing improvement in behaviorally deviant children: a preliminary investigation. *The American Journal of Psychiatry* 128: 1432–36.

Millichap, J. (1973). Drugs in management of minimal brain dysfunction. *Annals of the New York Academy of Sciences* 205:321–34.

Peters, J., Davis, J., Goolsby, C., Clements, S., and Hicks, T. (1973). *Physician's Handbook —Screening for MBD.* CIBA Medical Horizons.

Petersen, I., Eeg-Olofsson, O., and Sellden, U. (1968). Paroxysmal activity in EEG of normal children. In P. Kellaway and I. Persen, eds., *Clinical Electroencephalography of Children.* New York: Grune and Stratton.

Rapoport, J., Quinn, P., and Lamprecht, F. (1974). Minor physical anomalies and plasma dopamine-beta-hydroxylase activity in hyperactive boys. *American Journal of Psychiatry* 131:386–90.

Reitan, R., and Boll, T. (1973). Neuropsychological correlates of minimal brain dysfunction. *Minimal Brain Dysfunction* 205:65–89.

Rimland, B. (1972). Megavitamin treatment in children. In D. Hawkins and L. Pauling, eds., *Orthomolecular Psychiatry.* San Francisco: W. H. Freeman Co.

Robins, E., and Guze, S. (1970). Establishment of diagnostic validity and psychiatric illness: its application to schizophrenia. *American Journal of Psychiatry* 126:983–87.

Rutter, M. (1972). Relationship between the psychiatric disorders of childhood and adulthood. *Acta Psychiatrica Scandinavica 48:3–21.*

_____and Graham, P. (1968). The reliability and validity of the psychiatric assessment of the child. *British Journal of Psychiatry* 114, 563–80.

_____, Graham, P., and Yule, W. (1970). *A Neuropsychiatric Study in Childhood.* Lavenham, Suffolk: The Lavenham Press, Ltd.

Satterfield, J. (1973). EEG issues in children with minimal brain dysfunction. *Seminars in Psychiatry* 5:35–46.

Simmons, J. (1969). *Psychiatric Examination of Children.* Philadelphia: Lee and Febiger.

Schain, R. (1972). *Neurology of Childhood Learning Disorders.* Baltimore: The Williams and Wilkins Co.

Sprague, R., and Werry, J. (1974). Psychotropic drugs and handicapped children. In L. Mann and D. Sabatino, eds., *Second Review of Special Education.* Philadelphia: Raymond J. Balester & Lester Mann, Buttonwood Farms, Inc.

_____, Christensen, D., and Werry, J. (in press). Experimental psychology and stimulant drugs. *Excerpta Medica.*

Stewart, M., Pitts, F., Craig, A., & Dieruf, A. (1966). The hyperactive child syndrome. *American Journal of Orthopsychiatry* 36:861–67.

Sundby, H., and Kreyberg, P. (1969). *Prognosis in Child Psychiatry.* Baltimore: Wms. & Wilkins.

Tapia, F. *Diagnostic Interview in Child Psychiatry* (film). Univ. of Oklahoma, Okla. City.

Waldrop, M., and Halverson, C. (1971). Minor physical anomalies and hyperactive behavior in young children. In J. Hellmuch, ed., *The Exceptional Infant,* Vol. 2, New York: Brunner-Mazel.

Warren, R., Karduck, W., Bussaratid, S., Stewart, M., and Sly, W. (1971). The hyperactive child syndrome: normal chromosome findings. *Archives of General Psychiatry* 24:-161–63.

Werry, J. (1968). Studies on the hyperactive child. IV. An empirical analysis of the minimal brain dysfunction syndrome. *Archives of General Psychiatry* 19:9–16.

_____(1972). Organic factors in childhood psychopathology. In Quay and Werry, eds., *Psychopathological Disorders of Childhood.* New York: John S. Wiley & Sons.

_____, Minde, K., Guzman, A., Weiss, G., Dogan, K., and Hoy, E. (1972). Studies on the hyperactive child. VII. Neurological status compared with neurotic and normal children. *American Journal of Orthopsychiatry* 127:824–25.

Chapter Three

Natural History and Prognosis in the Hyperactive Child Syndrome

DENNIS P. CANTWELL, M.D.

Early investigators of the hyperactive child syndrome tended to emphasize that the syndrome was a time-limited condition which disappeared as the child grew older (Laufer and Denhoff, 1957; Bakwin and Bakwin, 1966; Eisenberg, 1966). However, while the *symptom* of hyperactivity may diminish with age (Rutter, 1968), it now seems that this initial optimism about the eventual outcome of hyperactive children was unjustified. This chapter will review the available research evidence pertaining to the natural history and ultimate prognosis of children with the hyperactive child syndrome and give some consideration to prognostic factors and the effect of different treatment modalities.

Initial suggestive evidence that hyperactive children did not simply "outgrow" their problem came from the clinical studies of Anderson and Playmate (1962) and Laufer and Denhoff (1957). The former investigators suggested that hyperactive children were prone to develop a variety of serious personality disorders as adolescents and adults. Laufer found that poor school performance, in the face of normal intellectual potential, characterized all of twenty previously hyperactive adolescents. They also had developed a variety of psychopathological symptoms as they grew older, but no consistent picture was described.

FOLLOW-UP STUDIES

The first systematic follow-up of hyperactive children was of eighteen children seen in the Johns Hopkins Hospital Child Psychiatry Outpatient Department between 1937 and 1946 (Menkes et al., 1967). All of the children were retrospectively diagnosed as hyperactive from clinic records on the basis of the presence of a defined behavioral syndrome. None of the patients had seizures, IQ's below 70, or a diagnosis of psychosis, but all did have indications of neurologic abnormalities of the "soft" type (poor coordination, speech impairment, visual motor dysfunction). The mean age at first clinic visit was seven years, with a range from two years, seven months, to fifteen years, six months.

Fourteen (eleven males, three females) of the original eighteen were followed up and eleven of these were personally examined by the authors. Those examined received a personal interview to determine interval history and current mental status, a neurological evaluation, and brief psychometric testing (Ammons, Bender-Gestalt). The follow-up interval ranged from fourteen to twenty-seven years, with a mean of twenty-four years, with the age of the patients at follow-up ranging from twenty-two to forty years. Clinical status at follow-up was as follows: eight were self-supporting, two were definitely retarded and entirely supported by their families, four were institutionalized psychotics. Four of the eight who were self-supporting at follow-up had spent some time in institutions, such as jails, juvenile halls and hospitals for the retarded. Eight of the eleven had definite evidence of abnormality on neurological examination and one had presumptive evidence. Three still demonstrated evidence of restlessness and distractibility, one at the age of twenty-four. Finally, psychometric testing revealed that only one patient performed at an average or above level on the Bender. Differences in the tests used at initial evaluation and at follow-up made the IQ testing difficult to interpret but it is worth noting that the follow-up IQ was more than 10 points lower than the initial IQ in five cases.

On all counts, then, the results of this retrospective study hardly call for optimism. The prospective studies that have followed are no more hopeful in their outlook. The Montreal group (Weiss et al., 1971; Minde et al., 1971; Minde et al., 1972) has reported several prospective follow-ups of overlapping groups of patients. Their initial communication (Weiss et al., 1971) presented the status of sixty-four hyperactive children (sixty boys, four girls) four to six years after their initial referral. When seen initially this group of children were between six and thirteen years of age, had no evidence of psychosis or major brain damage, and had WISC IQ's greater than 85. A wide variety of interviews, rating scales, psychometric and other evaluative techniques were used in initial and follow-up examinations. Follow-up results indicated that, as a group, the children had improved in the target symptoms of hyperactivity, distractibility, aggressivity and excitability. However, they were still rated as more disturbed in these areas than a normal control group matched for age, sex and IQ. Distractibility, rather than hyperactivity, was now the major complaint of the mothers.

Psychiatric examination revealed no cases of psychosis, though three did show marked schizoid personality traits. Fully one-quarter had a history of antisocial behavior, with 15 percent having been already referred to the courts. Nearly one-third had no steady friends. Emotional immaturity, lack of ambition and a severe lack of ability to maintain goals were the main pathological traits reported by the mothers. The examining child psychiatrists were also impressed by this lack of ambition and by the marked depression and low self-esteem demonstrated by the children at interview.

Educational retardation of a rather marked degree was present in a significant number of the children. Seventy percent had repeated at least one grade, 35 percent two or more grades. Ten percent were in special classes and 5 percent had already been expelled from school. Classroom behavior, as reported by teachers, confirmed that the children were more restless, more aggressive, more antisocial and less able to concentrate than their classmates.

Psychometric evaluation revealed no significant changes in the WISC performance IQ or in the Goodenough Draw-a-Person Test, a significant improvement in WISC Verbal IQ and a significant deterioration in the Lincoln-Oseretsky Motor Development scores.

Minde (Minde et al., 1972) also reported on the five-year follow-up status of 91 out of 104 children originally seen at the Montreal Children's Hospital (presumably including the sixty-four reported by Weiss). This larger group also showed a significant decrease in all target symptoms (hyperactivity, distractibility, excitability and aggressivity) over the five-year period, but still scored significantly higher on all target symptoms than normal peers. General psychiatric status was measured by the Peterson-Quay Symptom Checklist which yields separate scores for Neuroticism, Psychopathy and Immaturity. Despite a significant decrease in scores over the follow-up period, the hyperactive group still showed more symptoms in all three areas than the normal population. They were most deviant on the Psychopathic Scale and least on the Immaturity Scale. The only significant change in the battery of psychometric test scores was a drop in performance on the Lincoln-Oseretsky from the 31st to the 15th percentile. An overall judgment at outcome was made based on a combination of six factors: complaints at the time of follow-up, peer interactions, relationship to authority, antisocial behavior, object relations and sexual adjustment. Those twenty-eight children (30 percent) who scored as well-adjusted in five out of six of these categories were placed in the "good outcome" group, while those eighteen (20 percent) who scored as poorly adjusted in four out of six were placed in the "poor outcome" group. The remaining 50 percent belonged to neither of these two extreme groups. This report confirmed the preliminary findings of Weiss (Weiss et al., 1971) on a smaller subsample of these hyperactive children.

A third report (Minde et al., 1971) compared the academic performance of a subsample of thirty-seven of these children with the performance of thirty-seven same-sexed, non-hyperactive classmates. By the age of eleven, twenty-one of the hyperactive group, as opposed to six of the control group, had repeated one or more grades in school. The hyperative children scored significantly lower than the controls in ten out of twelve school subjects, with the hyperactive group equalling the performance of their peers only in "non-academic" subjects (physical activity, art and handiwork). This inferior performance held true even with careful matching for IQ. A detailed look at the battery of psychometric test results indicated that the hyperactive children had uneven cognitive patterns and a preponderance of verbal difficulties that made academic progress in a normal class setting unlikely, particularly when combined with their restlessness and inattention. Finally, an investigation of the school records and report cards of these children over a four-year period indicated that the hyperactive child's failure in school is a consistent phenomenon. They were doing as poorly in classroom performance four years after initial diagnosis as they had been one year after diagnosis.

Three other prospective studies of hyperactive children have been reported from different areas of the country. Mendelson (Mendelson et al., 1971) interviewed the mothers of eighty-three children between the ages of twelve and sixteen years who had been diagnosed as hyperactive two to six years earlier in a children's hospital in St. Louis. As a global judgment 55 percent of the group were felt to be improved, with 35 percent unchanged or worse. When outcome was assessed in three specific areas—presence of major symptoms, difficulties at home and difficulties at school—about half were reported improved in all three areas, 14 percent in the first two areas and 10 percent in the first area only, and about one-quarter were unchanged or worse in all three areas.

Although the intensity of the symptoms had often improved, the great majority of the children (over 75 percent) still demonstrated the cardinal symptoms of hyperactivity, distractibility, impulsivity and irritability. "Rebellious attitude" was now the most frequent chief complaint of the parents, half of whom were unable to think of a career for which their child would be suited. Forty percent of the parents had seriously considered sending their child to live away from home.

Antisocial behavior of a rather marked degree was a frequent finding at follow-up. Twenty-two percent of the children had long histories of such behavior and were considered likely to be sociopathic as adults. Nearly 60 percent had had some contact with the police, 17 percent on three or more occasions. Nearly a quarter had been referred to the juvenile court. More than a third had threatened to kill their parents, 7 percent carried weapons and 15 percent had set fires. Two-thirds were considered by their parents to be incorrigible. The emerging picture, then, is of children who have difficulty conforming to rules, whether set by society or by their families.

Very poor school performance was also a characteristic finding. One-quarter were attending some type of special school or class, nearly 60 percent had failed one or more grades, and nearly 20 percent two or more grades. Nearly three-quarters of the group still had concentration and attention problems in the classroom. Some 60 percent were considered by teachers to be a discipline problem, while 17 percent had begun truanting.

Finally, nearly half of the children were experiencing depressive symptoms at follow-up with frequent periods of low mood and poor self-image. Fifteen percent had either talked of or attempted suicide. Thus a significant number of these children were experiencing inner turmoil as well as having a disruptive influence on their environment.

Laufer (1971) and Denhoff (1973) have reported preliminary findings from a questionnaire follow-up of one hundred hyperactive children in a private practice in Providence, Rhode Island. Sixty-six patients returned the questionnaire. They ranged in age from three to thirteen (mean age, 8) at time of initial evaluation and from fifteen to twenty-six (mean age, 19.8) at follow-up. Hyperactivity was still present in two-thirds of the group. Some 30 percent reported symptoms of psychopathology such as mood swings, feelings of persecution and episodes of violence, but there were no reported suicide attempts. More than one-third had had subsequent psychiatric treatment, including 5 percent who had been hospitalized. Nine percent were receiving continuing psychiatric care at the time of follow-up.

Difficulty with the law was reported by 30 percent of fifty-five respondents but none were in jail. Drug experimentation was reported by about 5 percent and drug overdose by two of fifty-seven patients. Some 8 percent reported excess alcohol intake. Academic outcome was relatively good compared to other studies. Although fifty of the sixty-six had required some type of remedial education, of the forty-eight patients who answered questions regarding academic status some 47 percent were either in or had graduated from high school and 29 percent were either in or had graduated from college.

On the whole, then, the results of this study are slightly more optimistic than the others reported. This may be due to the fact that these were private patients of presumably higher social class who received more intensive and consistent treatment. However, the optimistic findings may simply be a reflection of several defects in the study: questionnaires only were used in the follow-up; nothing was said about the one-third who did not respond to the questionnaires; and not every question was answered by the two-thirds who did reply.

One other prospective follow-up study deserves mention, though the patient population was a select one. Dykman (Dykman et al., 1973) of the University of Arkansas originally compared eighty-two boys with "minimal brain dysfunction" with thirty-four controls. The MBD group was selected so that they also had learning deficits in one or more basic skills, and the original population contained twenty-nine who were hyperactive, nineteen hypoactive, and thirty-four normoactive as rated by teachers. They ranged in age from 9.5 to 12 years at initial evaluation. Thirty-one of the LD-MBD cases and twenty-two of the controls were followed up when each child had reached age fourteen. A wide variety of follow-up measures were used. Some of the most significant results are summarized below.

Initially the control group had been superior to the MBD group only in verbal IQ, but at follow-up this superiority included full-scale IQ as well. Over one-third of the MBD children declined 10 points or more in verbal IQ while more than one-half of the controls gained 10 points or more in performance IQ over the follow-up period. Academically, the patient group was several years behind the control group in reading, spelling and arithmetic, with their worst performance in oral reading. They seemed to be most deficient in conceptual, sequencing and symbolic abilities as indicated by their subtest patterns on the WISC.

Teachers rated the MBD group as still more of a problem in the classroom than the controls, but "hyperactivity" and "inattentiveness" per se no longer significantly discriminated the groups at follow-up. Parents also still rated the subjects as problem children, but the specific areas of problem behavior were not listed by the authors. The MBD group rated themselves as having more problems than the controls in nearly all areas measured by the Minnesota Counseling Inventory. However, a self-rating comparing themselves to their classmates on thirty items of classroom behavior failed to discriminate the groups.

Finally, the MBD group had a higher incidence of neurological abnormalities at follow-up, but had improved considerably from their initial evaluation. They also seemed less impulsive and had improved in visual motor skills.

Thus this study also highlights the poor academic performance of hyperactive children over time. But it should be noted that all of these children had learning deficits at initial evaluation, which is not true of all hyperactive children (Cantwell and Satterfield, in press). Moreover, not all of the MBD group were truly hyperactive, and the percentage of the MBD children who were in the hyperactive group at follow-up is not mentioned.

In summary, the studies reviewed above paint the following picture of the hyperactive child in adolescence: Hyperactivity per se seems to diminish with age, but the children are still more restless, excitable, impulsive and distractible than their peers. Attentional and concentration difficulties remain major problems. Chronic, severe underachievement in almost all academic areas is a characteristic finding. Low self-esteem, poor self-image, depression and a sense of failure are common. Antisocial behavior occurs in up to one-quarter and a significant number have had police contact and court referral.

The clinical picture of the hyperactive child as an adult remains unclear as there are no anterospective studies following hyperactive children into adulthood. There are isolated reports of young adults still requiring stimulant medication (Arnold et al, 1972; Oettinger, 1972). The Menkes (Menkes et al., 1967) study suggests that in some cases the syndrome may be a precursor to psychosis and other types of psychopathology in adulthood. Two family studies also support the notion that the hyperactive child syndrome is a precursor to the development of psychopathology in adulthood. Cantwell (1972) carried out a systematic psychiatric examination of the parents of fifty hyperactive and fifty matched normal control children. Eight of the fathers of hyperactive children were thought to have been hyperactive as children themselves. Six of these were given a diagnosis of alcoholism when they were seen as adults, one was given a diagnosis of sociopathy, and the eighth had an undiagnosed psychiatric illness with heavy drinking as one of the symptoms. One father in the control group who was thought to have been hyperactive as a child was also given a diagnosis of alcoholism when seen as an adult. Two of the mothers of the hyperactive children were considered to have been hyperactive as children and they were diagnosed as hysterics as adults.

In a similar study Morrison (Morrison and Stewart, 1971) systematically evaluated the parents of fifty-nine hyperactive and forty-one normal control children. They found that twelve parents of hyperactive children (nine fathers and three mothers) were felt to have been hyperactive as children. Of these nine fathers, five were diagnosed as alcoholic as adults, one was a sociopath, one had multiple depressive phobic and compulsive symptoms, and two were heavy drinkers who did not meet the diagnostic criteria for alcoholism. Of the three previously hyperactive mothers, one had a depressive illness as an adult and one qualified for both a diagnosis of alcoholism and a diagnosis of hysteria. One father and one mother of the normal control children were were thought to have been hyperactive as children. As adults the father was an epileptic with psychosis who had a drinking problem and the mother had bipolar affective disorder.

These data strongly suggest not only that is the hyperactive child syndrome a precursor to significant psychiatric and social pathology in adulthood but that alcoholism, sociopathy and hysteria are the likely psychiatric outcomes in adulthood. This suggestion is supported by the findings of the follow-up studies of hyperactive children that antisocial behavior (including drinking problems) is prevalent by adolescence. Moreover, retrospective studies of adults with antisocial behavior indicate that a significant percentage were hyperactive, aggressive and impulsive as children (Quitkin and Klein, 1969; Shelley, 1970). Data from the Cambridge-Sommerville youth study (McCord and McCord, 1960) and the Oakland growth study (Jones et al., 1960) indicate that alcoholic adults also were described as restless, aggressive and impulsive as children. While none of these studies is conclusive, they are strongly suggestive that the adult outcome of hyperactive children is likely to be as poor as one might predict from their fairly well established poor outcome in adolescence.

TREATMENT EFFECTS
The follow-up studies summarized above also provide some information on the effect of various treatment modalities on the long-term outcome of hyperactive children.

In the Menkes study (Menkes et al., 1967) four patients were seen on one occasion and three on only two occasions. The remainder were seen in the clinic for periods ranging from two to seven years. Apparently no child or family received intensive therapy of any type and no child received drug therapy. No correlation was found between the outcome and the amount of treatment the patient had received.

Sixty-six of the children in the Montreal population (Weiss et al., 1971; Minde et al., 1971; Minde et al., 1972) had received chlorpromazine up to 200 mg. daily, while thirty-eight had taken dextroamphetamine up to 20 mg. daily following their initial evaluation. Thirty-two had taken medication less than six months, thirty-seven remained on medication between one and three years, and twenty-two had taken it for three years or more. Only twelve were still taking any medication at the time of follow-up. Forty-six had discontinued medication because it was ineffective or because of side effects, and only fourteen because sufficient improvement had occurred. There was no significant correlation between psychological adjustment and length of time the patients had been maintained on medication. In fact there was a trend for those on medication the longest period of time to be more *poorly* adjusted at follow-up.

Fifty-four percent of the group had received some type of psychological treatment or counseling. Twenty children received less than ten hours, sixteen children between ten and twenty hours, and twelve children over twenty-five hours of individual or family therapy over the five-year period. The more aggressive, distractible children tended to receive more hours of psychotherapy and the treated children scored higher initially on the Neuroticism scale of the Peterson-Quay than did the untreated group. Although this initial high Neuroticism score dropped to a level comparable to the control group at follow-up, the other scale scores did not, and psychotherapeutic intervention did not differentiate the "good" and "poor" outcome groups at follow-up.

Over two-thirds of the children initially thought to have moderate to severe learning problems had received some form of remedial educational help. None of the children so treated showed improvement on any psychological test.

At the time of follow-up in the St. Louis study (Mendelson et al., 1971), 40 percent were still in treatment at the Children's Hospital and another 14 percent were in treatment elsewhere. Ninety-two percent had received stimulant medication coupled with supportive psychotherapy for the children and counseling for the parents in some cases. Sixty percent of the children were reported as improved for at least six months while on stimulants, 12 percent had deteriorated, and the outcome was equivocal in 28 percent. No attempt was made to assess the effect of the other treatment modalities on outcome.

Since the Rhode Island study (Laufer, 1971) was of a private-practice population, all patients by definition had received some form of treatment. All had been on either amphetamines or methylphenidate, with twenty-four taking medications less than six months and thirty-one from six months to five years. No other treatment is mentioned as being provided by the authors, although 35 percent reported receiving subsequent psychiatric help as noted above. None of the ten patients still taking any medication at follow-up was taking stimulants. No attempt was made to relate types of outcome to treatment.

All patients in the Arkansas study (Dykman et al., 1973) had received some form of remedial education in varying degrees in a variety of programs. Follow-up results indicated that this probably did help the patients but not enough to bring them up to the level of academic performance of the controls. This is in line with the results of a more controlled study by Conrad (Conrad et al., 1971) who randomly assigned sixty-eight hyperactive children matched for intelligence and degree of hyperactivity to one of four experimental groups: placebo/no tutoring; placebo/tutoring; dextroamphetamine/no tutoring; and dextroamphetamine/tutoring. Tutoring alone produced little benefit while those who received both tutoring and dextroamphetamine showed improvement in behavior and on a number of psychological tests. However, the dextroamphetamine-only group showed the most improvement. Most disappointing was the fact that only three of sixty-eight children made enough progress in a year's time to no longer need remedial help.

In summary, none of these studies has clearly demonstrated that treatment of any type significantly alters the prognosis of hyperactive children. However, the data are sparse, and none of the studies can be considered to involve children who were intensively and consistently treated over the course of the follow-up period.

PROGNOSTIC INDICATORS

Information regarding indicators of prognosis is limited and contradictory. Menkes (Menkes et al., 1967) found that initial IQ, definite evidence of brain dysfunction, and "favorable" or "unfavorable" home environment were not predictors of any type of outcome. However, both Mendelson (Mendelson et al., 1971) and the Montreal group (Weiss et al., 1971; Minde et al., 1971; Minde et al., 1972) found certain familial variables to be associated with an antisocial outcome. Those children with the most antisocial behavior at follow-up in the Mendelson study were more likely to have fathers who had learning or behavior problems as children and who had been arrested as adults. Weiss found that the families of the ultimately antisocial children had been rated as significantly more pathological at initial evaluation. Three specific items on the rating scale—poor mother-child relationship, poor mental health of the parents, and punitive child-rearing practices—distinguished the families of the ultimately antisocial children from the rest of the group. Weiss also found that the 20 percent who were succeeding at school on follow-up had higher initial full-scale IQ's. This was confirmed by Minde in a more detailed look at academic outcome of a small subsample of these children. Those least academically successful differed from those who were most academically successful in having lower WISC full-scale IQ scores and a greater verbal-performance discrepancy on the WISC, as well as evidence of verbal difficulties and visual-spatial problems. Dykman found those with less evidence of neurological abnormality to be less retarded academically at follow-up. The only significant predictors of "good" or "poor" outcome in the Minde (Minde et al., 1972) study were initial aggression scores and initial scores on the Psychopathic Scale of the Peterson-Quay check list. However, the "poor" outcome group did tend to have initially higher scores on most target symptoms as well as evidence of low initial IQ, a positive history of neurological abnormalities, lower socioeconomic status and more unfavorable ratings of their family environment. There were twenty children who could be said to have deteriorated over the period of follow-up. No clear-cut predictive characteristics of these children were found. However, it is worth noting that there were three children in the "poor" group at follow-up who at initial evaluation were considered well-adjusted. All three of these had definite schizoid tendencies.

SUMMARY
(1) Prospective and retrospective follow-up studies of hyperactive children indicate that they are prone to develop significant psychiatric and social problems in adolescence and later life.
(2) Antisocial behavior, serious academic retardation, poor self-image and depression seem to be the most common outcomes in adolescence.
(3) Alcoholism, sociopathy, hysteria and possible psychosis seem to be likely psychiatric outcomes in adulthood.

(4) Evidence for indicators of prognosis is limited and contradictory. (5) It has not been clearly demonstrated that treatment of any type significantly affects the long-term outcome of the hyperactive child.

REFERENCES

Anderson, C., and Playmate, H. (1962). Management of the brain damaged adolescent. *American Journal of Orthopsychiatry* 32:492–500.
Arnold, L., Strobl, D., and Weisenberg, A. (1972). Hyperkinetic adult: study of the "paradoxical" amphetamine response. *Journal of American Medical Association* 222:693–94.
Bakwin, H., and Bakwin, R. (1966). *Clinical management of behavior disorders in children.* Philadelphia: W. B. Saunders Co.
Cantwell, D. (1972). Psychiatric illness in the families of hyperactive children. *Archives of General Psychiatry* 27:414–17.
_____ and Satterfield, J. (in press). Psychopharmacology in the prevention of antisocial and delinquent behavior. *International Journal of Mental Health.*
Conrad, W., Dorkin, E., Shai, A., and Tobiessen, J. (1971). Effects of amphetamine therapy and prescriptive tutoring on the behavior and achievement of lower class hyperactive children. *Journal of Learning Disabilities* 4:45–53.
Denhoff, E. (1973). The natural life history of children with minimal dysfunction. *The Annals of the New York Academy of Sciences.* 205:188–206.
Dykman, R., Peters, J., and Ackerman, P. (1973). Experimental approaches to the study of minimal brain dysfunction: a follow-up study. *Annals of the New York Academy of Sciences* 205:93–108.
Eisenberg, L. (1966). The hyperkinetic child and stimulant drugs. *Developmental Medicine and Child Neurology* 8:593–98.
Jones, H., MacFarlane, J., and Eichorn, D. (1960). A progress report on growth studies at the University of California. *Vita Humana* 3:17–31.
Laufer, M. (1971). Long-term management of some follow-up findings on the use of drugs with minimal brain dysfunction. *Pediatrics* 39:55–58.
_____ and Denhoff, E. (1957). Hyperkinetic behavior syndrome in children. *Journal of Pediatrics* 50:463–74.
McCord, W., and McCord, J. (1960). *Origins of Alcoholism.* Stanford, Calif: Stanford University Press.
Mendelson, W., Johnson, J., and Stewart, M. (1971). Hyperactive children as teenagers: a follow-up study. *Journal of Nervous Mental Disorders* 153:273–79.
Menkes, M., Rowe, J., and Menkes, J. (1967). A twenty-five year follow-up study on the hyperkinetic child with minimal brain dysfunction. *Pediatrics* 39:392–99.
Minde, K., Lewin, D., Weiss, G., Lavigueur, H., Douglas, V., and Sykes, E. (1971). The hyperactive child in elementary school: a five-year, controlled follow-up. *Exceptional Child* 38:215–21.

_____, Weiss, G., and Mendelson, M. (1972). A five-year follow-up study of 91 hyperactive school children. *Journal of the American Academy of Child Psychiatry* 11: 595–610.

Morrison, J., and Stewart, M. (1971). A family study of the hyperactive child syndrome. *Biological Psychiatry* 3:189–95.

Oettinger, L. (1972). Proceedings of the workshop on evaluating long-term effects of stimulant drug treatment. Chevy Chase, Md.: Psychopharmacology Research Branch, National Institute of Mental Health, June 26, pp. 150–176.

Quitkin, F., and Klein, D. (1969). Two behavioral syndromes in young adults related to possible minimal brain dysfunction. *Journal of Psychiatric Research* 7:131–42.

Rutter, M. (1968). Lésion cérébrale organique, hyperkinesis at retard mental. *Psychiat Enfant* 11:475.

Shelley, E. (1970). *Syndrome of Minimal Brain Damage in Young Adults.* Read before Annual Meeting of American Psychiatric Association, San Francisco.

Weiss, G., Minde, K., Werry, J., Douglas, V., and Nemeth, E. (1971). Studies on the hyperactive child. VIII. Five-year follow-up. *Archives of General Psychiatry* 24:409–14.

PART II

The Hyperactive Child Syndrome: Research Aspects

Chapter Four

Neurophysiologic Studies with Hyperactive Children

JAMES H. SATTERFIELD, M.D.

It is fairly well recognized that hyperactive children differ from both normal and neurotic control children on behavioral measures at home and at school. Several studies have also found that hyperactive children differ from non-hyperactive children on measures which are indicators of central nervous system function.

Many studies have reported an increased incidence of EEG abnormalities in hyperactive children (Capute et al., 1968; Hughes, 1971; Klinkerfuss et al., 1965; Wikler et al., 1970; Wender, 1971). However, whether or not hyperactive children truly have an increased incidence of an abnormal EEG is not well-established because of the fact that there are so few investigations of the incidence of EEG abnormalities in blindly rated control groups. Two well-designed studies which utilized blindly rated control groups were conducted by Capute and by Hughes. Capute studied a group of children with minimal brain dysfunction, all of whom had soft neurologic signs, which made this sample a special one since only about half of nonselected MBD children have such signs. They reported that 43 percent of 106 children had mild to moderate EEG abnormalities, compared to 17 percent of mild to moderate EEG abnormalities in a normal control group. Hughes compared 214 children who were underachievers with a like number of normal controls. The incidence of EEG abnormalities in the underachiever group was 41.2 percent, significantly higher than in the control group, which had an incidence of only 29.8 percent (p < 0.007). However, in a study of twenty hyperactive children, twenty neurotic children and twenty normal children it was found that there were no group differences in the incidence of EEG abnormalities (Werry et al., 1972).

Two independent investigators have reported that evoked cortical response measures are significantly different in hyperactive children when compared with normal children. Satterfield et al. (1973) studied auditory evoked cortical responses in thirty-one hyperactive children and in twenty-one sex-age-matched normal control children. They found that hyperactive children have longer latencies and smaller amplitudes of the auditory evoked response. Buchsbaum et al. (1973) studied visual evoked response measures in twenty-four hyperactive children and in twenty-four sex-age-matched normal controls. They reported that hyperactive children had larger amplitude visual evoked responses.

Several investigators have studied autonomic function in hyperactive children. Yoss (1970) has found that 20 to 25 percent of hyperactive children have a narcoleptic-like pupillograph record. Dykman et al. (1971) found lowered autonomic responsivity to stimulation and no difference in resting skin resistance. Cohen and Douglas (1972) found lower specific electrodermal responsivity in hyperactive children but no difference in skin conductance levels between normals and hyperactive children. Satterfield and Dawson (1971) reported lower skin conductance levels and lower nonspecific electrodermal activity in hyperkinetic than in normal children. Satterfield et al. (1974), in a different study, reported higher skin conductance levels in hyperactive children. The two studies are difficult to compare since the experimental parameters differed in many respects. The authors suggest that opposite results found may be due to a greater reactivity to a more stimulating test environment in the second study (Satterfield et al., 1974).

Although several of the above studies have reported abnormalities in CNS function in hyperactive children, the amount of agreement across studies is discouragingly small. This is probably due in part to the heterogeneity within the groups as well as between the groups studied and to the differences in the experimental methodology among laboratories.

This report presents findings from four studies from the same laboratory in which the groups were more homogeneous and in which the experimental methodology was identical in three of the four studies. Between-group heterogeneity has been reduced due to a common set of selection criteria for subjects in the four studies and to the fact that the hyperactive group was further subdivided into two more homogeneous subgroups (good and poor responders). Findings that suggest that one subgroup of hyperactive children (those who respond best to stimulant medication) have low central nervous system arousal before treatment are presented (Satterfield and Dawson, 1971; Satterfield et al., 1974; Satterfield, 1973).

METHODS

The details of the specific methodology of all four studies have been previously reported and will not be repeated here. However, in general, all of these studies had in common the following methodology:

All patients were referred to the Gateways Hospital Hyperkinetic Children's Clinic for evaluation and treatment. To be included in these studies, a child had to be (1) male, (2) between the ages of six and nine years, (3) currently attending school, (4) tested normal vision and hearing, (5) at or above 80 in IQ on the Wechsler Intelligence Scale for Children (WISC full-scale), (6) medication-free for a period of at least three months prior to testing, (7) diagnosed independently by two child psychiatrists as a hyperactive child by behavioral criteria which required evidence of a chronic symptom pattern of hyperactivity, distractibility, excitability and impulsivity as reported by parents and teachers. Since all subjects were children, informed consent was obtained from the child's parents after the procedure had been fully explained. A structured interview with the child's parents covering the child's behavior and development and a psychological test battery, including the WISC intelligence test, were conducted for all subjects.

Treatment was carried out for a three-week period. The dosage of methylphenidate was adjusted upward at weekly intervals until a good clinical response was obtained or until side effects prohibited further increase. Teacher rating scales were obtained before and immediately after three weeks' treatment. The rating scale for teachers consisted of thirty items of classroom behavior arranged in a checklist form so that the teacher could check off whether each individual item of behavior was exhibited by the child (a)not at all; (b)just a little; (c)pretty much; (d)very much. These individual ratings were given numerical scores of 0, 1, 2 and 3, respectively, and then summed to give a total rating score on all behavioral items. Thus, higher scores on the teacher rating scale reflect more disturbed behavior. These scales have been shown to have high test-retest reliability, and to validly differentiate placebo from methylphenidate treatment groups (Satterfield et al., 1972).

Laboratory studies included power spectral analyses of the EEG, auditory evoked cortical responses and skin conductance level measures.

RESULTS

Some investigators have suggested that a high skin conductance level (SCL) indicates a high level of central nervous system arousal (Duffy, 1962). Since one characteristic of hyperactive children is a high level of behavioral excitation, it might be hypothesized that they would also have high levels of internal arousal as indicated by high skin conductance levels. This hypothesis was tested by a comparison of resting skin conductance levels in a group of twenty-four hyperactive children and in a group of twelve normal control children. Contrary to the hypothesis, twelve (50 percent) of the hyperactive children had abnormally *low* CNS arousal levels as indicated by low skin conductance levels, while only two (8 percent) had abnormally high arousal levels (Satterfield and Dawson, 1971). It was also found that stimulant medication raised these low CNS arousal levels as indicated by increased SCL. That is, the action of stimulant medication in these hyperactive children is to stimulate the CNS; it is not the often described "paradoxical" action inferred from its calming effect on behavior.

In a second study, in addition to skin conductance level, two other indices of CNS arousal level were measured: (a) the resting EEG and (b) the sensory evoked cortical response (Satterfield et al., 1972). All patients were treated with methylphenidate, as described above, and changes in teacher rating scales obtained before and after three weeks' treatment were used as a measure of improvement, also as described above. From the total group of fourteen hyperactive children, those children with 70 percent or more improvement (six best responders) were compared with those children who obtained 30

TABLE I
Comparison of Pre-Treatment CNS Arousal Measures

Laboratory Measure	Best Responders (N = 6)	Worst Responders (N = 5)
Mean skin conductance level		
(umho)	16.7	24.4
EEG background		
Mean amplitude (μv)	16.4*	13.2
Mean power (0–8 hertz)	255**	216
EEG movement artifacts	304*	163
Auditory evoked response		
Mean peak-to-peak amplitude		
(P_2–N_2) at slow rate (μv)	19.9*	10.9
Percent recovery		
P_1–N_1	27*	92
N_1–P_2	16*	108

Significance level
*$p < .05$ (Mann-Whitney U Test)
**$p < .01$ (Mann-Whitney U Test)

percent or less improvement (five worst responders). When compared before treatment, however, we found that those hyperactive children who obtained the best clinical response had lower CNS arousal levels, as indicated by lower skin conductance levels, higher mean EEG amplitudes, more energy in the low frequency band of the resting EEG, and larger evoked cortical response amplitudes, than did the poor responders. (See Table I.) These laboratory findings are all consistent with the hypothesis of low pre-treatment CNS arousal levels in those hyperactive children who later obtained the best response to methylphenidate. Furthermore, following methylphenidate treatment, the good responders showed a significant increase in CNS arousal, as indicated by changes in the above described electrophysiological measures. These results confirmed the finding of the previous study that there is a subgroup of hyperactive children with low CNS arousal and that methylphenidate acts like a CNS stimulant in this low arousal subgroup. Moreover, the low arousal subgroup of hyperactive children in this second study was also characterized by more movement artifacts in the laboratory and more disturbed behavior in the classroom. Both of these improved with medication. Thus methylphenidate was found to produce both a greater change in CNS arousal and greater behavioral improvement in these low aroused hyperactive children.

The third study was an investigation of the relationship between skin conductance levels and certain items of maladaptive behavior described by classroom teachers in eighteen hyperactive children (Satterfield et al., 1974). The previously described teacher rating scale was used by teachers to rate each child on thirty items of classroom behavior. It was found that the hyperactive children with the lowest arousal levels (lowest SCL) had the most overall classroom behavioral disturbance (correlation $r = .49$, $p < .05$). They also obtained the best clinical response to methylphenidate (correlation $r = -.44$, $p < .05$). Moreover, there was a significant negative correlation between SCL and individual items of maladaptive behavior. That is, those children who had the lowest SCL were rated by teachers as demonstrating more disturbance on items which reflect motor control (restlessness), distractibility (easily distracted), attention (does not follow directions) and impulsivity (talks a lot, irritable). (See Table II.)

In the fourth study, we utilized the presence of excessive slow wave activity in the clinical EEG as an indicator of low CNS arousal. The most common type of clinical EEG abnormality in hyperactive children, both in our population and as reported by others, is excessive EEG slowing (Satterfield et al., 1973). In the second study reported above, excessive slow wave activity, as measured by power spectral analysis of the EEG, was used as an indicator of low CNS arousal and was found to be associated with a good clinical response to methylphenidate (Satterfield et al., 1972). In the fourth study, the relationship between clinical EEG and response to methylphenidate

TABLE II

Point Biseral Correlation Values Between
Skin Conductance Level and Degree of Behavioral Disturbance

Behavioral Attribute	Correlation
Restless	$-.53^*$
Easily distracted	$-.50^*$
Does not follow directions	$-.58^{**}$
Talks a lot	$-.61^{**}$
Irritable	$-.48^*$

* $p < .05$ T Test
** $p < .01$

treatment was investigated in fifty-seven hyperactive children (Satterfield et al., 1973). The clinical EEG's were interpreted without knowledge of either the power spectral analysis or the response to treatment data. The fifty-seven hyperactive children were divided into three groups according to their clinical EEG findings: (a)normal, (b)borderline and (c)abnormal. Response to treatment was measured by the change in the teacher rating scales for each child. The abnormal EEG group had significantly more improvement than did the borderline group (p < .01) and also greater improvement than did the normal EEG group (p < .001).

The findings of the four studies reported here are summarized in Table III. The first study identified a subgroup of hyperactive chil-

TABLE III

Study	Number of Subjects	Characteristics of Good Responder Hyperactive Children
1	24	Low skin conductance level
2	14	Low skin conductance level Resting EEG *High amplitude **High low frequency energy Auditory evoked cortical response *Larger amplitude *Slow recovery Response to methylphenidate *Decrease in low frequency energy **Decrease in evoked response amplitude Behavioral measures High level of disturbed classroom behavior
3	18	+ Low skin conductance level + + High level of disturbed classroom behavior
4	57	**Clinical EEG abnormality (excessive slowing)

*Significant at p < .05 Mann-Whitney U Test
**Significant at p < .01 Mann-Whitney U Test
+ Significant at p < .05 Spearman Rank Order Correlation
+ + Significant at p < .01 Spearman Rank Order Correlation

dren who had low CNS arousal levels as measured by SCL. In this study it was also found that methylphenidate raised CNS arousal levels in these hyperactive children. In the second study, both of these findings were replicated utilizing two additional indicators of CNS arousal: evoked cortical response and resting EEG. The third study showed that low CNS arousal level was associated with a greater degree of behavioral disturbance in the classroom as well as with a positive clinical response to methylphenidate. In the fourth study it was found that those hyperactive children with excessive EEG slowing obtained the best response to treatment. Thus eight laboratory measures were found which were associated with a positive response to methylphenidate, and all are consistent with the hypothesis of low CNS arousal in "good responder" hyperactive children. None of the measures in any of the four studies produced results inconsistent with this hypothesis.

COMMENT

Following are the principal findings from the four studies reported above. (1)There is an identifiable subgroup of "good responder" hyperactive children who are found to have low CNS arousal. (2)The pre-treatment CNS arousal level is negatively correlated with the severity of the child's behavioral disturbance; in other words, the lower the child's CNS arousal level, the greater his problem with motor control, attention span and impulsivity. (3)Stimulant medication in these low arousal hyperactive children functions like a stimulant—it increases the CNS arousal level. (4)Those hyperactive children with greatest increases in CNS arousal level resulting from stimulant medication obtained the best clinical response as measured by teacher rating scales.

Additional support for the view that hyperactive children may have lower arousal levels comes from studies which have reported that children with poor concentration in school are characterized by lower task-relevant autonomic arousal (Dureman and Palshammer, 1968a, 1968b) and from autonomic studies which show an inverse relationship between motor impulsivity and autonomic responsivity (arousal level) in children (Jones, 1950). Knopp et al. (1972), utilizing electronic pupillography as an index of CNS arousal, reported that hyperactive children with low CNS arousal were found to be good responders to stimulant medication.

Assuming that there is a subgroup of "good responder" hyperactive children who have low CNS arousal, how does this low arousal explain the clinical picture of a behaviorally highly excited child before treatment? How does a low arousal theory explain improvement in motor and sensory functions following stimulant drug treatment?

It is our hypothesis that associated with the low CNS arousal levels in hyperactive children there is insufficient CNS inhibition and that CNS arousal and inhibition vary together. This neurophysiological model may be used to explain part of the symptom picture presented by the low aroused hyperactive child.

Insufficient inhibitory control over motor functions could be expected to result in the commonly observed excessive and inappropriate motor activity exhibited by these children. Consistent with this theory is our finding that the lower the arousal level, the greater was the restlessness as reported by schoolteachers (Satterfield et al., 1974). Also, the low arousal, good responder hyperactive children had excessive movement-generated EEG artifacts in the laboratory whereas the high arousal, poor responder group had even fewer movements than the normal control group (Satterfield et al., 1972).

Lack of inhibitory control over sensory function could be expected to result in easy distractibility, with the low aroused child responding to irrelevant stimuli as readily as to relevant stimuli. Consistent with this theory is our finding that the lower the arousal level, the greater were the child's difficulties with distractibility and problems of attention in the classroom (Satterfield et al., 1974).

To explain the change in the clinical picture of the hyperactive child in response to stimulant medication, we hypothesize that stimulant medication, which we found to increase CNS arousal (as measured by SCL, EEG and evoked potential changes), also raises inhibitory levels in hyperactive children. Increased inhibitory control over motor functions should enable the hyperactive child to reduce his non-goal-directed and inappropriate motor behavior which interferes with learning in the classroom. Consistent with this hypothesis are studies which report that stimulant drugs not only decrease the absolute amount of motoric activity but also increase the amount of motoric activity devoted to goal-directed behavior (Lytton and Knobel, 1958). Several clinical studies have reported that stimulant medication results in better integrated or more controlled performance and not simply an alteration of activity level (Knobel, 1959; Knobel et al.,

1959; Knobel, 1962). Increased control over motor response is also suggested by studies of continuous performance tests which demonstrate that stimulant drugs result in slower responding when it is more appropriate to do so in terms of the demands of the particular task (Conners and Rothschild, 1968). That stimulant drugs act to improve fine motor coordination as measured by the Lincoln Oseretsky scale is also consistent with the concept of improved control over motoric activity.

Increased arousal and the associated increased inhibitory control over sensory function should enable the child to inhibit nonmeaningful stimuli in order to selectively attend in a learning situation. A number of clinical studies using behavior rating scales have shown that stimulant medication does produce a significant positive effect on attention with an associated decrease in distractibility (Conners, 1972). Also consistent with the view of improved attention span are a number of studies which have shown that stimulants act to improve intellectual performance as measured by psychological tests. Conners (1971) has suggested that such improvement is due to enhanced attention to the task and/or increased arousal or motivation. The most consistent effects of amphetamine on human performance are the enhancement of vigilance, particularly when performance has been degraded by fatigue or boredom (Weiss and Laties, 1962). A study of hyperactive children found that stimulant medication resulted in improvement in a factor thought to reflect assertiveness and drive (Conners et al., 1967). In agreement with this finding of increased drive and assertiveness are studies which report an increased pupil-initiated positive pupil-teacher interaction in the classroom and an increase in verbalization following stimulant medication (Sprague et al., 1970; Creager and Van Riper, 1967). Thus stimulants appear to produce a more vigorous and determined performance in children, which would, in part, account for improvement in intellectual performance.

Several other lines of evidence lend support to our proposed neurophysiological model: (1)animal neurophysiological studies which suggest a relationship between reticular arousal level and the amount of corticofugal inhibitory influence on incoming sensory signals at synapses in sensory pathways, (2)those animal and human studies suggesting an association between reticular arousal level and level of cortical inhibition, (3)several animal neurophysiological studies suggesting that stimulant medication may produce increased inhibition of sensory signals by means of increased reticular inhibitory activity, and (4)neurophysiological studies in hyperactive children which have found low CNS inhibitory levels that are increased by administration of stimulant medication.

In studies which suggest a relationship between reticular arousal level and amount of corticofugal inhibitory influence of sensory signals, it has been found that stimulation of the ascending reticular activating system increases cortical arousal levels in wide areas of cerebral cortex (Moruzzi and Magoun, 1949). Further, stimulation of certain of these cortical areas has been found to result in inhibition of sensory signals at synapses in sensory pathways (Livingston, 1959; Satterfield, 1962). Therefore, increased reticular arousal produces increased cortical arousal which, via descending neural pathways, could be hypothesized to increase inhibition of incoming sensory signals at synapses in direct sensory pathways.

Several investigators of animal neurophysiology have postulated that reticular arousal and cortical inhibition vary together. It has been found that, as compared to the sleeping state, during waking there is a significant increase in cortical inhibition (as measured by cortical excitability cycle) (Evarts et al., 1960). Walley and Weiden (1973) have presented results from animal and human research which suggest that CNS arousal and cortical inhibition vary together. They have proposed that an increase in arousal enhances the focusing of attention by facilitating cortical recurrent inhibition during arousal. Some clinical evidence in humans also suggests that CNS arousal and CNS inhibition may vary together either due to normal changes in the physiological state or in response to medication. It is known that as a normal adult drifts into a light sleep, accompanied by a lowering of the CNS arousal level, his legs and arms may twitch and jerk, secondary to a concurrent lowering of cortical inhibitory control. Dextroamphetamine, which is well-established as a CNS stimulant —that is, as a drug which raises arousal level—may also, at the same time, increase cortical inhibition and has, in fact, been used as an adjunct therapy to reduce seizure activity in patients with epilepsy (Livingston and Pruce, 1972).

Animal neurophysiologists have found that the reticular formation functions both as an arousal center and as an inhibitory center. Stimulation effects at the reticular formation both increase cortical arousal and enhance the inhibition of sensory signals at synapses in the sensory pathways (Moruzzi and Magoun, 1949; Hernandez-Peon, 1961). An important site of action of stimulant drugs is the brain stem reticular formation (Killam, 1962). Thus stimulant drug effects could be expected to result in an increase in arousal (reticular and cortical) and an increased inhibition of sensory signals in sensory neuronal pathways.

Neurophysiological studies of hyperactive children have reported that they have low CNS inhibitory levels and that the action of stimulant medication is to raise these low inhibitory levels. Laufer et al. (1957) reported the most direct evidence for a low level of CNS inhibition in hyperactive children. They found that the photometrazol threshold was significantly lower in hyperactive children than in age-matched controls. These findings were interpreted as indicating a dysfunction of the reticular activating system, resulting in insufficient shielding of the cortex from irrelevant stimuli. Several investigators have found evidence that stimulant drugs increase CNS inhibition in hyperactive children. Laufer et al. (1957) have reported an increased photometrazol threshold in hyperactive children, and Shetty (1971) has reported an increased amount of alpha rhythms following dextroamphetamine administration. Conners and Rothschild (1973) have reported an increased habituation of peripheral responsivity following administration of stimulant medication.

The essence of the above proposed neurophysiological theory is one of low arousal and insufficient inhibitory controls over motor outflow and sensory input. This lack of inner control results in flooding of the brain by sensory signals arising from within or without, any of which may trigger a motor response. In such a state the child's behavior is controlled by stimuli, relevant and irrelevant, over which he has no control. He is not free to choose to conform or rebel, to learn or not to learn, but is instead driven from within and from without by stimuli which would be ignored (inhibited) by the normal child. From this perspective it is easy to understand why adults commonly fail to modify the hyperactive child's disruptive behavior and why psychotherapy and prescriptive tutoring have been found to be less beneficial than stimulant medication (Conrad et al., 1971; Eisenberg et al., 1965). Stimulant medication does not, as has been suggested, reduce the disturbing impulses. Rather, it restores the CNS to a more normal state in which the child can be in control of his sensory input and motor responses. The child can then begin to exercise control over himself and can begin to experience the world in a more normal manner.

The neurophysiological model presented here does not attempt to minimize the importance of environmental influences upon the hyperactive child's behavior. It does suggest that until the child's inner control systems are established other treatment modalities may not produce desired changes.

Stimulant medication alone is often insufficient. This is especially true in older hyperactive children who have experienced their own inability to cope with social expectations that they conform and learn. Without the controls necessary to do either, such children often develop secondary emotional and behavioral problems.

Children who repeatedly fail at tasks which they observe their peers accomplishing learn both at home and at school that they are "dummies" and "bad." They feel powerless, stupid and failures in the inevitable competitions of childhood. Peers reject them; teachers discipline them; parents punish them. The experience of impotence at self-control, the lack of mastery in normal tasks and the bewilderment of not being able to follow directions and of always "being wrong" lead such children to chronic depression based on poor self-image. Isolation, suspiciousness and failure to participate in the normal developmental tasks of latency, including cognitive functioning, result. These children are not motivated to try, because failure is so painful. Antisocial behaviors such as fighting, stealing and lying are easier. Such behaviors offer these children immediate, if erroneous, boosts to self-esteem and the sense of personal power. For such children psychotherapy and/or family therapy and counseling are critical to restoring self-confidence, improving self-image and alleviating the depression.

Many hyperactive children, when first seen, are two or more grade levels behind in at least one subject in school (Minde et al., 1971). Such children require remedial education to correct this type of deficit. Medication will not teach a child anything. Normalization of CNS function by use of medication in hyperactive children with longstanding behavioral and/or learning problems may be viewed as a necessary but insufficient procedure for achieving the desired improvement in behavioral and cognitive functioning.

Too often clinicians view treatment as an "either/or" decision process and recommend either medication or psychological treatment but not both. It is our opinion that the two forms of treatment facilitate one another and should be used together to obtain maximal benefit for many children.

REFERENCES

Buchsbaum, M., and Wender, P. (1973). Average evoked responses in normal and minimally brain dysfunctioned children treated with amphetamine. *Arch. Gen. Psychiatry* 29:764.

Capute, A. J., Niedermeyer, E. F. L., and Richardson, F. (1968). The electroencephalogram in children with minimal cerebral dysfunction. *Pediatrics* 41:1104.

Cohen, N. J., and Douglas, V. I. (1972). Characteristics of the orienting response in hyperactive and normal children. *Psychophysiology* 9:238–45.

Conners, C. K. (1971). Recent drug studies with hyperkinetic children. *Journal of Learning Disabilities* 4, 9:478–83.

_____ (1972). Pharmacotherapy of psychopathology in children. In H. C. Quay and J.S. Werry, eds., *Psychopathological Disorders of Childhood.* New York: John Wiley & Sons, pp. 319–24.

_____ and Rothschild, G. H. (1968). Drugs and learning in children. In *Learning Disorders,* Vol. III. Seattle, Washington: Special Child Publications, pp. 191–224.

_____ and Rothschild, G. H. (1973). The effect of dextroamphetamine on habituation of peripheral vascular response in children. *Journal of Abnormal Child Psychology* 1:16–25.

_____, Eisenberg, L., and Barcai, A. (1967). Effect of dextroamphetamine in children. *Arch. Gen. Psychiatry* 17:478–85.

Conrad, W. G., Dworken, E. S., Shai, A., Tobiessen, J. E. (1971). Effects of amphetamine therapy and prescriptive tutoring on the behavior and achievement of lower class hyperactive children. *Journal of Learning Disabilities* 4:45–53.

Creager, R. O., and Van Riper, C. (1967). The effect of methylphenidate on the verbal productivity of children with cerebral dysfunction. *J. Speech Hear. Res.* 10:623–28.

Duffy, E. (1962). *Activation and Behavior.* New York: John Wiley & Sons.

Dureman, I., and Palshammer, S. (1968a). Psychophysiological reactions in a serial approach-avoidance conflict situation: its relation to test anxiety and school motivation in children. Department of Psychology, University of Uppsala, Sweden (April).

_____ (1968b). The dynamics of psychophysiological activation in children performing under reward conditions involving an approach-avoidance conflict. Department of Psychology, University of Uppsala, Sweden (May).

Dykman, R. A., Ackerman, P. T., Clements, S. D., Peters, J. E. (1971). Specific learning disabilities: an attentional deficit syndrome. In H. R. Myklebust, ed., *Progress in Learning Disabilities,* Vol II. New York: Grune & Stratton.

Eisenberg, L., Conners, C. K., Sharpe, L. (1965). A controlled study of the differential application of outpatient psychiatric treatment for children. *Japanese Journal of Child Psychiatry* 4, 3:125–32.

Evarts, E.V., Fleming, T. C., Huttenlocher, P. R. (1960). Recovery cycle of visual cortex of the awake and sleeping cat. *Am. J. Physiol.* 199:373–76.

Hernandez-Peon, R. (1961). Reticular mechanisms of sensory control. In W. Rosenblith, ed., *Sensory Communication*. New York: MIT, pp. 497–520.

Hughes, J. R. (1971). Electroencephalography and learning disabilities. In H. R. Myklebust, ed., *Progress in Learning Disabilities*, Vol II. New York: Grune & Stratton.

Jones, H. E. (1950). The study of patterns of emotional expression. In M. L. Reymert, ed., *Feelings and Emotions*. New York: McGraw-Hill.

Killam, E. K. (1962). Drug action on the brainstem reticular formation. *Pharmacol. Rev.* 14:175–223.

Klinkerfuss, G. H., Lange, P. H., Weinberg, W. A., and O'Leary, J. L. (1965). Electroencephalographic abnormalities of children with hyperkinetic behavior. *Neurology* 15:-889.

Knobel, M. (1959). Diagnosis and treatment of psychiatric problems in children. *Arch. Gen. Psychiatry* 1:310–21.

———(1962). Psychopharmacology for the hyperkinetic child—dynamic considerations. *Arch. Gen. Psychiatry* 6:198–202.

———Wolmen, M. B., and Mason, E. (1959). Hyperkinesis and organicity in children. *Arch. Gen. Psychiatry* 1:310–21.

Knopp, W., Arnold, L. E., Andras, B. S., and Smeltzer, D. J. (1972). Electronic pupillography: predicting amphetamine response in hyperkinetic children. Presented at the American Psychiatric Association Meeting, Dallas, Texas (May).

Laufer, M. W., Denhoff, E., and Solomons, G. (1957). Hyperkinetic impulse disorder in children's behavior problems. *Psychosom. Med.* 19, 1:38–49.

Livingston, R. B. (1959). Central control of receptors and sensory transmission systems. In J. Field, ed., *Handbook of Physiology*, Section I, Vol. I. Washington, D.C.: American Physiological Society, pp. 741–60.

Livingston, S., assisted by Pruce, I. M. (1972). *Comprehensive Treatment of Epilepsy in Infancy, Childhood and Adolescence*. Springfield, Ill.: C. C. Thomas.

Lytton, G. J., and Knobel, M. (1958). Diagnosis and treatment of behavior disorders in children. *Dis. Nerv. Syst.* 20:1–7.

Minde, K., Lewin, D., Weiss, G., Lavigueur, H., Douglas, V., and Sykes, E. (1971). The hyperactive child in elementary school—a five-year controlled follow-up. *Except. Child* 38:215–21.

Moruzzi, G., and Magoun, H. W. (1949). Brainstem reticular formation and activation of the EEG. *Electroencephalogr. Clin. Neurophysiol.* 1:455–73.

Satterfield, J. H. (1962). Effect of sensorimotor cortical stimulation upon cuneat nuclear output through medial lemniscus in cat. *J. Nerv. Ment. Dis.* 135, 6:507–12.

——— (1973). EEG issues in children with minimal brain dysfunction. *Semin. Psychiatry* 5, 1:35–46.

———, and Dawson, M. E. (1971). Electrodermal correlates of hyperactivity in children. *Psychophysiology* 8:191.

———, Atoian, G., Brashears, G. C., Burleigh, A. C., and Dawson, M. E. (1974).

Electrodermal studies of minimal brain dysfunction children. In *Clinical Use of Stimulant Drugs in Children.* Excerpta Medica, The Hague, 87–97.

_____, Cantwell, D. P., Lesser, L. I., and Podosin, R. L. (1972). Physiological studies of the hyperkinetic child *I. Amer. J. Psychiatry* 128, 11:102–08 (May).

_____,Cantwell, D. P., Saul, R. E., Lesser, L. I., Podosin, R. L. (1973). Response to stimulant drug treatment in hyperactive children: prediction from EEG and neurological findings. *J. Autism. Child Schizo.* 3, 1:36–48.

Shetty, T. (1971). Alpha rhythms in the hyperkinetic child. *Nature* 234:476.

Sprague, R. L., Barnes, K. R., and Werry, J. S. (1970). Methylphenidate and thioridazine: learning, reaction time, activity, and classroom behavior. *Am. J. Orthopsychiatry* 40:615–28.

Walley, R. E., and Weiden, T. D. (1973). Lateral inhibition and cognitive masking: a neuropsychological theory of attention. *Physiol. Rev.* 80, 4:284–302.

Weiss, B, and Laties, V. G. (1962). Enhancement of human performance by caffeine —and the amphetamines. *Pharmacol. Rev.* 14:1–36.

Wender, P. H. (1971). *Minimal Brain Dysfunction in Children.* New York: Wiley & Sons.

Werry, J. S., Minde, K., Gusman, A., Weiss, G., Dogan, K., and Hoy, E. (1972). Studies on the hyperactive child. VII:Neurological status compared with neurotic and normal children. *Amer. J. Orthopsychiat.* 42(3).

Wikler, A., Dixon, J. F., and Parker, J. B., Jr. (1970). Brain function in problem children and controls: psychometric, neurological, and electroencephalographic comparisons. *Am. J. Psychiatry* 127:634.

Yoss, R. E. (1970). The inheritance of diurnal sleepiness as measured by pupillography. *Mayo Clin. Proc.* 45:426–27.

Chapter Five

Biochemical Research with Hyperactive Children

EDWARD R. RITVO, M.D.

In 1937, Bradley published for the first time in medical literature the remarkable observation that certain children with hyperactivity are calmed when given benzedrine (dl amphetamine), normally a stimulating drug. Many clinicians soon confirmed his finding with regard to benzedrine and other stimulants, and offered suggestions to explain this "paradoxical effect." None of these explanations, however, led to confirming experimentation, due mainly to our lack of knowledge of how and where drugs act within the central nervous system.

Fortunately, this situation has recently changed. Over the past decade much basic research has been conducted in laboratories throughout the world and our knowledge of neurobiochemistry and neuropharmacology is increasing at an exponential rate. In 1971, Paul Wender, M.D. published a book entitled *Minimal Brain Dysfunction in Children* (1971). In it he reviewed the results of recent neurobiochemical research and related them to a clinical analysis of children with minimal brain dysfunction and hyperactivity. He then formulated a set of hypotheses concerning central nervous system regulation of activity levels, and how drugs influence regulatory balance. These hypotheses have led to a series of clinically based experiments which appear to be breaking the logjam of our ignorance in this area.

In this chapter we shall begin by reviewing two recently established principles of neurobiochemistry and neuropharmacology. We shall then elaborate Wender's hypotheses within this context. In conclusion, the results of several clinical studies stemming from these hypotheses will be discussed.

PRINCIPLES OF NEUROBIOCHEMISTRY AND NEUROPHARMACOLOGY

By way of introduction, we must review and possibly update our thinking on two general principles of neurobiochemistry. The first has to do with the well-documented fact that there are chemicals within the central nervous system that transmit messages from one nerve cell (neuron) to the next. Most of us learned physiology in the grand old days, when things were "grand" by virtue of our ignorance. For example, I recall being taught that neurons fired "electrical impulses" from one to the next—and that a synapse, the junction between neurons, was a type of electrical switch. For decades, professors taught that an "action potential moved down a neuron and caused that neuron to become excited." Over the past decade much research has been done to disprove this old notion. It has now been shown that neurons synthesize chemicals within their cell bodies. The electrical energy about which we were taught, the "action potential," represents pollution, if you will, from the exhaust stacks of these factories operating with neurons. The factories manufacture specific chemicals called "neurotransmitters." When a neurotransmitter is found at the end of one neuron, it "stimulates" the next neuron to start chemical reactions. The neurotransmitters are then deactivated by other chemicals present at neuron junctions, which are manufactured there, or carried there by the bloodstream. Three principal chemical neurotransmitters within the central nervous system have been identified and studied extensively, although others may also exist. They are: (1)serotonin (5 hydroxytryptamine), (2)dopamine, and (3)noradrenaline. Understanding the role of neurotransmitters is crucial to understanding both how the central nervous system operates and the clinical research which has evolved with regard to the action of drugs on hyperactivity.

A second major principle is that the central nervous system contains systems which work in opposition to each other to modulate or regulate functioning. The old notion was that stimuli were not present at all times, and a message occurred only to signal an end organ to do something. For example, if one's arm hangs limply, the old notion was that no messages were coming to "raise" it. We have now learned that when one's arm hangs limply it is because the messages from the central nervous system to raise it are equally balanced by other messages to lower it. In more sophisticated neurophysiological parlance, modulating systems exist which are referred to as "facilitating" and "inhibiting." Action in end-organ systems (e.g., muscles) occurs when facilitation overrides inhibition. This concept of modulating systems helps to explain the clinical observation that a drug can result in facilitation or inhibition, depending upon its level of concentration.

THEORETICAL FORMULATIONS

In my opinion, Paul Wender, M.D., Assistant Professor of Pediatrics and Psychiatry, Johns Hopkins Hospital, has made the most significant theoretical contribution to our understanding of hyperactive children to date. In *Minimal Brain Dysfunction in Children* he suggests the following: "(1)Children with minimal brain dysfunction have an abnormality in the metabolism of monoamines: serotonin, noradrenaline, or dopamine. (2)This biochemical abnormality affects behavior by impairment produced in (a)the reward mechanism of the brain and (b)the activating system of the brain." So that it is clear, let me restate his hypotheses again in his words: "Minimal brain dysfunction children are characterized by two abnormalities: (1)an apparent increase in arousal, accompanied by an increased activity level and a decreased ability to concentrate, focus attention, or inhibit response to the irrelevant, and (2)a diminished capacity for positive and negative affect."

These hypotheses attempt to explain the clinical fact that the majority of children with minimal brain dysfunction, when given amphetamines, demonstrate decreased motor activity, increased attentiveness and increased responsiveness to social demands. A small minority, however, are not slowed down by amphetamines nor do they show the other effects. Wender also notes that in general the stimulant drugs have a bi-phasic effect on the majority of minimally brain damaged children; in lower doses they are calmed and in higher doses they are activated. In normal children their effect seems to be consistently activating. As the dose is increased in normal children, they become increasingly irritable. If we assume that both the inhibiting and excitatory arousal systems are mediated by the monoamines, and both respond to amphetamines, we can then postulate that the inhibitory system is less active at a low level of monoamine activity and that it increases its activity more rapidly with increasing levels of monoamines and peaks sooner. Thus, if the *excitatory* system is at a *higher* level of activity, the child is *excited*. If the *inhibitory* system is *more* active, he appears *sedated*.

Wender goes on to suggest that the effects of the monoamine may be directly on the reticular activating system and/or associated areas which feed into it, such as the caudate nucleus. However, as he points out, no experimental data yet exist to support this point.

He also draws upon interesting inferential evidence to help explain the fact that there are changes in the monoamine systems which occur with maturation. For example, he cites animal studies which show that brain levels of serotonin and noradrenaline increase progressively with age. If confirmed in humans, this data could explain the clinical observation that some signs of minimal brain dysfunction such as hyperactivity decrease with age. Thus, if the syndrome is partly caused by decreased reactivity of monoamines, one would expect an amelioration of symptoms as the levels increase with age. He cites another interesting study done on rats that showed that testosterone administration increases the activity of the monoamines. Increased androgenic activity normally occurs at the time of puberty and could thus increase the level and/or functional activity of the monoamines, further helping to explain why some symptoms decrease at puberty.

CLINICAL STUDIES

In this section the experimental studies of Rapoport, Coleman and Arnold will be reviewed. The first study to be discussed was conducted by Rapoport, Lott and Alexander at the National Institute of Health in 1970. They designed an experiment based on Wender's hypothesis that hyperkinetic behavior in children with minimal brain dysfunction may be related to a focal depletion of monoamines in the central nervous system. Nineteen hyperactive boys, ages five to ten years, were observed during ten-minute playroom sessions and at two-week intervals. Each was given a placebo, dextroamphetamine and chlorpromazine. Qualitative ratings of distractibility and overall playroom activity were made by two observers. Twenty-four-hour urine specimens were obtained to evaluate the excretion of adrenaline and noradrenaline. An age- and sex-matched control group of six boys was also used.

The results indicated that playroom activity was significantly decreased by dextroamphetamine but not by chlorpromazine or placebo. The average twenty-four-hour urinary adrenaline and noradrenaline excretion did not differ between the nineteen hyperactive boys and the six controls. There was, however, a significant inverse relationship found between noradrenaline excretion and the global activity ratings in the pre-drug period within the inpatient group. This inverse relationship did not exist for adrenaline. In other words, the most active children had a significantly lower level of noradrenaline excretion than the least active. They concluded "the findings of an inverse relationship between urinary noradrenaline and the degree of hyperactive behavior and an inverse relationship between urinary noradrenaline and the improvement of symptoms of hyperactivity during dextroamphetamine administration provides some support for the hypothesis that a disturbance in noradrenaline metabolism may be associated with a sub-group of hyperactive children. Furthermore, the pre-drug noradrenaline values predicted significantly the decrease in playroom activity and distractibility obtained with dextroamphetamine but not with chlorpromazine."

These findings lend some support to Wender's hypothesis and suggest that a prediction tool may become available. Should such predictions prove valid, they would allow us to be more specific in prescribing amphetamine treatment for that group of hyperactive children most likely to respond.

Two interesting and highly relevant studies relating to measures of serotonin concentration in the blood of hyperactive children have been conducted by Dr. Mary Coleman. She carefully prefaces her remarks by noting that whole blood serotonin is manufactured by cells in the gastrointestinal tract whereas serotonin in the brain is probably manufactured by the nerve cells themselves, and thus her conclusions can be considered only inferential. She also notes that a further problem in studying serotonin levels in whole blood is the fact that they are altered in other conditions besides hyperactivity. Thus she emphasizes that any findings related to serotonin in the blood of hyperactive patients may be nonspecific to the disorder.

Bearing these and other cautions in mind, she reported (1971) finding a low blood concentration of serotonin in 88 percent of twenty-five children—ages four to twelve years with a diagnosis of hyperactivity and without evidence of gross organic brain disease by neurologic examination or EEG. She states in her discussion, "the hyperactive children studied in this paper undoubtedly are not a homogeneous group—the low concentrations of serotonin reported here suggest that hyperactivity may be a clinical sign with many underlying causes, but they have a common mechanism which is reflected in lower than normal blood concentrations of serotonin."

In a second and as yet unpublished study entitled "The relationship of hyperactive behavior to blood serotonin levels: a biochemical basis for drug selection" (personal communication), she reported on twenty-nine individuals, most of whom were retarded, between four and thirty-nine years, residing at Rosewood State Hospital in Maryland. All these patients had increased motor activity, poor attention span, low frustration tolerance and emotional lability. Outpatient controls were obtained from the community and were matched for age and sex. Her results indicated that base-line whole blood total serotonin levels were depressed in 83 percent of the patients. Elevation of the blood serotonin levels to within the normal range by the administration of a variety of psychoactive agents was associated with the disappearance of the hyperkinetic syndrome. Those patients who remained hyperactive continued to have low serotonin levels. Also, return of hyperactivity upon withdrawal of medication in patients previously controlled was associated with a fall in blood serotonin. Dr. Coleman discusses the difficulty inherent in this study in terms of patient population, the drugs used and the clinical parameters she attempted to measure. She then suggests in her conclusion: "(1)factors related to the release and storage of serotonin are important in the pathogenesis of the hyperkinetic syndrome in a significant proportion of patients; (2)whole blood serotonin levels may be useful as a basis for selecting drugs in the treatment of hyperactivity."

The third series of research studies to be reviewed were conducted by Arnold and his co-workers (1972, 1973) on the possible role of monoamines in hyperactivity. Amphetamine is a racemic or mixed compound since it has molecules which turn to the right and to the left. Dextroamphetamine is a purified form in which the molecules turn just to the left. Arnold and his group wished to study separately the effect of these two isomers, dextroamphetamine and levoamphetamine, in eleven hyperkinetic children. They were also interested in discovering if there was a difference in relevant potency of the amphetamine isomers with regard to specific symptoms. This was prompted by animal studies which indicated for some behaviors elicited by amphetamines, such as locomotor stimulation, dextroamphetamine is ten times as potent as levoamphetamine, while for other behaviors, such as stereotyped gnawing in rats, the two isomers have similar potencies. It has also been reported in man that dextroamphetamine is considerably more potent as a central nervous system stimulant than levoamphetamine, while the two have similar potencies in producing amphetamine psychosis.

A well-controlled cross-over experiment utilizing placebos, a teacher rating scale, a parent rating scale and a weekly quantification of selected symptoms was conducted. The results indicated that both drugs were significantly more effective than the placebo. Dextroamphetamine was consistently superior to levoamphetamine, in improving general clinical ratings, though not to a statistically significant degree. Levoamphetamine was slower starting, showing significant benefit on target symptoms only after three weeks, whereas dextroamphetamine showed its maximum benefit after the first week of treatment. Of particular interest was the observation that levoamphetamine was better for hyperactivity and aggressiveness than for inattentiveness, whereas dextroamphetamine seemed equally beneficial for all three. The fact that certain target symptoms —namely, hyperactivity and aggressiveness—were affected differently from other target symptoms—namely, inattentiveness—allowed the authors to speculate that these drugs might have a differential effect on the dopamine neurotransmitter systems in the brain.

Following up these initial and admittedly inconclusive findings, Arnold and his co-workers next carried out experiments in animals. Four hyperkinetic, aggressive and untrainable dogs were given both levoamphetamine and dextroamphetamine and their behaviors monitored. Although both drugs were equally effective in suppressing aggression, the duration of the effects was different. While the same amount of dextroamphetamine kept the dogs quiet for seven hours after administration, levoamphetamine lasted only half as long. In another experiment using the same drugs, elimination of all signs of hyperkinetic behavior required three to four times as much levoamphetamine as dextroamphetamine. They concluded from these experiments (1)that levoamphetamine has a shorter duration of action than dextroamphetamine, and (2)that, during the period of maximum drug effect, levoamphetamine and dextroamphetamine seem to be approximately equal in their aggression-controlling potency, but dextroamphetamine is three to four times as potent in calming hyperactivity. These results suggest that the beneficial effects of amphetamines on aggressive behavior and on hyperactivity may operate through different biochemical mechanisms.

Encouraged by these findings, the authors went back to reexamine the clinical data accumulated in the 1972 study. Eleven patients' records were reviewed. They were divided into two diagnostic subgroups: an unsocialized, aggressive group and an overly anxious, hyperkinetic group, according to the criteria of Dr. Barbara Fish. They found that the unsocialized, aggressive group had responded as well to levoamphetamine as to dextroamphetamine, and both of these drugs had been significantly better than placebo. In contrast, for the overly anxious, hyperkinetic group, the levoamphetamine had been no better than placebo, even though dextroamphetamine proved significantly better. In discussing these results, the authors point out that apparently aggressive, hostile behavior may be a distinct (even separable) part of the overall syndrome of hyperactivity. Aggression seemed to have been helped by levoamphetamine as much as by dextroamphetamine, in contrast to anxiety and overactivity, which appeared to have been helped significantly more by dextroamphetamine.

Extending these observations to possible biochemical mechanisms, they postulate that aggression may be controlled by dopamine-mediated pathways which are more sensitive to levoamphetamine. In contrast, hyperactivity may be controlled by noradrenaline mediated pathways that are more sensitive to dextroamphetamine.

DISCUSSION

In conclusion, we have reviewed the theoretical speculations of Paul Wender, M.D. and several clinical studies which they have generated. The evidence to date indicates that there well may be specific neurobiochemical dysfunctions within the central nervous system of certain children which cause hyperactivity. Hopefully, further research will allow us to identify these patients on a laboratory basis.

We would then be closer to the goal of ideal medical intervention—namely, to be able to diagnose at a molecular level, and to design specific rational therapeutic interventions to correct underlying pathogenic processes.

REFERENCES

Arnold, L. E., Kirilcuk, V., Corson, S. A., and Corson, E. D. (1973). Levoamphetamine and dextroamphetamine: differential effect on aggression and hyperkinesis in children and dogs. *American Journal of Psychiatry* 130:165–70.

————, Wender, P. H., McCloskey, K., and Snyder, S. H. (1972). Levoamphetamine and dextroamphetamine: comparative efficacy in the hyperkinetic syndrome. Assessment by target symptoms. *Archives of General Psychiatry,* 27:816–22.

Coleman, M. (1971). Serotonin concentrations in whole blood of hyperactive children. *Journal of Pediatrics* 78:985–90.

Rapoport, J. L., Lott, I. T., Alexander, D. F., and Abramson, A. U. (1970). Urinary noradrenaline and playroom behavior in hyperactive boys. *Lancet* 2:1141.

Wender, P. (1971). *Minimal Brain Dysfunction in Children.* New York: Wiley-Interscience.

Chapter Six

Familial-Genetic Research with Hyperactive Children

DENNIS P. CANTWELL, M.D.

In contrast to the other psychiatric disorders of childhood, there has been little investigation of familial factors in the hyperactive child syndrome, probably due to the assumption of some "organic" etiology. However, what little information there is suggests that familial and genetic factors may play a significant role in the pathogenesis and prognosis of this disorder. This chapter will review the currently available research evidence relating to families of hyperactive children.

PSYCHIATRIC ILLNESS IN THE FAMILY

Based on clinical observation and historical data a number of investigators have suggested that there is an increased prevalence rate for psychiatric illness in the families of hyperactive children. Wender (1971) felt that parents of hyperactive children had an apparent increase in the prevalence of mixed psychopathology (schizophrenia, affective disorders, sociopathy). Satterfield et al. (1974) found that parents of hyperactive children had a markedly greater incidence of neurosis, antisocial behavior, "nervous breakdown," suicide, attempted suicide and alcoholism when compared to parents of matched control children. In their original clinical description of thirty-seven hyperactive children in St. Louis, Stewart et al. (1966) found that over half had one first- or second-degree relative whose behavior led to serious legal or employment problems or required psychiatric treatment. Presumptive psychiatric diagnoses of these relatives included eight with affective disturbance, five with alcoholism or other addictions, and six with other disorders. At the time of follow-up, of eighty-three of the St. Louis population (Mendelson et al., 1971) 22 percent of the fathers and 4 percent of the mothers were having significant marital, legal or employment problems related to heavy drinking. Nearly a quarter of the fathers, 10 percent of the mothers and 37 percent of the siblings had behavior or learning problems as a child.

These clinical and historical data have now been confirmed by two systematic family studies of the hyperactive child syndrome. Cantwell (1972) carried out a systematic psychiatric examination of the parents of fifty hyperactive children and fifty matched normal control children. Most of the parents of children in the control group were free of any psychiatric illness, whereas nearly half of the parents of the hyperactive children had some psychiatric diagnosis. The fathers in both groups tended to be ill more than the mothers. The specific differences between the groups were in the greater prevalence of alcoholism, sociopathy, hysteria and probable hysteria in the parents of hyperactive children. Thirty percent of the fathers of hyperactive children were diagnosed as alcoholic and 16 percent were given a diagnosis of sociopathy. Eight percent of the mothers of hyperactive children were diagnosed as alcoholic and 16 percent were given a diagnosis of hysteria or probable hysteria. No other psychiatric disorders were found to have an increased prevalence rate in these parents.

Eight (16 percent) of the fathers of hyperactive children were thought to have been hyperactive as children themselves. Six of these were given a diagnosis of alcoholism when they were seen as adults, one was given a diagnosis of sociopathy, and the eighth had an undiagnosed psychiatric illness with heavy drinking as one of the symptoms. Only one of the fathers of the normal control children was thought to have been a hyperactive child, and he too was given a diagnosis of alcoholism when seen as an adult.

Two (4 percent) of the mothers of hyperactive children were thought to have been hyperactive as children. As adults one was felt to be a hysteric and one was given a diagnosis of probable hysteria. No mothers of the normal control children were thought to have been hyperactive children.

In a similar study, Morrison and Stewart (1971) systematically evaluated the parents of fifty-nine hyperactive and forty-one normal control children. One-third of the parents of the hyperactive children had some psychiatric diagnosis, while over 80 percent of the parents of the control group were free of any psychiatric illness. As in the Cantwell study the specific differences between the groups were in the greater prevalence of alcoholism, sociopathy and hysteria in the parents of the hyperactive children. Twenty percent of the fathers of hyperactive children were given a diagnosis of alcoholism and 5 percent were given a diagnosis of sociopathy. Five percent of the mothers of hyperactive children were diagnosed as alcoholic and 10 percent were given a diagnosis of hysteria.

Morrison and Stewart also found that twelve parents of hyperactive children (nine fathers and three mothers) were felt to have been hyperactive as children. Of these nine fathers, five were diagnosed as alcoholics as adults, one was a sociopath, one had multiple depressive, phobic and compulsive symptoms, and two were heavy drinkers but not alcoholic. Of the three previously hyperactive mothers, one had a depressive illness as an adult and one qualified for both a diagnosis of alcoholism and a diagnosis of hysteria.

One father and one mother of the normal control children were thought to have been hyperactive as children. As adults the father was an epileptic with psychosis who had a drinking problem and the mother was manic-depressive.

ENVIRONMENTAL ASPECTS

The data reviewed above strongly suggest that hyperactive children are likely to grow up in families where one or more members is psychiatrically ill. This puts them "at risk" for the development of psychopathology (Rutter, 1966; Graham et al., 1973). This risk may be due to genetic factors, to environmental factors, or to a combination of both.

Surprisingly little information is available on the family environment of hyperactive children and even less on the effect of this family environment on the ultimate prognosis of the hyperactive child. Menkes et al. (1967) rated the home environment as "unfavorable" in thirteen out of eighteen of their cases but the family environment did not seem to play a role in long-term prognosis. Conrad and Insel (1967) reported that hyperactive children whose parents were "grossly deviant" or "socially incompetent" tended to respond less well to amphetamine therapy. Close inspection of their criteria for "grossly deviant" and "socially incompetent" reveals that these terms were used to describe parents who were either mentally ill, alcoholic or sociopathic. Mendelson et al. (1971) found that fathers who demonstrated antisocial behavior as adults and who had learning or behavior problems as children had children who were the most antisocial among a group of hyperactive children. Weiss et al. (1971) also found that those hyperactive children demonstrating significant antisocial behavior came from "pathological families" characterized by poor parental mental health, punitive child-rearing practices, and a poor mother-child relationship. Minde et al. (1972) rated five separate aspects of family functioning (marital relationship, child-rearing practices, maternal deprivation, emotional climate at home, parental mental health) in the families of hyperactive children. None of these significantly differentiated "good" and "poor" outcome groups at the time of initial evaluation but the families of "good outcome" children improved over time while those of "poor outcome" children deteriorated. The authors interpreted these data in a "child to parent" direction; that is, they felt that the children in the "poor outcome" group had a negative effect on family interaction and emotional climate in the home. However, the data could also be interpreted in a "parent to child" direction; i.e., those hyperactive children reared in homes with a poor emotional climate and poor child-rearing practices have the poorest outcome.

GENETIC ASPECTS

Adoption Studies
The data from the two family studies reviewed above suggest that the hyperactive child syndrome is a familial disorder that passes from generation to generation and that there is a familial relationship between the hyperactive child syndrome and three adult psychiatric disorders: alcoholism, sociopathy and hysteria. The data do not explain whether the possible mechanism of transmission of the hyperactive child syndrome is a genetic or environmental one. Nor do they explain whether the familial relationship between the hyperactive child syndrome and the three adult psychiatric disorders is genetic or environmental.

Morrison and Stewart (1973) and Cantwell (in press b) used the adoption study method to test the following hypotheses:

(1) The hyperactive child syndrome is genetically transmitted from generation to generation.

(2) There is a genetic relationship between the hyperactive child syndrome and three psychiatric disorders of adulthood: alcoholism, sociopathy and hysteria.

To test these hypotheses, both investigators conducted a systematic psychiatric examination of the *non-biologic* parents of *adopted* hyperactive children. If the non-biologic parents and their extended families do not show the same increased prevalence rates for the hyperactive child syndrome and the other psychiatric disorders found in the biologic parents, then a strong argument could be made for a genetic factor operating in the syndrome.

In both of these studies, the hyperactive child syndrome was found to a much greater degree in the biologic first- and second-degree relatives of hyperactive children than in the relatives of the adopted children. The prevalence rates for the syndrome found in the adopting relatives were not significantly greater than those found for the relatives in the control group and were less than the generally accepted prevalence rates for the syndrome found in the general population. These data are consistent with the hypothesis that there is a genetic transmission of the hyperactive child syndrome from generation to generation.

The data from these studies is also consistent with the hypothesis that the familial relationship between alcoholism, sociopathy and hysteria in parents and the hyperactive child syndrome is a genetic one. Systematic psychiatric examination of the adopting parents did not reveal the high prevalence rates for alcoholism, sociopathy and hysteria that had been found in the biologic parents. Nor were increased prevalence rates found for these conditions in the non-biologic second-degree relatives of adopted hyperactive children.

Another type of adoption study was conducted by Safer (1973), who studied the full and half sibs of seventeen index cases with "minimal brain dysfunction." Ten of the nineteen full sibs were considered likely to manifest minimal brain dysfunction, whereas that diagnosis was given to only two of twenty-two half sibs. These data are also consistent with a genetic mechanism of transmission of the syndrome.

Twin Studies

Comparing identical with fraternal twin pairs where at least one member of each pair manifests the condition under investigation has been a traditional method for evaluating whether genetic factors play an important role in that condition. Unfortunately, twin studies of the hyperactive child syndrome have been limited. Lopez (1965) found a 100 percent concordance rate for the hyperactive syndrome in his four monozygotic twin pairs. Only one of his six dizygotic twin pairs was concordant for the syndrome. However, sex differences between the monozygotic and dizygotic twin pairs cloud the interpretation of the data (Omenn, 1973).

A larger twin study has been reported by Willerman (1973). The mothers of ninety-three sets of same-sexed twins rated their children on the Werry-Weiss-Peters Activity Scale (Werry et al., 1970). There were twenty-eight monozygotic and twenty-eight dizygotic male pairs and twenty-six monozygotic and eleven dizygotic female twin pairs. The heritability estimate was .82 for the males, .58 for the females, and .77 for males and females combined. These data suggest a substantial genetic component to *activity level*. However, this in itself says nothing about genetic factors in the hyperactive child syndrome. Willerman arbitrarily defined children with scores on the activity scale in the top 20 percent as "hyperactive." There were eight monozygotic and sixteen dizygotic twin pairs with activity scores in this range. The heritability estimate for this group was .71. If scores in this range on the Werry-Weiss-Peters scale can be considered as evidence that these children manifest the hyperactive child syndrome, then the Willerman twin study is also consistent with the notion that genetic factors play an important role in the hyperactive child syndrome.

Mechanism of Genetic Transmission

The mechanism of the possible genetic transmission can only be hypothesized at present. Genetic models to be considered include a chromosome anomaly, simple autosomal dominant and simple autosomal recessive transmission, sex-linkage and polygenic inheritance. The only reported chromosome study of hyperactive children failed to find any evidence of sex chromosome aneuploidy or other chromosome abnormality (Warren et al., 1971). If the mechanism were a simple autosomal dominant gene, one of the parents of a hyperactive child should also manifest the disorder; there should be no significant sex differences in the prevalence of the disorder; and there should be no skipping of generations. None of these three conditions appear to be met in the hyperactive child syndrome; thus a simple autosomal dominant gene does not appear to be a realistic model for this disorder (Cantwell, in press a).

With a simple autosomal recessive gene model, each of the parents would carry the gene but neither would be affected. This model predicts that 25 percent of full sibs of the proband children would manifest the disorder. Although clinical experience (Wender, 1971; Omenn, 1973) indicates that the syndrome does occur in siblings, more systematic data are needed on a larger population to determine if the prevalence rate in full siblings approaches the 25 percent predicted by a recessive model. However, the high percentage of parents manifesting the syndrome (Morrison and Stewart, 1971; Cantwell, 1972) would seem to rule out this model also.

The excess of males with the disorder might suggest a sex-linked gene. However, this model also appears unlikely due to the high degree of apparent transmission from father to son (Morrison and Stewart, 1971; Cantwell, 1972).

The last possible model to be considered is that of polygenic inheritance. In essence, this model states that more than one gene is involved in the transmission of a disorder and the proband manifests the disorder only when correct number or combination of genes are present. This model is very difficult to prove or disprove due to its complexity. Morrison (1973; Morrison and Stewart, 1973) has offered preliminary evidence in favor of a polygenic model in two separate studies. The first study tested the following two consequences of the polygenic model: (1)"The greater the number of individuals in a family who manifest a disorder, the greater the risk factor in the family." Thus, if alcoholism is linked with the hyperactive child syndrome, then families with multiple cases of the hyperactive child syndrome should have higher prevalence rates for alcoholism than families with only one index case of the syndrome. (2)"Families with both an index case and a first-degree relative manifesting the syndrome may be presumed to have a greater concentration of the necessary genes." Thus they should also be more likely to have extended family members affected. Both such consequences were found to be true in Morrison's first study.

In his second study, Morrison used Slater's method (1966) of analysis of ancestral cases in an attempt to distinguish a possible polygenic model from a dominant gene transmission with reduced penetrance. Slater's method states that in the instance of a single dominant gene, one would expect secondary cases to occur exclusively, or nearly so, on one side of the family. In the cases of polygenic transmission, one would expect a significant number of probands to have both paternal and maternal ascendant relatives affected. Morrison's data on families in which two or more relatives had the hyperactive child syndrome were congruent with a polygenic model using Slater's method.

DISCUSSION
Taken together, then, the available evidence for genetic factors operating in the hyperactive child syndrome is tentative but strong. The family studies reviewed strongly suggest that the syndrome is a familial disorder. However, both of these family studies were done "non-blind." That is, the investigators knew whether they were interviewing the parent of a hyperactive child or a control child. Thus interviewer bias could have influenced the diagnosis of the adult psychiatric state and the retrospective diagnosis of hyperactivity in the parents. Moreover, it could be argued that parents of a hyperactive child are more "sensitized" to the diagnosis than the parents of a normal child, and thus are more likely to describe themselves as having been hyperactive as children.

Finally, all of the hyperactive children had been raised by their natural parents and one could explain the development of the syndrome in these children by several environmental mechanisms (Cantwell, in press b).

The two adoption studies offer answers to some of these objections. All of the adopted hyperactive children had been separated from their natural parents in the first few months of life and had had no further contact with them. The adopting parents had raised the children from the first few months of life and thus should be equally likely to be sensitive to the diagnosis. The failure to find increased prevalence rates for the hyperactive child syndrome or other psychiatric disorders in the adopting parents and second-degree relatives argues against a purely environmental mechanism of transmission of the syndrome. However, both adoption studies suffer from the fact that no information was available about the *biologic* parents of the *adopted* hyperactive children. Comparison of the biologic parents of *one* group of hyperactive children with the adopting parents of *another* group of hyperactive children was a necessary compromise. A study of the biologic and adopting parents of the *same* group of hyperactive children is needed for more conclusive evidence.

As noted above, a properly conducted twin study on a clinically diagnosed population of hyperactive children has not yet been done. However, even a "perfect" twin study would be subject to certain criticisms. The basic assumption underlying twin studies is that any difference between monozygotic (MZ) twins is due solely to environmental factors, while differences between dizygotic twins (DZ) are due to both genetic and environmental factors. Thus the extent to which monozygotic twins resemble each other more than dizygotic twins is held to reflect the strength of the genetic contribution to a characteristic. Nevertheless, this basic assumption can be criticized on a number of grounds.

There is evidence from several studies that MZ and DZ twins may not have equivalent environmental experiences (Partanen et al., 1966; Mittler, 1971). Family and friends may treat MZ twins more alike than they do DZ twins, thus exposing MZ twins to greater environmental similarity. Spurious support will be given to a genetic hypothesis by any environmentally created similarities which would tend to reduce intrapair differences in MZ twins. Moreover, MZ twins are more vulnerable than DZ twins to pre- and perinatal abnormalities (Mittler, 1971). Since such abnormalities may play an etiologic role in some hyperactive children, nongenetic factors may spuriously elevate the concordance rate in MZ twins. Finally, twins are in many respects not a representative sample of the general population. Thus data obtained from one twin study may apply to that particular population only, and generalization to another twin population, much less to the general population, can be hazardous.

Phenotypic diagnosis is as much a problem in genetic studies of the hyperactive child syndrome as it is in genetic studies of all psychiatric disorders. In the absence of specific laboratory tests for psychiatric disorders, the phenotypic diagnosis is made on the basis of a clinical picture. There is ample evidence of lack of agreement in psychiatric diagnosis in both adults and children (Rutter et al., 1973; Shepherd et al., 1968; Kendell et al., 1971). Shields and Gottesman (1972) have shown how differences in diagnostic criteria among clinicians can lead to marked differences in heritability estimates in adult schizophrenia. Moreover, even perfect agreement in diagnosis of a particular condition among investigators does not assure that all probands presenting with the same clinical picture do in fact have the same condition. This is particularly likely with the hyperactive child syndrome. Studies of response to stimulant drugs have shown that there are some hyperactive children who respond dramatically to medication and others who are made worse (Fish, 1971). Follow-up studies indicate that the natural history of the disorder is not a uniform one (Menkes et al., 1967; Weiss et al., 1971; Mendelson et al., 1971). Neurologic and neurophysiologic studies also indicate that hyperactive children are a heterogeneous group (Satterfield et al., 1972). It is likely, then, that if there is a genetic component to the syndrome, it is operating in one subgroup of these children, or there may be several genetically distinct subgroups. Future genetic investigations should concentrate on various subgroups of hyperactive children—for example, "drug responsive" versus "non-drug responsive" children—in an attempt to obtain a more homogeneous proband group.

Finally, it must be noted that the crucial genetic studies of the hyperactive child syndrome have not yet been done. Although the various types of studies reviewed here (family studies, adoption studies, twin studies) may *suggest* a genetic component, they cannot *prove* it. Genetic mechanism precisely defined is the only way to prove a genetic component. Segregation and linkage studies are the only analyses that can precisely define a genetic mechanism. Segregation studies are difficult to do in humans. Newer, mathematical models will hopefully allow detailed pedigree analysis over multiple generations (Spence, 1973). Linkage studies will require the discovery of a "genetic marker" associated with the hyperactive child syndrome. Recent investigations of linkage of the Xg blood group and color-blindness with bipolar affective disorder in adults offer a model for such studies (Winokur et al., 1969; Winokur and Tanna, 1969; Fieve et al., 1973).

An even more fruitful area of investigation might be the effect of the family environment on response to treatment and ultimate prognosis in the hyperactive child syndrome. Data reviewed previously suggest that the hyperactive child syndrome may be a precursor to alcoholism, sociopathy, hysteria and possibly psychosis in adulthood. What is not known is whether it is the hyperactive children with antisocial, alcoholic, hysteric or psychotic parents who themselves develop these or other psychiatric disorders in adulthood. This is likely to be the case when one considers that hyperactive children with psychiatrically ill parents are exposed to "double doses" of the factors, whether genetic or environmental, that predispose to disturbed behavior in childhood and later life. The meager evidence available at the present time does suggest that the presence of a psychiatrically ill parent and other familial variables do play a role in response to treatment and in the determination of certain types of outcome in the hyperactive child syndrome. But much more in the way of systematic research is needed in this area.

SUMMARY

(1) Systematic psychiatric studies of the biological families of hyperactive children have revealed that:

   (a) A significant number of the parents of hyperactive children were themselves hyperactive as children.

   (b) The parents have increased prevalence rates for certain psychiatric illnesses as adults: alcoholism and sociopathy in the fathers, hysteria and alcoholism in the mothers.

   (c) These increased prevalence rates for hyperactivity, alcoholism, sociopathy and hysteria are also found in the second-degree relatives of hyperactive children.

(2) The hypothesis that genetic factors play an important role in the hyperactive child syndrome is supported by adoption studies and twin studies.

(3) The hypothesis that there is a genetic relationship between the hyperactive child syndrome, alcoholism, sociopathy and hysteria is supported by family studies and adoption studies.

(4) Very little evidence is available on the effect of the family environment on the hyperactive child. What little evidence there is suggests that certain familial variables do affect the long-term outcome of children with the syndrome.

REFERENCES

Cantwell, D. (1972). Psychiatric illness in the families of hyperactive children. *Archives of General Psychiatry* 27:414–17.

———— (in press a). The hyperkinetic syndrome. In M. Rutter and L. Hersov, eds., *Recent Advances in Child Psychiatry*. London: Blackwell.

———— (in press b). Genetic studies of hyperactive children. *American Psychopathology Association Annual Report.*

Conrad, W., and Insel, J. (1967). Anticipating the response to amphetamine therapy in the treatment of hyperkinetic children. *Pediatrics* 40:96–99.

Fieve, R., Mendlewicz, J., and Fleiss, J. (1973). Manic-depressive illness: linkage with Xg blood group. *American Journal of Psychiatry* 130:1355–59.

Fish, B. (1971). The "one child, one drug myth" of stimulants in hyperkinesis: importance of diagnostic categories in evaluating treatment. *Archives of General Psychiatry* 25:193–203.

Graham, P., Rutter, M., and George, S. (1973). Temperamental characteristics as predictors of behavior disorders in children. *American Journal of Orthopsychiatry* 43: 328, 339.

Kendell, R., Cooper, J., Gourlay, A., Copeland, J., Sharpe, L. and Gurland, B. (1971). Diagnostic criteria of American and British psychiatrists. *Archives of General Psychiatry* 25:123–30.

Lopez, R. (1965). Hyperactivity in twins. *Canadian Psychiatric Association Journal* 10:-421–26.

Mendelson, W., Johnson, J., and Stewart, M. (1971). Hyperactive children as teenagers: a follow-up study. *Journal of Nervous Mental Disorders* 153: 273–79.

Menkes, M., Rowe, J., and Menkes, J. (1967). A twenty-five-year follow-up study on the hyperkinetic child with minimal brain dysfunction. *Pediatrics* 39:392–99.

Minde, K., Weiss, G., and Mendelson, M. (1972). A five-year follow-up study of 91 hyperactive school children. *Journal of the American Academy of Child Psychiatry* 11:-595–610.

Mittler, P. (1971). *The Study of Twins.* Penguin Science of Behaviour. Middlesex, England: Hazel Watson and Viney, Ltd.

Morrison, J. and Stewart M. (1973). Evidence for polygenetic inheritance in the hyperactive child syndrome. *American Journal of Psychiatry* 130:791–92.

———— and Stewart, M. (1971). A family study of the hyperactive child syndrome. *Biological Psychiatry,* 3:189–95.

———— and Stewart, M. (1973). The psychiatric status of the legal families of adopted hyperactive children. *Archives of General Psychiatry* 28:888–91.

Omenn, G. (1973). Genetic issues in the syndrome of minimal brain dysfunction. *Seminars in Psychiatry* 5:5–19.

Partanen, J., Bruun, K., and Markkanen, T. (1966). *Inheritance of Drinking Behavior.* New Brunswick, N.J.: Rutgers University Center of Alcohol Studies.

Rutter, M. (1966). *Children of Sick Parents.* London: Oxford University Press, Inc.

————, Shaffer, D., and Shepherd, M. (1973). Preliminary communication: an evaluation of the proposal for a multi-axial classification of child psychiatric disorders. *Psychological Medicine* 3:244–51.

Safer, D. (1973). A familial factor in minimal brain dysfunction. *Behavior Genetics* 3: 175–87.

Satterfield, J., Cantwell, D., Lesser, L., and Podosin, R. (1972). Physiological studies of the hyperkinetic child. I. *American Journal of Psychiatry* 128:1418–24.

_____, Saul, R., Cantwell, D., Lesser, L., and Podosin, R. (in press). Central nervous system arousal in hyperactive children. *Journal of the American Academy of Child Psychiatry.*

Shepherd, M., Brooke, E., Cooper, J., and Lin, T. (1968). An experimental approach to psychiatric diagnosis: an international study. *Acta Psychiatrica Scandinavica.* Suppl. 201:44.

Shields, J., and Gottesman, I. (1972). Cross-national diagnosis of schizophrenia in twins. *Archives of General Psychiatry* 27:725–39.

Slater, E. (1966). Expectation of abnormality on paternal and maternal sides: a computation model. *Journal of Medical Genetics* 3:159–61.

Spence, M. (1973). Current research on the genetics of autism. Read before the University of California extension course on autistic children.

Stewart, M., Pitts, F., Craig, A., and Dieruf, A. (1966). The hyperactive child syndrome. *American Journal of Orthopsychiatry* 36:861–67.

Warren, R., Karduck, W., Bussaratid, S., Stewart, M., and Sly, W. (1971). The hyperactive child syndrome: normal chromosome findings. *Archives of General Psychiatry* 24: 161–162.

Weiss, G., Minde, K., Werry, J., Douglas, U., and Nemeth, E. (1971). Studies on the hyperactive child. VIII. Five-year follow-up. *Archives of General Psychiatry* 24:409–14.

Wender, P. (1971). *Minimal Brain Dysfunction in Children.* New York: Wiley-Interscience.

_____, Epstein, R., Kopin, I., and Gorson, E. (1971). Urinary monoamine metabolites in children with minimal brain dysfunction. *American Journal of Psychiatry* 127:141–45.

Werry, J., Sprague, R., Weiss, G., and Minde, K. (1970). Some clinical and laboratory studies of psychotropic drugs in children: an overview. In W. L. Smith, ed., *Drugs and Cerebral Function.* Springfield, Ill.: Charles C. Thomas.

Willerman, L. and Plomin, R. (1973) Activity level in children and their parents. *Child Development* 44:854–58.

Winokur, G., and Tanna, V. (1969). Possible role of X-linked dominant factor in manic-depressive disease. *Diseases of the Nervous System* 30:89–93.

_____, Clayton, P., and Reich, T. (1969). *Manic Depressive Illness.* St. Louis: C. V. Mosby Co.

PART III

Management of the Hyperactive Child Syndrome

Chapter Seven

Stimulant Drug Treatment of Hyperactive Children

BARBARA FISH, M.D.

It is popular to allege that a "stimulant is the drug for the hyperactive child" (Fish, 1971). Certainly there *are* many hyperactive children who are helped by a central nervous system stimulant. When it works, it provides economical and rapid treatment which can return the child to more normal functioning both in and out of school.

The danger of this dictum is that it oversimplifies a very complex diagnostic and therapeutic problem. To perpetuate the simplistic idea that all hyperactive children simply require stimulant medication is to neglect the fact that many of these children require specific remediation for learning disabilities, that others require more potent medication, and that still others need attention to social and psychological problems which are impeding normal growth and development.

To put these issues into proper perspective, it will be necessary to discuss the limitations as well as the indications and therapeutic action of stimulant medication. Contrary to the "one child, one drug" myth, there is no one hyperactive child and stimulants are not the drug of choice for all of them. We will have to examine the diagnostic subgroups of hyperactive children and define what is meant by "hyperactive behavior disorder" and "minimal brain dysfunction." Finally, it will be necessary to discuss other pharmacologic treatments for these children and a practical regimen for this important aspect of their treatment.

DO STIMULANTS WORK?

First, to the question "Do stimulants really work?" the answer is "Yes, they do work"—perhaps the only simple statement one can make in the course of this discussion. After the newspaper reports of large numbers of children in Omaha being put on stimulant drugs, apparently without adequate medical indications or supervision, there was a Congressional investigation and finally in 1971 the Department of Health, Education and Welfare and the Office of Child Development convened a blue-ribbon panel to put the issues into proper perspective. Many different fields of expertise and all shades of opinion were represented. The panel's report (Freedman, 1971) arrived at a balanced point of view regarding the problems that had arisen, as well as recommendations. What came out of it was that, if one surveys all the studies, one finds that in about 60 to 70 percent of hyperactive children, the hyperactivity will respond to stimulant medication. This refers to the very heterogeneous group of children brought to clinics, eliminating those who are mentally retarded or psychotic, or who have specific neurologic disorders. The more recent controlled studies (Conners and Eisenberg, 1963; Conners et al., 1969; Weiss et al., 1968) confirm the earliest clinical studies, done in the late 1930's and early 1940's by Bradley (1937; Bradley and Bowen, 1941) and Bender and Cottington (1942), so that things have not greatly changed in thirty-five years.

However, the fact that stimulants are effective is only the beginning of the story. (1)First of all, there are many different kinds of hyperactive children, and one must subdivide the group, diagnose the children and treat them appropriately. (2)Stimulants are the drug of choice only for certain of these children. (3)Most of these children who come to anyone's attention also need some kind of educational remediation. Stimulants alone are not going to do the job, and this is one of the key issues that was highlighted by the Omaha affair. The problem arises when people simply prescribe stimulant medication as if this were a cure-all for everything and everybody. (4)Whereas stimulants are the drug of choice for some of these children, there are others for whom stimulants do not work. In fact, some of them are made worse, and many of these children need more potent medication. This is often neglected when stimulants are used as if they could cure every hyperactive child.

There are still other complications. (5)Stimulants do not only help children with hyperactivity, they also help many children who are not hyperactive. In fact, I think they are even better for those children than for some of the hyperactive children. (6)Furthermore, stimulants can also help some children who have specific neurological disorders, as well as those with so called minimal brain dysfunction and those with no signs of neurologic disorders.

WHAT STIMULANTS DO

Let us consider first what stimulant drugs do when they do work. When they are effective, one sees a symtomatic improvement. I think the critical target symptom for the stimulants' action is the short attention span, rather than the hyperactivity. The restlessness is either associated with, or may even be a result of, decreased attention span. Table I is taken from the very early classic papers mentioned above and one can see that the effects of treatment have not changed. Bradley's paper in 1937 was on Benzedrine, the very first study of about fifteen to twenty children, followed by a larger study (Bradley and Bowen, 1941), in a residential treatment center. Bender and Cottington's 1942 study was of children hospitalized at Bellevue.

Both studies found, in terms of the symptomatic improvement, that the most striking change occurred in school activities on the first day of treatment. This is the first important point: the change is very rapid when it works, and one doesn't have to keep children on

TABLE I
Clinical Changes with Amphetamine

Change	Bradley (1937 and 1941)	Bender & Cottington (1942)
1	"Most striking change . . . in school activities the first day"	"Response immediate and dramatic"
2	"Great increase of interest"	"Stimulating interest . . . increase in attention span"
3	"Drive to accomplish"	"Drive in learning"
4	"Subdued emotional response . . . sense of well-being . . . subdued in a social rather than physiological sense"	"The majority became quieter, more cheerful, and relaxed"
5	"Some decrease of motor-activity"	"Overactivity was reduced"
6	"Cried more easily, agitated"	"Increasingly tense, irritable"

medication for a long time to find out whether it is the right drug or not. The response was immediate and dramatic, with an increase in attention span. Secondly, they both found that there was a great increase in interest in the children, particularly in school activities, and that there was a drive to accomplish, and increase of motivation in learning.

The next point which makes for confusion is what Bradley called "subdued emotional responses, a sense of well-being, subdued in a social rather than a physiological sense." In other words, children became quieter, calmer. Bradley emphasized that this was not physiological slowing down. Similarly, according to Bender, the majority became "quieter," but it was in the sense of being more cheerful and more relaxed. In other words, they were less irritable, less tense, less upset. But it has been the so-called calming action that many people have misunderstood. They assume it is a slowing down, and wonder what is this "paradoxical sedative effect" with a stimulant drug. It isn't really sedation at all, in the pharmacologic sense of decreased central nervous system arousal. Bradley did say that there was some decrease of motor activity, and Bender also found that when overactivity was present it was reduced.

Both authors also found the same kinds of toxic symptoms. In certain children, sometimes even small doses turned out to be too much. As Bradley put it, some of them cried more easily and some became agitated. Bender found the same thing—that many of them became tense and irritable.

These are basically the same kinds of effects that we find now. Conners and Eisenberg, in some of the more recent controlled studies, referred to many of the same changes (Conners and Eisenberg, 1963; Conners et al., 1969). They said the children became less apathetic, much like the earlier reports of increased interest and drive. This affected the children who were not hyperactive; these were often inhibited, overly quiet children. The decrease in tension and in impulsivity obviously is also the same as the earlier findings, as is the decrease in disorganized behavior and hyperactivity.

In addition to these studies, which were mostly focused on children who were selected because of hyperactivity or learning problems, there have been beneficial effects found in other types of children. In my own earlier work in private practice, I used amphetamines. In my experience with Dr. Bender, I had not been impressed with the effectiveness of amphetamine in severely disturbed hyperactive children (Fish, 1971) and therefore used it primarily with phobic, inhibited, neurotic children, in whom it seemed to have done the most good at Bellevue. In these children, when it works, amphetamine will often reduce anxiety and tension and loosen up some of their inhibitions. That action more closely resembles what one sees in adults.

No "Paradoxical Effects"

I indicated above that the action of stimulants is not "paradoxical" in children. The confusion occurs when people slip from the *behavioral* description of quieting and decreased activity to the assumption that there is a *pharmacological* sedative action, a damping of central nervous system activity. But these are not synonymous. One can get behavioral quieting and decreased hyperactivity without having a sedative action in terms of the physiological response in the central nervous system. Only if the stimulants were sedative in the pharmacologic sense would their action be paradoxical.

The problem is that adults tend to be very "adultamorphic" about children. If we were as active as these children, it would mean that we had a lot of excess energy and drive. We slow down when we feel tired or depressed. So adults assume when they see children being overactive that they must feel exuberant and full of energy. Some children do; that is the normal state for children.

But many hyperactive children do not feel that way at all. Before we had physiological data, I used the analogy of normal infants. When they get tired, they become more excitable, more irritable. They cry and scream and are very active. They thrash around and often have difficulty in "turning off" and dropping off to sleep. Or, an analogy even closer to home: when young children get overtired at five o'clock, unlike their parents who are ready to collapse, the children get excited, scream, yell and run around, instead of slowing down and dropping into a chair and wanting to be quiet the way their parents do. They are often really tired, just like the infants. Normal children will often act more irritable and more excitable when they're tired, and they get more easily upset by little things. We cannot assume that their nervous systems are truly in a stimulated state when they are acting hyperactive, excitable and irritable.

The scientific data supporting this have been reviewed by Dr.

Satterfield in Chapter Four. This work is critical in pointing out that physiologically many of the hyperactive children do not have a para- doxical response to stimulants. These are children whose central nervous systems are under-aroused and the drugs do exactly what they do in adults—stimulate and bring up central nervous system activity to a normal level. Then the children act calmer and less restless. Studies by Knopp and others also point out the same thing (Knopp et al., 1973). They used a different physiological technique, looking at the contraction of the pupil, and they found that in many hyperactive children there was a "tuning down" of the nervous sys- tem and that stimulants brought this activity back up to normal. They did find a small group of children where the opposite was true. Although the results are still preliminary, it appears that there was a small group who were physiologically "overstimulated" to start with, and in these the amphetamines did bring them down to a normal level. So there is a small subgroup that may be responding in a *truly* paradoxical fashion. In general, the basic response to stimu- lants is a heightening of central nervous system activity. The increase of interest and drive is exactly what occurs in adults unless they are oversensitive and become more agitated, tense and nervous. This, also, is the way some of the children respond.

One has to remember this stimulant action of these drugs not only because of these common toxic effects. Some children, especially those who are more excitable and more disturbed to start with, but who may look similar to other hyperactive children, become much worse if they are put on stimulants. They become very much more disturbed, and often overtly psychotic, even though they were not apparently psychotic before. We think from what we have seen that these are often children who have borderline psychotic symptoms even before they are given medication. Sometimes after such a re- sponse, someone will think, "He's worse, therefore he needs more drugs." They increase the dose and the child gets still worse. The reaction is reversible. As soon as the medication is stopped, they get better. At Bellevue we saw too many children who had been put on stimulants and actually became psychotic enough to need admission to the hospital, then became better when the medication was stopped (Fish, 1971). Stimulants were being misused in these children. Instead of continuing to use the same drug at higher doses, other drugs should have been tried.

WHAT STIMULANTS DO NOT DO

One also has to discuss what stimulants *do not do.* They can change drug-susceptible symptoms such as attention, interest, drive, restlessness, etc. They do not change patterned activity of a child. No drug really changes that. If a child has a problem in social interaction, possibly secondary to his hyperactivity and aggressivity, the drug could change only the excitability that made him act aggressive. But if he has already gotten into difficulties with other children, he will still feel badly about himself and other children. The drug is not going to take the place of giving him help for these feelings.

In the same way, a drug is not going to take care of the patterned problems which constitute the learning disability in many of these children. A large percent—well over half, depending on the particular group one is discussing—have very specific perceptual problems that enter into their educational difficulty. Some of the reports on stimulants give the impression that the children were all better at school after medication. Perhaps they did do somewhat better when they were only given medication. If they had poor attention and perceptual problems before, at least when their attention improved they could look at the things that were difficult, could listen a little better to the teacher and learn some of the material, if the perceptual problems were not too severe. But a drug will not clear up those perceptual problems. Some tests reflect an improvement in impulsivity (Conners et al., 1969), but none of the tests have shown changes in what I would consider the structured, patterned disabilities of these children. They will still need very specific remedial help, depending upon what kind of educational disability they have.

It is poor treatment if children are given medication without having had an adequate diagnostic evaluation for the educational problems—if they are given drugs as if that were going to do the whole job.

DEFINING "HYPERACTIVITY"

Another problem is that even though stimulants work, one cannot predict when they are going to work and when they are not. In order to discuss this, we must define what we mean by hyperactivity, hyperactive behavior disorder and minimal brain dysfunction. The confusion arises because the term hyperactivity is used interchangeably for many different kinds of things. It is only a symptom; it describes only a piece of behavior and nothing more. But it gets used as if it were a specific label for a disease or even for a particular group of children. Unless we define this much more carefully, it will continue to create confusion. "Hyperactive child" is often used interchangeably with "minimal brain dysfunction." What do these terms mean? One can't straighten this out unless one distinguishes the diagnosis of the mental disorder from the other terms.

Table II shows the diagnostic grid presented in an earlier paper (Fish, 1971).The terms used in the official psychiatric glossary of mental disorders (*Diagnostic Manual*, 1968) are listed in the vertical column on the left. These terms refer to a *total personality picture, a medical diagnosis.* These are different from *symptoms* listed horizontally across the top of the table.

The *symptom of hyperactivity* is listed in the horizontal row on top. Any child may be overactive or not overactive. This symptom of hyperactivity can occur in any one of the psychiatric disorders that occur in children. In the top row are the most severe disorders, the *psychotic reactions.* These include schizophrenic children and children who have a psychosis with a specific organic brain disorder. Psychotic children may be hyperactive.

In the next row are listed the moderately disturbed children who have the so-called *behavior disorders.* They aren't really neurotic, because children's disorders are much more fluid and flexible. They may have a little flavor of neurosis and these are the children with an "overanxious behavior disorder." Or, children may have some personality difficulty with less evidence of anxiety. They deny that they are worried or anxious inside, even when one can find out eventually that there is something troubling them. These are children who have to deny problems and have to see everything as something that happens outside of themselves. They need to blame problems on circumstances, or on other people. They have great difficulty being introspective about themselves. They don't have anything as fixed as an adult character disorder, although many of them do when they are grown up. These children have what are called "unsocialized aggressive behavior disorders." The neurotic, overanxious children can be overactive or not. They are overly conforming, overanxious and overdependent, just the opposite of the unsocialized aggressive children who say, "Let me handle it my way, don't interfere. I don't need

TABLE II
Diagnostic Scheme for Mental Disorders in Children with or without Developmental Disorders*

Diagnosis	Symptom of Hyperkinesia — None Present / Motor disturbance (306.3)	Developmental Disorders: Cognitive Dysfunction — None Minor / Learning disturbance (306.1)	Cognitive Dysfunction — Major / Mental retardation (310–315)	Other Cerebral Dysfunction — None Minor / Psychomotor disorder (306.3)	Other Cerebral Dysfunction — Major / OBS (292–294, 309)
Mental disorders					
Schizophrenia, childhood type (295.8)					Rarely, both diagnoses coexist
Psychosis with OBS (292–294)					Psychosis with OBS (292–294)
Behavior disorders:					
Hyperkinetic reaction (308.0) (immature, inadequate-labile type only)					Nonpsychotic OBS (309)
Withdrawing reaction (308.1)					Nonpsychotic OBS (309)
Overanxious reaction (308.2)					Nonpsychotic OBS (309)
Unsocialized aggressive reaction (308.4)					Nonpsychotic OBS (309)
Transient adjustment reaction (307.1)					Nonpsychotic OBS (309)
No mental disorder (318)					Nonpsychotic OBS (309)

*Numbers in parentheses are from the *DSM II*.

to be taught. I can read." The aggressive children may also be hyperactive or not.

Within the behavior disorder category are also the children who now are designated by the term *"hyperactive behavior disorder,"* a specific mental disorder. The way this is described in the official APA glossary is very inadequate. It mentions only overactivity, restlessness and decreased attention span, which does not differentiate these children from any of the other types of behavior disorders when the latter are also overactive. When we studied hyperactive children on the Bellevue inpatient service and tried to rate the severity of their disturbance, we found we couldn't compare them until we split them into four distinct types of children (Fish and Shapiro, 1965). We could compare the children to each other within each of these groups and then rate their disturbance. One group was very disorganized and completely fragmented. These are in the psychotic category in Table II. Two groups of children were well organized. They were either overanxious and overdependent, or they denied anxiety and got into difficulty because they acted too independently. These are now called the "overanxious" and the "antisocial aggressive" behavior disorders. Then there were children who were not fragmented and sick, as the really psychotic children were, but they certainly weren't as well put together as the other two groups. They didn't have one specific way of coping. Sometimes they were overanxious and dependent; sometimes they were fighting to be independent and were very negative and aggressive. Sometimes they were very clinging and very babyish. We called this the *immature, inadequate, labile* group. They were inadequate in the sense that they were not grown up enough and organized enough to have already developed some particular style of coping with their problems. They were certainly immature in this sense. And they were very labile. They looked very different from one day to the next in the way they related and behaved. It is this kind of child for whom I would prefer to reserve the term "hyperactive behavior disorder." They acted differently from the other types of behavior disorders, even though the other children were also hyperactive.

The immature, inadequate, labile group responded differently to medication. When all the children were given placebo, a fairly large number of the well-organized children responded. Even though they were sick enough to require hospitalization, they could respond to the general demands of a structured inpatient service. The hyperactive, inadequate, labile children just couldn't change. They would try, but they couldn't try long enough and they just couldn't cope. They didn't seem to have sufficient maturity. We suspect that this is partly neurological in a very broad sense. They did not have a specific organic brain disease, but functioned like much younger children, although they were not mentally retarded. They did not respond to milieu treatment when on placebo, but had to have an effective medication before they could improve.

The APA glossary of mental disorders (*Diagnostic Manual*, 1968) should add a description of inadequate, immature, labile behavior to the criteria for the "hyperactive behavior disorder," to differentiate these children from hyperactive children with other behavior disorders. Jenkins, who wrote the final version of this section of the glossary, said that these were the children the term was intended for. Without the more specific description, the "hyperactive behavior disorder" becomes a wastebasket for any hyperactive child who is not psychotic but severe enough to need some kind of help. This is one of the major diagnostic problems.

Finally, at the bottom of Table II are the children who are milder than the behavior disorders. They have either mild disorders or no mental disorder. The mild disorders are called *transient adjustment reactions*. In other words, these children have no crystallized personality problem. They are responding only to an immediate stress. As soon as this is removed, they are fine. That term is often misapplied to children with more chronic behavior disorders, because there is some reactive element. Every child has some reactive problems, including schizophrenic children. "Adjustment reaction" should be reserved for children whose *only* difficulty is an acute reaction. For example, the three-year-old who goes into the hospital and suddenly starts to bed-wet again should not be treated with drugs. All he needs is to be removed from the stressful situation and then he gets better. A child with this type of reaction, particularly the younger child under stress, can develop transient hyperactivity.

Hyperactivity as a Symptom
Hyperactivity as a symptom is really a sign of immaturity. It is one of the few ways children have of responding to problems. Children are normally "hyperactive" compared to adults, and tend to be some-

what impulsive. They run around much more and we marvel at their energy. The very young child always has problems stopping and starting. His mother says "no" and he stops for a second. He knows what "no" means and he knows what is going to happen if he doesn't listen, but he has trouble with his brakes. He hasn't refined all the necessary equipment. So hyperactivity is a normal response for the child. If he is under stress, he may get more hyperactive. Hyperactivity as a symptom is a very nonspecific response—a more primitive response, if you will, than the kinds of symptoms adults have, such as anxiety or depression. Children have to be more grown up before they can express their distress in such differentiated feelings as anxiety, fearfulness, worry or depression and sadness. Their unhappiness has a much more undifferentiated quality and is all mixed up with being angry.

Hyperactivity, or overactivity, is just as nonspecific as a symptom as anxiety or depression is in adults. Just as there are normal adults with no mental disorder who feel anxious or sometimes depressed, so children can sometimes be overactive without having any mental or personality disorder. Adults with neurotic disorders or psychoses can also be anxious or depressed. In order to treat the adult, we have to make a psychiatric diagnosis of how well put together his total personality is. We have to do the same thing with children. One sees the symptom of hyperactivity and then has to evaluate how well put together this individual is in terms of total personality organization. The diagnosis is simply the psychiatrist's way of categorizing this severity of disorganization and estimating how well the individual is likely to respond to treatment.

Learning Disorders and "Minimal Brain Dysfunction"

There are other problems that get confused with hyperactivity as a symptom. Table II indicates that children with any personality diagnosis may have no cognitive problems and no problem in learning. Or they may have a minor cognitive problem with a lag in a specific area of learning, like children with reading disabilities, arithmetic problems or speech disorders. Or they may have a major cognitive disorder with mental retardation.

Learning disorders occur with all diagnoses and also with no mental disorder. Some children with "hyperactive behavior disorders" have no cognitive disturbance. However, because of their general immaturity, there is a higher incidence of learning disorders and minimal neurological symptoms in this group of children than in the "overanxious" or the well-organized, "antisocial," "aggressive" children. But they can have learning disorders, too, as can psychotic children.

Obviously the treatment of the learning disorder must be different, depending on how severe the personality problem is. All of them will need specific educational help. If a child has no personality problem, he can meet the teacher halfway on the educational problem. If he is very immature, he will have additional difficulties and his teacher and others will have to handle his educational problem accordingly. In the same way, medication will work differently on these different kinds of children and affect the attention disturbance differently, depending on how severe the personality disorder is.

Finally, "other cerebral dysfunctions" are listed on the horizontal line of symptoms in Table II, to include the perceptual disorders or specific motor disabilities and other neurologic problems. Children with any diagnosis may be totally without such signs, even the immature, inadequate, "hyperactive behavior disorders." Or they may have minor signs with so-called "minimal brain dysfunction" or they may have severe, very specific neurologic disorders. There may be a child with a major neurologic disorder who has no personality disorder, or he may have any one of these personality types.

The so-called *minimal brain syndrome* is another one of these wastebaskets. At times the diagnostic criteria are not even specified. At times the term is used as if it were synonymous with the "hyperactive behavior disorders," but it isn't. I would limit it to children who have some sign of *cerebral dysfunction* that is minor. This could include any one of specific patterns of motor, perceptual or cognitive disturbance. It might be associated with any kind of psychiatric personality disorder or with no personality problem, whereas the "hyperactive behavior disorder" refers to a particular type of personality organization, which may or may not be associated with perceptual or cognitive symptoms.

WHEN TO GIVE MEDICATION

To start with, we see a child whose problems seem severe enough to require medication. This problem continues wherever he goes, even out of the immediately stressful situation, and even when we begin to handle his learning disorder. Even when we give him one-to-one remedial help of the kind he seems to need, he still has problems of attention. So we add medication to this program to see whether a drug can help him focus his attention any better.

If he needs specific remedial help, his remedial teacher ought to try working with him first, to see what he is like without a drug, so that she has some base line against which to measure improvement without relying on the classroom situation where he has been frustrated. It is quite possible that when he gets enough attention, and the teacher helps him focus and he isn't in a distracting situation, he may have no problem with attention. But he still may have some problem with attention in the overstimulating classroom setting and he also needs to function there. At least then we would know that his disorder is not severe enough to show up in a one-to-one situation, although it does show up in the group.

I would try a drug if, under ordinary conditions, a child continued to show some kind of *attention difficulty that did not subside within two to four weeks,* and which significantly interfered with his academic or social functioning. Generally children are very changeable. If a child is able to respond to an optimal teaching situation without the physiological help of a drug, he does so very quickly. If it takes a long time, even if eventually one can modify his behavior, it is too much of a strain on the child to have to change without some pharmacologic help. I feel it is kinder to the child to add medication very early, if it's going to accelerate his improvement even a little.

Medication can be stopped at the point when the child's behavior and his learning have caught up. He has repatterned, with the help of medication, so he can now cope with learning in the way that he will have to cope with it every day without the help of a drug. Then one stops the medication. Preadolescent children do not become addicted. At least we have never seen it so far. They usually want to stop the medication long before we think they are ready to. They do not tend to be dependent on the drug. The problem is rather that they don't see the need for it in the first place.

DRUG POTENCY
In order to discuss the indications for drug treatment, one should first rank drugs in terms of potency from the mildest to the most potent.

I would classify the *stimulants as the mildest of the drugs.* The kinds of changes they produce, beneficial as well as toxic changes, are milder than the other drugs. I also believe that they are useful for milder types of symptoms and for children with generally milder forms of the behavior disorders (Fish, 1960, 1968).

Also in the mild category are the *minor tranquilizers,* but for children we tend not to use the same tranquilizing drugs that are used in adults. Phenobarbital does not usually help prepubertal children. In general, drugs such as meprobamate are not as effective in preadolescent children as are other drugs, although one sometimes uses them. The most effective minor tranquilizer for children is Benadryl. It does not seem to sedate children under the age of nine or ten. After ten, it acts as it does in adults, and children begin to feel a little tired or even sleepy during the daytime. What happens before ten years is that it seems to have a more normalizing effect on the restlessness and hyperactivity especially, but also on some of the anxiety symptoms as well. It helps some children who are even more disturbed than those who respond well to amphetamines (Fish, 1960, 1968).

The most potent drugs are the so-called *major tranquilizers,* those used for adults with severe personality and neurotic disorders, but primarily for the psychotic disorders. These include chlorpromazine (Thorazine), trifluperazine (Stelazine), haloperidol (Haldol) and thiothixene (Navane).

WHICH DRUG FOR WHICH CHILD?

We still don't always know which drug is going to be best for a particular child. The physiological tests are still a research tool and are too cumbersome for everyday use in any case. The simplest procedure is to use a trial of several drugs, starting with the mildest and working up to the more potent.

Even if I think a child is more severe, that is, higher up on my grid (Table II), and even though he will probably need a stronger drug, I would still start with a trial of the milder drugs just to make certain. It is the children in the milder range of the behavior disorders for whom I think the stimulants work best. As one goes higher up on the scale of severity, children generally need something stronger. However, I would always give them the benefit of the doubt and start off with the *stimulants.* One can tell if they respond within two hours; if it isn't enough, one can increase the dose the next day and titrate it up until there are signs of too much drug.

All this is discussed with the child. One tells him, "Any medicine can make you feel too sleepy, too tired, too washed out or too tense and too jumpy. I don't know how you are going to feel and I want you to tell me if it makes you feel too dopey or too jumpy." The child may begin to be a little too fretful or become a little more cheerful. He may not even think it's the drug. Children tend to attribute anything bad that happens to them physically to the drug. Any thing good that happens to them they feel is just themselves; they don't think it's the drug. So the child will often tell you very quickly, "That medicine makes me very cranky; it makes me feel bad and I've been crying a lot and having trouble sleeping." He probably won't mention his trouble eating, unless you ask him, so one must monitor the weight of children on stimulants. They can show rapid drops in weight and this should obviously always be discussed with the parents to make certain the children don't get too much medication. Some say children get over the loss of appetite, but I have yet to see it. Apparently it takes a long time and I have never kept a child on stimulants that long.

Even if the symptoms improve with stimulants and the attention improves, unless the child becomes absolutely like a normal child and is free of any symptoms that may be susceptible to drug treatment one should try something else to see if it helps more. This assumes one has pushed the dose up sufficiently so one knows that this is the best this drug can do. A higher dose only makes him feel worse. Then one takes him off the drug to see what he is like without anything. He may have already changed somewhat on the first drug.

I would then try him on the next more potent drug, which would be *Benadryl.* One titrates this up the same way, starting with a lower dose and gradually building it up until the point where it seems like a little too much. Younger children don't get sleepy on Benadryl, but often they get a sense of fullness in the head, they have deeper rings under their eyes, or their face looks a little too tense. At that point, we know the dose is too much, and can determine what the next lower dose was able to do.

In my private practice series, each child was his own control. There were sixteen children in the behavior disorder group whom I tried on stimulants. Fourteen showed some improvement. However, of that fourteen there were only five that did so well on stimulants, losing their symptoms completely, that they didn't need a trial on any other drug. These were the children with school phobias (Fish, 1960). The psychiatric diagnosis was "overanxious behavior disorder." On stimulants, their symptoms melted away completely and they returned to school. When I withdrew the drug, they continued to be fine and never needed a trial on anything else. Most of the other children with behavior disorders, especially the "immature, inadequate" ones, did better on Benadryl than they did on stimulants. We still need a controlled study of stimulants versus Benadryl. There are studies of stimulants versus chlorpromazine (Weiss et al., 1968), but this is a big jump. One should test something in-between. I consider Benadryl less toxic than the stimulants, because children don't get sleepy and they don't develop poor appetite and irritability. When I got to Bellevue and began doing controlled studies, the children there were too severely ill and needed more potent medication. It wasn't an appropriate population to test on amphetamine.

If a child continued to have disabling problems on Benadryl, even though he was not psychotic, I would try him on a major tranquilizer starting with *chlorpromazine*, which is still the standard. One would titrate this up in exactly the same way as the previous drugs. It is even more obvious when there is too much chlorpromazine because the children get sleepy and one can readily see when to decrease the dose. When children with severe behavior disorders respond to chlorpromazine, they usually don't need doses that are so high that one has to worry about the serious long-term toxic effects. The effects of chlorpromazine on the liver, eyes and skin occur in adults on very high doses. Usually children with behavior disorders do not need much more than 100 mg. a day, and this is a relatively small, safe dose. It is only the extremely psychotic children, whose symptoms don't disappear even with the strongest drugs we use, who need high doses. They always have some residual symptoms, and one has to weigh the toxicity with the benefits given the child by a given dose. I would not hesitate to use a major tranquilizer if the child did better on it than on any other medication, as long as it was monitored carefully. More specifics about other drugs and the management of medication will be found in the references (Fish, 1960, 1968), including toxic effects and how one monitors these.

The public health problems that the HEW-OCD panel addressed

itself to still exist. There sometimes is inadequate medical supervision of these children. Pressed by the number of children needing help, stimulants may be prescribed as if they could do the whole job and some are prescribed when they are not indicated. Good medical care requires a thorough diagnostic evaluation of the personality disorder, of neurologic, psychological and educational impairments, followed by an adequate trial of appropriate educational remediation, and then a careful evaluation of which drug is most helpful. This thorough a program is not as readily available to all children as it should be.

REFERENCES

Bender, L., and Cottington, F. (1942). The use of amphetamine sulfate (Benzedrine) in child psychiatry. *Amer. J. Psychiat.* 99:116–21.

Bradley, C. (1937). The behavior of children receiving Benzedrine. *Amer. J. Psychiat.* 94:577–85.

———— and Bowen, M. (1941). Amphetamine (Benzedrine) therapy of children's behavior disorders. *Amer. J. Orthopsychiat.* 11:92–103.

Conners, C. K., and Eisenberg, L. (1963). The effects of methylphenidate on symptomatology and learning in disturbed children. *Amer. J. Psychiat.* 120:458–64.

————, Rothschild, G., Eisenberg, L., Schwartz, L., and Robinson, E. (1969). Dextroamphetamine sulfate in children with learning disorders: effects on perception, learning and achievement. *Arch. Gen. Psychiat.* 21:182–90.

Diagnostic and Statistical Manual of Mental Disorders (1968). 2nd ed. Washington, D. C.: American Psychiatric Association.

Fish, B. (1960). Drug therapy in child psychiatry: pharmacological aspects. *Compr. Psychiat.* 1:212–27.

———— (1968). Drug use in psychiatric disorders of children. *Amer. J. Psychiat.* 124 (Feb. Suppl):31–36.

———— (1971). The "one child, one drug" myth of stimulants in hyperkinesis. Importance of diagnostic categories in evaluating treatment. *Arch. Gen. Psychiat.* 25:193–203.

———— and Shapiro, T. (1965). A typology of children's psychiatric disorders: I. Its application to a controlled evaluation of treatment. *J. Amer. Acad. Child. Psychiat.* 4:32–52.

Freedman, D. X. (1971). Chairman: Report of the conference on the use of stimulant drugs in the treatment of behaviorally disturbed children. Sponsored by the Office of Child Development and the Office of the Assistant Secretary for Health & Scientific Affairs, Dept. Health, Educ. & Welfare, Washington, D. C. (January 11–12).

Knopp, W., Arnold, L. E., Andras, R. L., and Smelzer, D. (1973). Predicting amphetamine response in hyperkinetic children by electronic pupillography. *Pharmakopsychiatrie/Neuro-Psychopharmakologie* 6:158–166.

Satterfield, J. H., Cantwell, D. P., Lesser, L. I., and Podosin, R. (1972). Physiological studies of the hyperkinetic child, I. *Amer. J. Psychiat.* 128:1418–24.

Weiss, G., Werry, J. S., Minde, K., Douglas, V., and Sykes, D. (1968). Studies on the hyperactive child. V:The effects of dextroamphetamine and chlorpromazine on behavior and intellectual functioning. *J. Child Psychol. Psychiat.* 9:145–56.

Chapter Eight

Behavioral Management of the Hyperactive Child

JAMES Q. SIMMONS, III, M.D.

This chapter is intended to briefly discuss behavioral strategies which can be employed directly with children who are hyperactive. No effort will be made to become immersed in the differential diagnostic problems of minimal brain dysfunction, specific learning disabilities or other problems related to hyperactivity in children. The purpose is to generally redefine for the reader the cardinal principles of behavior modification and describe their application to the hyperactive child in different configurations, which in no way excludes the application of other treatment modalities to this complex problem. It is not intended as an in-depth discussion of the general field of behavior therapy and its principles, nor is it intended to be a specific guide for behavioral intervention. Hopefully it will present some guidelines for thinking about one type of strategy for the management of this problem area.

With regard to the hyperactive child there are three major reasons for looking beyond medication and considering behavioral strategies. The first reason generally relates to the problems of drugs themselves and, in particular, side effects and the long-term effects of stimulant drugs on physical growth, the possible development of a pattern of drug-dependent behavior, and problems of learning which may be state-dependent and thus may affect the transfer of learning from the drug state to the non-drug state (Solomons, 1973; Millichap, 1973; Wender, 1971).

The second area of concern centers on the behavioral repertoire of hyperactive children and the types of environmental responses they have elicited over the course of their lifetime. It is clear from the histories of children with hyperactive behavior that considerably more is involved than hyperactivity and a short attention span (Laufer, 1973). The children are a part of a complex interactive microcosm (the family) and macrocosm (the general social surroundings) in which any one of the three components periodically serves as a trigger mechanism for maladaptive behavior. Therefore, not only does the hyperactive child require management (whether pharmacological or behavioral), but also the environment (family, peers and school) needs some degree of management with regard to expectations of, rewards and punishments to, and adaptive responses to the hyperactive child.

The third reason for consideration of the need for behavioral management techniques is the fact that a significant number of hyperactive children do not respond to medication (Jacob et al., 1973), which essentially mandates some form of behavioral control strategies. Various psychotherapeutic approaches have been taken to achieve some degree of amelioration of the problems occasioned by the presence of a hyperactive child in the home and school. Hope is usually highest for some sort of short-term, unidimensional method of treatment, but it is obvious on the basis of experience that the disorder is multifaceted. Although pharmacological agents reduce hyperkinesis and are extremely useful in the population that does respond to the medication, there still remain a large number of problems under environmental control, and thus marginally suitable target symptoms for drug management. These include hyperactive behavior not responsive to drug effect, all aspects of task performance from initiation, to maintenance and completion, social conformity, play rules, peer interaction, and habit training, to name a few.

Since so many of these behaviors are under precise environmental control, it appears profitable to consider a functional analysis of behavior approach to their identification and the nature of maintaining events, and to apply reinforcement learning principles to their alteration.

CHARACTERISTICS OF A BEHAVIORAL APPROACH

The behavioral approach to human problems is an example of the direct translation of findings from the animal and human laboratory to the solution of these problems. The greatest impetus for this approach to human problem-solving has come from the extensive laboratory explorations of B. F. Skinner (1953) and a small but significant first and second generation of his students, who applied behavioral technology to a host of human problems. The basic contribution has been not necessarily in the actual management of a given condition, but in the establishment of a systematic approach to identifying problems and objectives, which leads to effective intervention. In order to understand more clearly the examples of the treatment approaches to be discussed below, it should prove useful to briefly describe, in a systematic fashion, five steps involved in the method of analyzing a problem and the selection of tactics for effecting change.

The first step involves the *identification and definition of behaviors to be established or modified.* Simple as it may sound, in this era of accountability it is essential to avoid global characteristics of behavior to be changed (such as ego strength, character and personality) and focus more precisely on clearly defined behaviors which can be easily described and reliably measured. In the case of the hyperactive child, this might mean sitting-in-chair behavior in school, percent time in attention to task, number of appropriate interactions with peers, or number of aggressive incidents per unit time, to mention just a few.

Step two involves the *analysis of the behaviors to be established or modified in the environment where they occur.* Although this essential ingredient of treatment has been inherent in residential management, it has been more implicit than explicit. Nevertheless, the evaluation of maladaptive functioning within the environment that generates it has usually been a part of the diagnostic process. However, more recently it has become a much more highly refined part of the art to analyze maladaptive behavior in the context of interaction with siblings (Brown, in press), peers (Clement, 1973; Patterson et al., 1965) and the dominant social environment. This approach not only analyzes the operations of the identified patient, but establishes in part the behavioral norms for the group, as well as identifies key triggering events or agents in the environment.

The next step is to *establish a change motivator.* Obviously with highly motivated, socially effective individuals there is a whole series of motivators ranging from the primary reinforcer to extremely unique intrinsic reinforcers. The exact nature of the latter is often difficult to determine. Thus the effective individual is performing at a high level under the influence of multiple complex stimuli and responses. However, as one moves to the maladaptive population such as the hyperactive child, the search for significant stimuli and effective reinforcers becomes somewhat more critical. Since reinforcers are unique to the individual, they may not be the same as those motivating other members of the peer group. It is conceivable, for example, that some of the behavior of the hyperactive child is intrinsically reinforcing (hyperactivity) and thus difficult to bring under control. Nevertheless, the general principles of reinforcement manipulation are applicable to the problem, and range from a search for primary reinforcers (e.g., food) used in a continuous reinforcement schedule, to somewhat more subtle reinforcement paradigms such as response cost (Mann, 1972), the Premack principle (Premack, 1965), token systems (Ayllon and Azrin, 1968), peer control systems (Clement, 1972) and ultimately self-control systems (Simmons and Wikler, 1972). The key feature of any reinforcement system other than aversive stimulation is the fact that success depends upon the reinforcement preferences of the patient and thus the best constructed objectives cannot be obtained if they are not supported by personally acceptable reinforcers.

After defining behaviors, establishing the environment within which they are to be studied and selecting a reinforcement system, the *next step* in practical management consists of *a measuring system,* which will provide reliable indicators of change (assuming that change is the objective of the intervention [Clement, 1972]). The critical agendas in this aspect of behavioral intervention involve the establishment of base lines on behavior, demonstrating a change over base line under the influence of treatment, and at times demonstrating a return to base line when treatment variables are removed. The very fact of measurement forces reliable definition of the behavior to be modified. Thus it becomes clear why time at task performance, time in seat, number of hitting incidents, frequency of foul language, and task performance itself, are the types of behaviors which command the attention of the behavior therapist. The measuring techniques themselves vary from simple frequency counts made with a hand counter or simple check list, to much more complex frequency and duration assessments utilizing a multiple-event recorder or even videotape recording which is then available for playback.

Step five in behavioral management requires *the definition of the change agent.* It is becoming more apparent with the passage of time that vast skill resources exist within various professions, the families and the peer culture which have not been traditionally utilized in effecting adaptive change in hyperactive children's behavior. With the introduction of behavioral technology, which can be transmitted in somewhat more parsimonious terms than traditional psychotherapeutic information, it is possible to greatly expand the number and educational levels of individuals who can be considered responsible change agents. The realization of this possibility is witnessed by the proliferation of reports concerning the use of teachers (Forness, 1970), parents and peers (Clement, 1973; Patterson et al., 1965), siblings (Brown, in press) and the self (Simmons and Wikler, 1972) as active participants in the treatment of children with behavioral disorders.

Somewhat related to the designation of change agents is the identification of the environment within which change is to take place. In the not too distant past, many children with severe behavioral problems were treated in the artificial climate of a therapist's office, a hospital or a clinic, with the hope that there would be an extension of newly acquired adaptive behaviors into other environments such as the home and school. Although some degree of generalization of treatment results from these somewhat artificial situations into other social areas does occur, more often than not if family, peers and school are not at least partially reprogrammed, treatment runs the serious risk of being defeated by forces outside the control of the therapist. It is this kind of thinking which has led to a considerable shift in interest and practice from the office to the environment within which the child must function.

These steps essentially represent the cornerstones of a behavioral approach to the management of hyperactive children. Obviously any further definition involving such areas as the problems of reliability, schedules of reinforcement, reversal and multiple base-line designs, in-depth discussion of independent and dependent variables and the details of measurement techniques is considerably beyond the scope of this paper. However, for the interested reader a variety of excellent texts is available (Kanfer and Phillips, 1970; Ferster & Perrott, 1968; Bandura, 1969).

CASE APPLICATIONS

Three clinical cases will be used to demonstrate the application of the principles described above. These actually represent approaches to single patients which make use of the therapist and family, the peers in a school setting, and the self in a hospital environment as control agents.

Case I

This child is a seven-year-old boy of normal intelligence, clinically diagnosed as "hyperkinetic reaction of childhood." The procedure utilized was developed by Lovaas and Willis (1974) and will be discussed in detail in a forthcoming manuscript.

The boy was early described as an active, restless infant. After age nine months, he was characterized as being "into everything." As he grew older he was unable to remain at one thing or in one place for any length of time. This inability to remain quiet eventually impaired his capability to maintain attention to tasks, or to pay attention to verbal instructions. A prominent feature of his social development was aggressiveness in his interaction with people and with objects. In addition, he was a demanding child who could not delay gratification and, when frustrated, responded with crying and whining or full-blown temper tantrums. In substance he had extreme difficulty with control which impaired his functioning at home, with his peers and in school. The impairment in school was both behavioral and academic.

Utilizing the five major categories of consideration described above, Lovaas and Willis (1974) approached the problem as follows: The treatment was carried out in three separate locations, beginning with the laboratory, then successively extending into the home and finally to the school. In the laboratory the primary focus was on task performance, which consisted of two simple math problems. Attendant behaviors necessary to accomplish these tasks were compliance to simple demands and a certain amount of in-seat behavior. The parents were selected as change agents and were instructed in the basic principles of behavior modification and referred to Patterson and Gullion's *Living with Children* (1968) for outside preparation. Through behavioral rehearsal, recognition training and on-the-spot instruction using "bug in the ear" technology, the parents were taught to define appropriate and inappropriate behaviors, to manipulate reinforcement contingent on the behaviors actually produced and to monitor their success or failure on the basis of behavioral change. During the laboratory phase of treatment, the reinforcers consisted of social praise, a play corner with various toys available and a "time out" corner.

The positive reinforcers were obviously used to increase the rate of compliance behavior and the "time out" corner was used to reduce noncompliant behavior. "Time out" was backed up by physical aversion in the form of spanking.

After the completion of the brief clinic phase of the program, the therapeutic activity was shifted to the home. The child was observed by the parents with the aid of one therapist. Behavior was recorded on a checklist and mainly included those items which were a constant problem to the parents. These included verbally refusing to obey, tantrums, refusing to obey a command within an arbitrary five-second period, biting and striking others, and yelling and screaming at the parents. These behaviors were monitored for short periods of time (five minutes), six times a day (three in the morning and three in the evening). The reinforcement medium was tokens backed up by items within the preference hierarchy of the boy himself. These included TV-watching, swimming and roller-skating. Adaptive behaviors such as self-care, home chores and others were rewarded with blue tokens (Sr^+), and unacceptable behaviors resulted in response cost in the form of red tokens ($Sr-$) discriminative for "time out" and its back-up, spanking.

Within a short period of time (six training sessions) there was a marked change from a high rate of noncompliance and at the same time there was also a marked decrease in demanding behavior on the part of the parent. When only blue tokens were given, although adaptive performance increased, maladaptive behaviors also remained at a high rate. With the introduction of a response cost stratagem (red tokens), adaptive behavior remained high while maladaptive behavior dropped to zero.

Subsequent to successful treatment within the home, the program was moved to the classroom, where selected behaviors associated with academic performance were identified. They included attention to task, completion of assignment and correctness. These were rewarded with blue checks which were exchanged at home for blue tokens. Again a response cost contract was introduced by the simple device of red checks for inappropriate behavior such as out-of-seat without permission, aggressive behavior and inappropriate posture. These were backed up at home by the red token system discriminative for "time out" and spanking. Again the level of academically adaptive behavior increased significantly and maladaptive behavior decreased to zero.

Case II

A second approach to this problem is epitomized in the rather creative work of Paul Clement (1973), who has utilized peers as behavior therapists in the modification of socially deviant behavior. Clement worked with a five-year-old boy not specifically described as hyperactive, but whose social behavior was provocative and teasing, and resulted in constant friction with his peers. In addition, classroom attention was impaired. Since the problems seemed to be interactive and to center on physically aggressive behavior and the lack of cooperative play, these were chosen as the target behaviors. Clement reasoned that maladaptive behavior in children is quite often generated and maintained by peer response to that behavior. Also, treatment is often successful in the isolation of a clinic or laboratory, but upon return to a previously programmed environment the maladaptive behavior immediately reasserts itself. Therefore, his strategy with this particular child was to obtain consent from the parents of several significant peers to utilize those peers as therapeutic aids in the intervention. The total procedure covered a period of approximately thirty weeks and was divided into two major segments: (1)treatment in the clinic, and (2)treatment in the school.

A two-week base line of classroom behaviors such as walking around in the classroom, disrupting others and physical aggression was taken prior to the beginning of treatment. Subsequently the patient and four peers were brought into the clinic, and another week of similar base-line study was carried out. In all instances, it was found that the patient's walking around and disruptive behavior (interrupting others' activities) was high, and that physical aggression toward him by his peers was also quite high, but his own aggression physically directed at his peers was low. Clement then began a thirteen-week period of intervention. Approximately ten weeks of the procedure involved rotating each child (including the patient) into the position of being "chief for the day" and having the responsibility of rewarding all the other children for cooperative play. The "chief" was aided by verbal instructions given to him through the use of the "bug in the ear" device. At the end of each session, the "chief" received the average number of tokens earned by each child in the group. These tokens were then exchanged for candies or small toys. The amount of cooperative play increased markedly and the previously existing maladaptive behaviors of the patient dropped to near zero levels. After ten weeks, the procedure was altered somewhat. The "chief" was given a "beeper" which was activated by the therapist. When this occurred, the "chief" registered points on a point counter whenever any of the children were involved in cooperative play with the patient. Again points were backed up with reinforcers obtainable at the store after each session. This variation, which produced the same effect noted during the initial intervention, was developed as an adaptation more suitable for the classroom, where the next phase of the program was to be carried out.

With parent and teacher consent, the program was moved into the patient's classroom, which was a somewhat more complex environment than the observation room of a clinic. The class of twenty-five students was divided into two teams, each with a captain. In both instances the captain was a child with a history of a high level of maladaptive interaction with the patient. For a fifteen-week period, the teams alternated two times a week playing the game of cooperative play with the patient. The game was carried out for a twenty-minute period during free time on as many days as possible for the duration of the program. The team captains were responsible for scoring points for their teams if someone in the group was interacting with the patient whenever the therapist activated a signal to the captain's beeper. At the end of each week the team with the highest score was given the privilege of special snacks at snack-time on Friday. Although a total of eighteen behaviors were analyzed involving the patient (ten), the class (four) and the teacher (four), the significant results consisted primarily of diminished walking around in the classroom and diminished disruptive behavior on the part of the patient, and a highly significant reduction in aggression toward the patient by his peers.

Case III
A third approach to this type of patient, carried out at the Neuropsychiatric Institute, UCLA, was depicted in a twenty-minute film seg-

TABLE I

Authors	Step I Identifying & Definition of Behaviors To Be Changed	Step II Environment Where Behavioral Analysis Was Carried Out
LOVAAS AND WILLIS	(a) Simple math problems (b) Compliance to simple demands (c) In-seat behavior (d) Tantrums (e) Yelling at parents (f) Attacking others (g) Self-care and chores (h) Attention to & completion of task (i) Correctness (j) Aggression (k) Out-of-seat behavior	(a) Laboratory (b) Home (c) School
CLEMENT	(a) Physical aggression (b) Cooperative play (c) Disrupting others (d) Physical aggression by peers (e) Walking around (f) Assertion	(a) Clinic (b) Home (c) School
SIMMONS AND WIKLER	(a) Aggression toward objects & people (b) Pouting (c) Profanity	(a) Hospital ward (b) Intramural school (c) Home

ment (Simmons and Wikler, 1972) involving a self-management program with a ten-year-old boy. In this instance the patient presented a major management problem because of violently aggressive behavior directed toward people and objects, pouting behavior which usually precipitated an aggressive episode, and profanity of an intolerable degree. Because of the intensity of this boy's behavior, plus the

TABLE I *(cont.)*

Step III	Step IV	Step V
Change Motivator	Measuring System	Change Agent
(a) Check marks (b) Tokens (c) Toy play (d) "Time out" (e) Spanking (f) Social praise (g) Social activities (h) TV-watching (i) Response cost	(a) Multiple event recorder (b) Check list	(a) Parents (b) Therapist
(a) Tokens (b) Points (c) Candies (d) Toys (e) Snacks in classroom (f) Social praise	(a) Check list (b) Point counter	(a) Selected peers (b) Classroom peers (c) Family
(a) Stars (b) Chips (c) Social activities (d) One-to-one (e) Response cost (f) "Time out"	(a) Check list (b) Wall chart	(a) Self by contract (b) Ward therapist (c) Family (?)

resistance of the family toward participating in the intervention, it was necessary to separate him from home and carry out the treatment in the hospital.

The choice of a self-management approach was settled upon because the family had difficulty in participating as therapists, despite dynamic family therapy and behavioral instruction, but rather seemed to view the child as a "bad boy." Since he continuously played this role to the hilt to meet family expectations (irrespective of which came first), the strategy decided upon was one in which the child would take the lead in effecting change in the total system. The initial approach to the boy himself was more in the nature of a contract, starting with an agreement on which behaviors he would like to bring under control. It was decided that the two most significant behaviors were the pouting and physical aggression. Pouting was identified as more significant than the swearing because it was usually an antecedent to physical aggression and the swearing was an accompaniment of the physical aggression. Therefore, the intervention was usually attempted early in the chain of behaviors to increase the likelihood that the appearance of the later behaviors in the chain would be reduced. The reinforcers agreed upon were primarily denoted by stars on a chart which earned tokens. These tokens could then be exchanged for treats which usually consisted of a period of time 1:1 with his therapist in a situation such as a walk, a hamburger in a local restaurant, or any other similar choice within our capability. The technique of assessment was basically a combination of self-observation plus observation by others in his environment. He was responsible for maintaining a self-scoring system, posting each waking hour in which none of the maladaptive behaviors appeared. He was given a special watch which could be set for a period of up to one hour. If that hour passed without any of the maladaptive behaviors appearing, he scored it as such on a master chart maintained under his control. These stars then earned tokens which could be exchanged at will for the privileges mentioned above. If he did have a self-reported or other-reported period of pouting, physical aggression or swearing during any hour of the waking day, he failed to receive a star and thus his token earnings were reduced. In addition, for physical aggression he was placed in a short "time out" and when the behavior was under control his clock was reset for the next hour beginning immediately upon release from "time out." Although his maladaptive behavior came under fairly rapid control, it was marked by several testing episodes, particularly around "time out" for aggressive behavior. He could neither earn during "time out" nor could he exchange tokens for reinforcers, but he did not lose any tokens already earned. The program was carried out over a period of eight weeks, during which time it was extended into the home. Despite the family's resistance to actively participating in the program even while in family therapy, the child's behavior was so different under his self-management program that the number of incidents where the family triggered off the behaviors at home was markedly reduced.

DISCUSSION

These three programs exemplify the behavioral approach to the kind of problems seen in the hyperactive child. The basic steps described for analysis of the problem and development of the intervention strategy for each of the cases is recapitulated briefly in Table I for the reader's convenience. Although only one child was diagnosed as a "hyperactive child," all three had behaviors characteristic of this group: physical aggression, disruption and academic inadequacy. Even though a variety of maladaptive behaviors can be brought under control using behavioral techniques, this in no way contraindicates the use of pharmacologic agents in those instances where they have been shown to be effective. Nevertheless, even those children who do respond to drugs show many maladaptive patterns which persist even when the hyperactive behavior is reduced. This finding obviously necessitates the development of a strategy to reduce or eliminate these maladaptive behaviors. The most parsimonious seems to be that of behavior modification.

There are many concerns relative to the use of behavior control measures, but a discussion of these is not germane to the basic purpose of this paper. It is perhaps sufficient to remember that the behaviors targeted for control are usually consensually agreed upon by teachers, parents, peers and, in many instances, the children themselves. Assuming that this consensual agreement contains some element of wisdom, the strategies used for change should be those which most economically focus in on the target behavior and can be demonstrated to effectively reduce it, in the case of maladaptives, or increase it, in the case of socially acceptable behavior. In two of the three clinical examples given, the treatment variable was removed (reversal) and the incidence of unacceptable behavior returned toward base line, while the number of adaptive behaviors began to diminish.

One element of the behavioral approach to these problems does come into question repeatedly. This generally relates to the use of punishment procedures or "time out" in achieving behavioral control (Simmons and Lovaas, 1969). An in-depth discussion of this is obviously also beyond the scope of this paper, but there is evidence that positive reinforcement alone does not always achieve the desired results (Mann, 1972). What is sometimes found is that positive reinforcement will increase the frequency of a newly acquired adaptive behavior to a certain point, but unless it is essentially competing with the predominant maladaptive behavior, the latter will still occur with a high frequency. This necessitates the use of a "time out" or response cost procedure which will operate somewhat independently on such things as temper tantrums, swearing, physical aggression and the like.

This paper has generally been slanted toward a clinical approach to the types of behavior seen in the hyperactive child. The descriptions of procedures used has dwelt not on the refinements of research design, but rather on the practical approach to the management of these problems. Although these clinical descriptions do not suffice to cover all of the vicissitudes of management, and are not mutually exclusive of other approaches, they do offer an insight into a method of treatment of demonstrated effectiveness.

REFERENCES

Ayllon, T., and Azrin, N. (1968). *The Token Economy: A Motivational System for Therapy and Rehabilitation.* New York: Appleton-Century-Crofts.

Bandura, A. (1969). *Principles of Behavior Modification.* New York: Holt, Rinehart and Winston.

Brown, N. (in press). Siblings as behavior modifiers. To be published in *Behavioral Counseling Methods* by J. Krumholtz and C. Thoresen.

Clement, P. (1972). *The Self-Management of Behavior* (13-minute segment of film), directed, produced and distributed by Phillip R. Blake, UCLA Neuropsychiatric Institute, Mental Retardation and Child Psychiatry Media Unit.

——— (1973). Children as behavior therapists. In *Therapeutic Techniques: Working Models for the Helping Professional.* Fullerton, Calif.: California Personnel and Guidance Association, 11–48.

Ferster, C. B., and Perrott, M. C. (1968). *Behavior Principles.* New York: Appleton-Century-Crofts.

Forness, S. (1970). Behavioristic approach to classroom management and motivation. *Psychology in the Schools* 7:356–63.

Jacob, R. G., O'Leary, K. D., and Price, G. H. (1973). *Behavioral Treatment of Hyperactive Children: An Alternate to Medication.* Unpublished manuscript.

Kanfer, F. H., and Phillips, J. S. (1970). *Learning Foundations of Behavior Therapy.* New York: John Wiley & Sons, Inc.

Laufer, M. W. (1973). Psychiatric diagnosis and treatment of children with minimal brain dysfunction. In, F. De La Cruz, B. Fox and R. Roberts, eds., *Minimal Brain Dysfunction.* Annals of the New York Academy of Sciences 205:303–09.

Lovaas, O. I., and Willis, T. (1974). *Behavioral Control of a Hyperactive Child.* Unpublished manuscript.

Mann, R. (1972). Behavior-therapeutic use of contingency contracting to control and adult behavior problem: weight control. *Journal of Applied Behavior Analysis* 5:99.

Millichap, J. G. (1973). Drugs in management of minimal brain dysfunction. In F. De La Cruz, B. Fox and R. Roberts, eds., *Minimal Brain Dysfunction.* Annals of the New York Academy of Sciences 205:321–34.

Patterson, G. R., and Gullion, M. E. (1968). *Living with Children: New Methods for Parents and Teachers.* Champaign, Ill.: Research Press.

———, Jones, R., Whittier, J., and Wright, M. A. (1965). A behavior modification technique for the hyperactive child. *Behavior Research and Therapy* 2:217–26.

Premack, D. (1965). Reinforcement therapy. In D. Levine, ed., *Nebraska Symposium on Motivation.* Lincoln, Neb.: University of Nebraska Press.

Simmons, J. Q., and Lovaas, O. I. (1969). The use of pain and punishment as treatment techniques with schizophrenic children. *American Journal of Psychotherapy* 23:23–36.

——— and Wikler, L. (1972). *The Self-Management of Behavior* (20-minute segment of film). Directed, produced and distributed by Phillip R. Blake, UCLA Neuropsychiatric Institute, Mental Retardation and Child Psychiatry Media Unit.

Skinner, B. F. (1953). *Science and Human Behavior.* New York: Macmillan Co.

Solomons, G. (1973). Drug therapy: initiation and follow-up. In F. De La Cruz, B. Fox and R. Roberts, eds., *Minimal Brain Dysfunction.* Annals of the New York Academy of Sciences 205:335–44.

Wender, P. H. (1971). *Minimal Brain Dysfunction in Children.* New York: John Wiley & Sons, Inc.

Chapter Nine

Videotape Training for Parents as Therapeutic Agents with Hyperactive Children

ANN FEIGHNER, M.S.W.

Average estimates are that from 3 to 6 percent of all school-age children are suffering from hyperactivity in varying degrees (Stewart, 1966; Werner, 1968; *Report,* 1971). Despite increasing evidence that hyperactivity is a chronic, multifaceted problem (Mendelson et al., 1971; Menkes et al., 1967; Weiss et al., 1971b), the diagnosis and treatment of this disorder continues to be oversimplified as a clinical problem (Fish, 1971). Unidimensional programs which use exclusively traditional individual psychotherapy, pharmacotherapy or behavior therapy ignore the full spectrum of psycho-social and biological components of this disorder (Chess, 1960; Eisenberg, 1966; Werry, 1968). This chapter outlines a multi-modality treatment program and discusses in depth the use of videotape techniques in training parents to be effective behavior modifiers of their hyperactive children.

EVALUATION

A thorough, systematic evaluation is a critical phase of the program. Each child is assessed with developmental histories, behavioral questionnaires from both parents and teacher(s), reports from professionals in other agencies who have been involved with the child, and interviews with the parents and child. From this information, current functioning is assessed and specific problem areas are pinpointed in terms of personal behaviors, family relationships and school performance. After careful screening, systematic methods of treatment can then be selected, utilizing a multidiscipline attack on all problem areas. The various treatment modalities should then be used in a complementary manner as dictated by the clinical needs of each case.

TREATMENT

Classroom Management and Curriculum Counseling

School-age children diagnosed as hyperactive (Stewart et al., 1966) usually require some type of intervention in the classroom. Here the role of the therapist as coordinator of a treatment program is most important as an effort is made to promote consistency of expectations and methods of behavioral reinforcement between the home and the school to further reinforce desirable non-hyperactive behaviors (Doubros and Daniels, 1966; Carlson et al., 1968). When accompanying learning problems exist, the therapist can help the parent find the most appropriate resource for the deficit, in either the school or the community. The whole educational process is important to the development of the child's self-image and future success, and if left untreated other efforts to help the child will certainly be made more difficult, if not futile.

Pharmacotherapy

It is not the purpose of this chapter to discuss the complexities of pharmacotherapy in the treatment of hyperactive children. (See Chapter Seven.) On the basis of previous studies, most children diagnosed as being hyperactive are placed on medication primarily to improve attention span, cognition and learning, and to decrease hyperactive behaviors (Conners and Eisenberg, 1963; Fish, 1968; Knights and Hinton, 1969; Krakowski, 1965; Laufer et al., 1957; Millicap, 1967; Safer et al., 1972; Satterfield et al., 1972; Steinberg et al., 1971; Weiss et al., 1968, Weiss et al., 1971a). With this multimodality treatment approach, we recognize that drug therapy does not permanently alter maladaptive behavior patterns, but can significantly enhance school performance and responsiveness to other treatment modalities. Early in the treatment process, parents and teachers are cautioned not to expect "miracles" with pharmacotherapy and are taught behavior management utilizing behavior modification techniques.

Behavior Modification as Taught in Education Groups
One method for teaching parents the principles of behavior modification involves a series of six group sessions where the phenomenology
of hyperkinesis and the specific method of using behavior modification techniques are taught (Hawkins et al., 1966; Smith and Smith,
1970; Stewart, 1970). These group sessions appear not only more
efficient in terms of cost and therapist time, but more constructive
than individual counseling as the group process acts as a behavior
modifier to help parents to accept new methods of behavior management.

Videotape
Once the parents have some intellectual understanding of the process
of behavior modification, its practical application is taught directly
by the use of videotape feedback (Bernal, 1969; Furman and
Feighner, 1973). This treatment method reinforces what the parents
have learned in group, and directly treats established negative behaviors in the child and maladaptive reinforcement patterns in the parents. The videotape feedback technique is designed for the parents
of the hyperactive child to enhance their own capacity to cope effectively with their youngster's affliction.

Longitudinal studies indicate that even after the basic hyperactivity has run its course, the patient is left with maladaptive traits
that seriously impair his overall adjustment (Mendelson et al., 1971;
Menkes et al., 1967; Weiss et al., 1971b). If a parent is inept in coping
with his child's chronic maladaptive behavior, the long-term result
can be reduced self-esteem in the affected youngster and subsequently could increase his tendencies toward antisocial behavior,
depression and other pathological manifestations.

This treatment approach combines the following three established
techniques: (1)videotape confrontation, (2)the use of parents as "surrogate therapists," and (3)the teaching and application of behavior
modification principles.

The use of videotape feedback presents the therapist with the
opportunity to record the segment of typical interaction between the
parent and child and immediately to confront the parent with his
own patterns of reaction. The actual use of videotaping is, of course,
not new and has been made famous by television's "instant replay,"
where significant plays in different sports are replayed immediately
for the benefit of the viewing audience. This is used to add interest

and visual impact to whatever game is being played, and the principle is the same in a therapeutic regime. The use of videotaping is widespread in a teaching capacity on both industrial and university levels. Except for the work with Bernal (1969), videotape has not been widely reported in parent training, although it has been successfully used and reported as being a method of adjunctive psychotherapy with groups, individuals and couples (Bailey, 1970; Berger, 1970; Boyd and Sisney, 1967; Danet, 1968, 1969; Geertsma and Reivich, 1965; Holzman, 1969; Moore, 1965; Resnikoff et al., 1970). Whatever the modality, videotaping provides therapy with highly relevant and appropriate data available immediately after its occurrence, which greatly enhances the learning impact.

Videotaping heightens a subject's sensitivity for his own behavior. When so many behaviors are deeply ingrained and nearly automatic, it is difficult merely by words for a therapist to describe a patient's behavior to him, and then how he might change it in enough detail that will be sufficient for him to actually gather specific details which will enhance his ability to change. Videotaping eliminates the need for a long monologue by the therapist, as the patient can see the point that the therapist is making by the use of this visual aid. Sometimes videotaping provides a shock to the viewer when confronted with his own behavior, and motivation for change is often increased by the person's own desire to present himself as someone with a positive self-image both to himself and to the therapist. Often when parents first come for help they are frustrated and tend to think of their child's behavior in vague, negative terms; the use of videotape helps the therapist direct the attention of the parents to focus on a few specific problem areas, thereby increasing chance for actual change. The parents who have total disbelief that there is any chance of effecting change in the child's behavior is also helped by this method, as the videotape provides a measurement from one session to another which can be replayed to the parents as many times as necessary to show how changes in their own methods have, in fact, elicited changes in their child's behavior. In addition, the videotape method forces the resistant parent to deal with reality by confrontation of his own behavior. The videotaping also ensures patient participation and greater involvement in the therapeutic process. It provides the therapist with a reproduction of what is actually happening between the parent and child and minimizes distortion.

Through their training as behavior modifiers, in effect the parents are being trained to be the child's therapist (Lindsley, 1966; Wahler et al., 1965). The parent is directly instructed by the use of videotape feedback on the application of behavior modification principles to eliminate undesirable behaviors and encourage positive behavior on the part of the hyperactive child. As is outlined in Chapter Eight, behavior modification is useful in eliminating specific maladaptive behaviors, and the instruction places primary emphasis on the selection and definition of rules, constancy of limit setting and utilization of positive reinforcement for acceptable behaviors. Behavior modification is used to teach the parent how to control the child, as the therapist uses positive reinforcement to shape the parental behaviors toward the child. The goal of behavior modification taught in these parent training sessions by videotape, therefore, is to provide consistency of environmental controls to facilitate internalization of control by the child. Parents can achieve considerable success in this role because their proximity to the child gives them the opportunity to reinforce behaviors with more regularity than any other person in the child's natural environment. In our program we have found few parents inappropriate for this kind of training and have found it successful with families of every socioeconomic level. Parent characteristics which have been indicators for success have been the presence of motivation and cooperation for change and a lack of severe interference from a spouse (or other significant person) which would make consistency difficult.

The simultaneous use of the parents as auxiliary therapist, videotape feedback and behavior modification principles to train the parents to affect their child's behavior represents a relatively unique combination approach compared with those in the general literature.

Method of Videotape Feedback

In preparing a family for videotape feedback, it is explained that this is a method for which we will concentrate on any complaint presented by the parent or child as being a problem and that we will encourage on-camera discussion of the more recently troublesome areas. Although it is preferable that both parents have the opportunity for several taping sessions, we have found that it is too overwhelming for more than one parent to work with the child at a time. Fifteen- to twenty-minute segments of interaction are videotaped and used immediately as a basis for discussion with the parents. Invariably, these brief taping sessions provide more than enough material to be used as a basis for instructing the parent on principles of coping with their child's behavior. In each session, with the children of about seven years and above, the taping period is begun by attempting to probe for and elicit some recent emotionally laden experience or problem that will serve as a basis for involving the parent and child in a discussion while on camera. In working with the younger child, who is usually not as verbal, the therapist helps structure a number of on-camera play interactions and the negative reactions the parents describe will usually follow. Generally, for either the older or younger child groups, this takes only a few minutes of preliminary discussion and by prearrangment the interviewer excuses himself and the remainder of the session is recorded with the parent and child alone. As soon as they get involved in the discussion or the play activity, both parent and child seem to ignore the camera. During the playback session, the child is usually sent back to the waiting- or playroom after he views himself on the tape for a few minutes. The parents are instructed in privacy since not having to cope with the child's presence seems to heighten their receptiveness for confrontation and learning. At this point, the tape is played back to the parent on the monitor, first for the general reaction of the parent and then for specific segments of interaction. The therapist, who has monitored the session in a separate room, then points out and instructs the parents how to recognize and eliminate "target symptoms." These are observable on-camera behaviors which the therapist feels are disruptive to the parent-child relationship.

Despite the variety of content or problems discussed in the sessions, a number of "target behaviors" repeat themselves. For instance, few parents and children, initially, have good eye contact when they talk; many parents ask questions without waiting for an answer; many children are able to sidetrack or distract a parent from continuing to discuss an important point by twisting in their chair, making fun of something or starting an argument about some vague, unrelated detail. A common communication problem that is obvious on tape is that it is difficult for many parents to allow for their child's involvement in discussions which depend on the child's cooperation. Another common occurrence is that most of the parents spend most of their time reacting to their child's negative behaviors and rarely notice anything positive. From these "target behaviors" and many others, behaviors are selected which are critical to the communication and ongoing relationship between the parent and child.

Parents are then given homework assignments which will ensure that they practice their new behavior modification skill. The process is repeated ten days to two weeks later. The beginning of each replay session is spent with the therapist positively reinforcing parents for any accomplishments they have made toward eliminating the target behavior and improving communication. The rest of the session is spent shaping that particular skill so that it is even more effective and then selecting one or two more basic target behaviors. Usually no more than two to three sessions with each parent are necessary to introduce and maintain significant change in the parent-child relationship.

CASE EXAMPLES
The following are three case examples to lend understanding to the variety of problems in which this treatment approach is effective.

Case I
Andy, age five, met the criteria for hyperactivity. Although he had adequate trials on methylphenidate and was doing better in kindergarten, he was doing poorly at home. His school performance and peer relationships had improved but many behavior patterns had remained unchanged. His parents complained that he always had a stomach ache which "prevented him from doing anything that they wanted," and that he was sassy, quick-tempered, stubborn and immature. Some target behaviors in playback sessions were the lack of parental consistency in what they expected of Andy, and inappropriate responsiveness to Andy's whining and complaints. Within three sessions, which took place over a six-week period, most of the complaints were gone. A five-month follow-up revealed that communication was better than ever before, that the parents had continued to firmly enforce basic rules, and that Andy was being positively reinforced for the first time for good behaviors. He was doing even better socially in school and seemed happier. There had been no complaints of abdominal pain after four and a half months.

Case II

Larry, age thirteen, had been treated with methylphenidate by his family doctor for about two and a half years when he was referred to the Center. His history of hyperactivity was typical, with the additional factor of severe education lag. With special education classes he was gradually catching up in school and his hyperactivity had improved, but the tensions in the family, due to years of poor communication, persisted.

Larry was described as stubborn, refusing to talk to his parents, lying, having temper flare-ups, and isolating himself from the family or doing bad things just to get attention. Although the parents were intelligent and reasonable people, their approach to Larry was inconsistent and they often repeated, "We've tried everything and nothing works." The first session revealed the father as excessively critical and offering no positive reinforcement for good behavior, which, when it was present, he had always taken for granted. By use of the videotape, the father noted this trait in himself and reduced his harshness considerably. A schedule of rules with reasonable positive and negative consequences was worked out that permitted many of the minor misbehaviors to be ignored. Because of the parent's lifelong tendency to respond only to negative behavior they were asked to keep a written diary of Larry's positive behavior, to heighten their awareness of what he actually did well. Subsequent interviews showed a gradual reversal of parental response patterns and replacement of emphasis on the child's assets rather than on his faults. The follow-up showed that both parents and child were pleased with themselves and each other.

Case III

Paul, age eleven, was referred to the Center by the family physician, who had treated the boy's hyperactivity with partial success using methylphenidate. However, Paul's problems in getting along with others in school had continued and tensions were worse in the home. His parents were polarized in how to treat him, the father getting stricter as the mother became more lenient. They knew this approach was poor and they couldn't seem to do much about it. Initial contact revealed that Paul was withdrawn and sullen and had begun fighting, stealing, swearing and lying, and frequently was leaving home without permission. In the initial replay, the father quickly recognized his gruffness and overbearing manner, and the fact that he was over-whelming this boy into sullen silence. The initial target behavior was getting Paul to talk. The parents were coached on more appropriate ways of listening which included being able to wait through silences and phrasing questions in such a way that allowed Paul to be in-volved in decision-making. Thereafter, other features of the prob-lems were dealt with as they emerged from the more verbal young-ster. After a series of six sessions, three with each parent, the parents reported very few of the former misbehaviors and that they were for the first time enjoying their relationship with Paul. In this case, it is of particular interest to note that the teacher was introduced into the videotape feedback phase of the treatment program. While all youngsters' progress in school is monitored on a regular basis, via check-list questionnaires and phone contact, this boy's sullen atti-tude was provoking all his teachers into response patterns similar to the parents. With two additional sessions of feedback, the teacher was also trained not to play into his sullen silence.

DISCUSSION

It should be remembered that this is a method used to modify parent behavior and thereby teach them appropriate methods of child man-agement. It is designed to give the parents actual on-camera observa-ble data of the child's behavior as well as their own. By replaying brief sections of the tape, pertinent material is quickly provided the therapist. One of the major advantages of applying this type of therapeutic approach is the availability of the existing relationship between the parent and child. The parents' extended exposure to the child gives them the potential for having a sustained influence on their child. Even though the relationship contains pathological fea-tures, the fact that the close relationship already exists and does not need to be created speeds the course of therapy. This contrasts markedly with the problem of the outside therapist who must build his own relationship before he can be effective in therapy; more important, the therapist does not have this same extended exposure to the child. The fact that this technique offers change in a remark-ably short period of time (three to ten sessions) further commends it, so it is not only effective but efficient in terms of the therapist's time and total cost to the family. Another very important reason for exploiting this type of therapeutic approach is that there is a vast discrepancy in numbers of professionals trained to do family and child therapy in relation to the number of problems that exist. With the current emphasis on providing adequate mental health care for everyone, we are forced to seek other methods than the more traditional long-term, one-to-one psychotherapeutic techniques. Another attractive feature to this technique is that many parents, by the time they have decided to seek treatment for their child at a psychiatric center, are so frustrated in their attempt to manage their child that their desire to see change is very high. If, initially enthusiastic, the parents did not gain some type of control and success rapidly, we would predict that many people would discontinue therapy. This method is clear, relatively uncomplicated, and we find few people threatened by the procedure after the initial session. We also find most parents take a degree of pride in being the therapist themselves and seem to enjoy being taught how to treat their child, as opposed to turning the treatment over to someone else.

In choosing a "target behavior" and training the parents by a behavior modification method to change that one behavior, we expect that if the parents can learn to modify this one behavior, they can then generalize the same principles to other target behaviors. We have found that this generalization of learning does occur, and once parents have gone through two to three target behaviors, they have adopted a method of behavior modification toward other behavioral difficulties.

While this treatment approach is effective in teaching many parents how to cope with their hyperactive child, it is not effective with all families. Parents in a psychotic or severely dysfunctional phase of a psychiatric illness do not learn from this method. Research indicates there is increased evidence of psychiatric illness in families of hyperactive children (Cantwell, 1972; Morrison and Stewart, 1971), and when parents are having severe difficulties themselves, they should get help for themselves before they can be effective with their children.

Although most parents who come voluntarily to a psychiatric center are sincerely motivated to get help, occasionally there is a parent who is so angry at his child that he refuses even to give the method a sincere try. Further explorations with this type of parent usually reveal that what they are really after by coming to the center is, in fact, placing their child outside the home.

There are relatively few studies which statistically validate the use of this method. It is for this purpose that, in the research which is being conducted, we have defined our population of children as those with hyperactivity. Although there are many other groups of behavior problem children where a similar approach is helpful, for research purposes we have stayed with the hyperactive population which is readily identifiable using Stewart's criteria (Stewart et al., 1966).

SUMMARY

A comprehensive program for treatment of hyperactive children has been presented, with an in-depth discussion of the use of videotape as a procedure to train parents to be effective behavior modifiers for their own children. This multi-modality program follows a course of comprehensive evaluation which provides a basis for intensive but short-term intervention into numerous problem areas. Treatment interventions with the child, family and school have been outlined with the emphasis on the combined usage of pharmacotherapy, behavior modification, curriculum counseling and parent-child videotape sessions.

A parent is trained to modify his child's maladaptive behaviors, as well as to correct longstanding communication difficulties between himself and his child by adding to the usual program several sessions of videotape feedback. After as few as three and not more than ten videotape sessions, parents comment on the lessening of tension in the family. The youngsters themselves recognize that things are "better at home," even though they cannot be more specific about what kinds of changes have occurred. Most important, parents, often for the first time, begin to enjoy their child and see him as an individual with positive qualities.

REFERENCES

Bailey, K. G. (1970). Audiotape self-confrontation in group psychotherapy. *Psychol. Rep.* 27:439–44.
_____ and Sowder, W. T., Jr. (1970). Audiotape and videotape consultation in psychotherapy. *Psychol. Bull.* 74:127–37.

Berger, M. M. (1970). *Videotape Techniques in Psychiatric Training and Treatment.* New York: Brunner/Mazel.

Bernal, M. (1969). Behavioral feedback and the modification of brat behaviors. *J. Nerv. Ment. Dis.* 148:375–83.

Boyd, H. S., and Sisney, V. V. (1967). Immediate self-image confrontation and changes in self-concept. *J. Consult. Psychol.* 31:291–94.

Cantwell, D. P. (1972). Psychiatric illness in the families of hyperactive children. *Arch. Gen. Psychiatry* 27:414–17.

Carlson, C. S., Arnold, C. R., Becker, W. C., and Madsen, C. (1968). The elimination of tantrum behavior of a child in an elementary classroom. *Behav. Res. Ther.* 6:117–19.

Chess, S. (1960). Diagnosis and treatment of the hyperactive child. *N.Y. State J. Med.* 60:2379–85.

Conners, C. K., and Eisenberg, L. (1963). The effects of methylphenidate on symptomatology and learning in disturbed children. *Am. J. Psychiatry* 120:458–64.

Danet, B. N. (1968). Self-confrontation in psychotherapy reviewed. *Am. J. Psychother.* 22:245–57.

––––––– (1969). Videotape playback as a therapeutic device in group psychotherapy. *Int. J. Group Psychother.* 14:433–40.

Doubros, S. G., and Daniels, G. J. (1966). An experimental approach to the reduction of overactive behavior. *Behav. Res. Ther.* 4:251–58.

Eisenberg, L. (1966). The management of the hyperkinetic child. *Dev. Med. Child Neurol.* 8:593–99.

Fish, B. (1968). Drug use in psychiatric disorders of children. *Am. J. Psychiatry* 124 (Feb. suppl.): 31–36.

––––––– (1971). The "one child, one drug" myth of stimulants in hyperkinesis. *Arch. Gen. Psychiatry* 25:193–202.

Furman, S., and Feighner, A. (1973). Video feedback in treating hyperkinetic children: a preliminary report. *Am. J. Psychiatry* 130:792–96.

Geertsma, R. H., and Reivich, R. S. (1965). Repetitive self-observation by videotape playback. *J. Nerv. Ment. Dis.* 141:29–41.

Hawkins, R. P., Peterson, R. F., Scheid, E. and Bijou, S. W. (1966). Behavior therapy in the home. *J. Exp. Child Psychol.* 4:99–107.

Holzman, P. S. (1969). On hearing and seeing oneself. *J. Nerv. Ment. Dis.* 148:198–209.

Knights, R. M., and Hinton, G. G. (1969). The effects of methylphenidate (Ritalin) on the motor skills and behavior of children with learning problems. *J. Nerv. Ment. Dis.* 148:643–53.

Krakowski, A. J. (1965). Amitriptyline in treatment of hyperkinetic children: a double blind study. *Psychosomatics* 6:355–60.

Laufer, M. W., Denhoff, E., and Solomons, G. (1957). Hyperkinetic impulse disorder in children's behavior problems. *Psychosom. Med.* 19:38–49.

Lindsley, O. E. (1966). An experiment with parents handling behavior at home. *Johnstone Bulletin* 9:27–36.

Mendelson, W., Johnson, N., and Stewart, M. (1971). Hyperactive children as teenagers: a follow-up study. *J. Nerv. Ment. Dis.* 153:273–79.

Menkes, M. M., Rowe, J. S., and Menkes, J. H. (1967). A twenty-five-year follow-up study on the hyperkinetic child with minimal brain dysfunction. *Pediatrics* 39:393–99.

Millicap, J. G. (1967). Treatment of minimal brain dysfunction syndromes. *Pediatr. Clin. North. Am.* 14:767–73.

Moore, F. J., Schernell, E., and West, M. J. (1965). Television as a therapeutic tool. *Arch. Gen. Psychiatry* 12:217–20.

Morrison, J. R., and Stewart, M. A. (1971). A family study of the hyperactive child syndrome. *Biol. Psychiatry* 3:189–95.

Report of the conference of the use of stimulant drugs in the treatment of behaviorally disturbed young school children (1971). *Psychopharmacol. Bull.* 7 (3) :23–29.

Resnikoff, A., Kagan, N., and Schauble, P. G. (1970). Acceleration of psychotherapy through stimulated videotape recall. *Am. J. Psychother.* 24:102–11.

Safer, D., Allen, R., and Barr, E. (1972). Depression of growth in hyperactive children on stimulant drugs. *N. Engl. J. Med.* 287:217–20.

Satterfield, J. H., Cantwell, D. P., Lesser, L. I., and Podosin, R. L. (1972). Physiological studies of the hyperkinetic child. *Am. J. Psychiatry* 128:1418–24.

Smith, J. M., and Smith, E. D. (1970). *Child Management: A Program for Parents and Teachers.* Ann Arbor, Mich.: Ann Arbor Books.

Steinberg, G. G., Troshinsky, C., and Steinberg, H. R. (1971). Dextroamphetamine-responsive behavior disorder in school children. *Am. J. Psychiatry* 128:174–79.

Stewart, M. A. (1970). Hyperactive children. *Sci. Am.* 222:94–98.

———, Pitts, F. N., Craig, A. G., and Dieruf, W. (1966). The hyperactive child syndrome. *Am. J. Orthopsychiatry* 36:861–67.

Wahler, R. T., Winkel, G. H., Peterson, R. F., and Morrison, D.C. (1965). Mothers as behavior therapists for their own children. *Behav. Res. Ther.* 3:113–24.

Weiss, G., Minde, K., Douglas, V., Werry, J., and Sykes, D. (1971a). Comparison of the effects of chlorpromazine, dextroamphetamine, and methylphenidate on the behavior and intellectual functioning of hyperactive children. *Can. Med. Assoc. J.* 104:20–25.

———, Minde, K., Werry, J. S., Douglas, V. I., and Nemeth, E. (1971b). The hyperactive child. VIII: Five-year follow-up study. *Arch. Gen. Psychiatry* 24:409–14.

———, Werry, J., Minde, K., Minde, K., Douglas, V., and Sykes, D. (1968). Studies on the hyperactive child. V: The effects of dextroamphetamine and chlorpromazine on behavior and intellectual functioning. *J. Child. Psychol. Psychiatry* 9:145–56.

Werner, E., Bierman, J. M., French, F. E., Simonian, K., Connor, A., Smith, S., Campbell, M. (1968). Reproductive and environmental casualties: a report on a ten-year follow-up of children of the Kauai pregnancy study. *Pediatrics* 42:112–27.

Werry, J. S. (1968). The diagnosis, etiology, and treatment of hyperactivity in children. *Learning Disorders* 3:173–90.

Chapter Ten

Educational Approaches with Hyperactive Children*

STEVEN FORNESS, ED.D.

Since most of the papers in this monograph are devoted to medical aspects of hyperactivity, it is important to bear in mind a certain paradox. While biomedical explanations of the problem of hyperactivity are extensive and may ultimately be shown to possess scientific validity, their current relevance to the education of hyperactive children has yet to be clearly demonstrated. Indeed, given the inchoate state of knowledge regarding neurological dysfunction in children, one must be cautious in imputing too great a role to the physician. Keogh (1971) has reviewed the hypothesis that hyperactivity and learning problems are both symptoms of underlying neurological deficit and concludes that the evidence for this position is very conflicting and uncertain. Werry (1968) goes so far as to suggest that the EEG and neurological work-up does very little credit to a complex problem and bears little relevance to treatment.

The concern is that overemphasis on medical bases of hyperactivity will lead teachers to view hyperactivity as a medical problem. Considering it so, they may then be led to view the hyperactive child primarily as a physician's *patient* and not as a *learner* who is ready to learn and profit from classroom instruction at least at some level.

Even the implications of such labels as "hyperactive" are a matter

*Preparation of this paper was supported in part by the U.S. Office of Education Grant #OEG–0–70–296(603) and NICHD Grants HD–04612, 00345 and 05615.

of grave concern. In terms of educational programs and school progress, there is no assurance that hyperactive children constitute a homogeneous group; nor can a teacher be certain that hyperactive children actually learn any differently in certain classroom situations than other types of exceptional children (Forness, in press). While pediatric neurologists, psychiatrists and psychologists may find it useful to speak of a "hyperactive syndrome," it is not altogether clear that this term is useful to teachers. After reviewing literature on the nine major diagnostic categories currently used in special education, Hewett and Forness (1974) conclude that multiple classroom groupings and a wide range of educational options should be the rule for each exceptional child. Indeed, each hyperactive child should be dealt with according to his or her own level of readiness for regular classroom functioning. Options would range from full-time placement in a special class to enrollment in a regular classroom with supportive assistance to the child's teacher. The fact that a child is hyperactive does not necessarily preordain him to a particular approach. Curriculum materials and techniques developed with mentally retarded children or children with sensory defects have, in fact, been effectively applied to children labeled hyperactive and vice versa.

Despite these disclaimers, it is still useful to speak of specific problems which the so-called hyperactive child may demonstrate in school even though these problems overlap those of other exceptional children. Before doing so, it is important to stress that the sheer level of a child's motor activity, as the term hyperactivity denotes, need not necessarily be an issue in school learning. For example, while there is a relatively high negative correlation between activity level and IQ (Grinsted, 1939), hyperactive children have been shown to form and learn concepts just as well as normal children under proper conditions (Freibergs and Douglas, 1969). It is also interesting that no differences were found between a group of hyperactive kindergarten children and their normal classmates when sheer level of motor activity was measured during free play (Maccoby, 1965). Distinctions must be made regarding when the behavior of the hyperactive child is problematic and when it is not. Turnure (1970) has illustrated, for example, how a certain type of overactivity such as frequent glancing around during a task may actually be a form of purposeful information-seeking. It has been suggested, in fact, that much of the touching and manipulative behavior of a hyperactive child may actually be an attempt to make sense out of what he perceives as a very disordered world (Wedell, 1970). It is therefore the quality and specificity of the child's activity which is of prime concern. How and when he is hyperactive is more important than the fact of hyperactivity itself, a contention which is abundantly apparent to anyone who has attempted to teach a hyperactive child.

The specific difficulties of hyperactive children which seem to be of importance are discussed herein in three selected areas: (a)attentional deficits, (b)impulse control, and (c)motivation. Educational approaches in each of these areas will also be discussed.

ATTENTIONAL DEFICITS

One hypothesis regarding the learning problems of hyperactive children suggests a deficit in the area of attending behavior (Keogh, 1971). The nature and extent of the hyperactive child's motor activity causes him to attend to tasks at a very low level, and thus he fails to acquire the necessary information to complete a task successfully. Part of this hypothesis implies that he has a very low threshold for attention which causes him to attend to everything in sight and not just to the task at hand. Such distractibility would supposedly put the hyperactive child at a serious disadvantage in the regular classroom with its myriad sources of stimulation.

Attending behavior does seem to be a primary concern in classroom performance. As Hewett (1968) has suggested, it is the critical beginning level in any form of classroom learning. In a study of twenty-four boys undergoing psychiatric evaluation for problems in classroom learning and behavior (Forness and Esveldt, in press), observation over a six-day period in their regular elementary schools indicated that low attending behavior was the primary distinguishing factor between these subjects and their peers in the same classroom. Another study of over 600 educationally handicapped children in California indicated that "difficulty in attending" was the problem which regular classroom teachers mentioned most frequently as a reason for referral of these children to special programs (Keogh et al., 1974).

That the hyperactive child indeed has such attentional deficits was the major assumption behind the first systematic attempt to design a comprehensive classroom program for hyperactive children

(Cruickshank et al., 1961). In this classroom, considerable effort was made to reduce distracting stimuli to a minimum. Space was increased between student desks to reduce distraction from other children's activities, and there were enclosed study cubicles to which children could be assigned for nearly total seclusion. Walls of the classroom were painted neutral colors; extraneous stimuli such as bulletin boards and posters were eliminated; and teachers wore smocks of neutral color. Classroom schedules were kept to a precise, predictable routine. Within this structured, nonstimulating atmosphere, materials and lessons to be learned were heightened in stimulus value. Letters and numbers were presented in brightly colored, three-dimensional form, and single words or sentences were presented one page at a time. In general, the possibility was increased that the child would attend to the task at hand and ignore irrelevant details.

Despite this prodigious attempt to engineer the classroom environment, there were only modest gains after one year in academic achievement between hyperactive subjects assigned to experimental classrooms and hyperactive children in control classrooms with traditional classroom environments. The point should be made, however, that *some* hyperactive children clearly benefited under the experimental approach, suggesting that at least some of its elements were effective. It is not clear that reducing distraction is the critical factor here. Cruse (1962), for example, studied vigilance and reaction time of hyperactive subjects in a room filled with toys on the floor, mirrors on the wall and balloons hanging from the ceiling blown about by a fan. He found no differences between the performance of hyperactive subjects in this situation and hyperactive subjects in a bare cubicle. It should be noted that his subjects had relatively low IQ and that distractibility might more easily be demonstrated in subjects of normal intelligence.

The question of stimulant medication is a crucial one here. If a particular drug is successful in regulating the child's hyperactivity, does it follow that attention to task or learning is increased? The answer is not clear. In a review of studies on the effects of medication, Freeman (1969) indicated that twenty-two of forty-five studies reported an improvement in behavior as a result of medication but that only ten of thirty-two reported improvement in learning. Typical of such studies was that by Conners and Rothschild (1968), who reported that dextroamphetamines improved attention, new learning and school behavior (as rated by teachers); however, no increase was reported in auditory perception, motor inhibition or short-term memory. Such mixed results suggest that one is rarely able to specify exactly how and under what conditions a particular drug will improve attention and learning.

Drugs, when they do work, probably make it possible for a child to do two things. First, he or she is able to make a measured and correct response for perhaps the first time in an academic situation. Second, and more importantly, the child gets a chance to feel some measure of success in that task, and this feeling of success as a learner carries over into new situations. The pattern of chronic failure and frustration is momentarily interrupted, and a new pattern temporarily emerges which a teacher can hopefully nurture and cause to generalize. The task, however, quickly becomes one of capitalizing on this initial success experience such that reliance on medication alone can gradually be attenuated.

It is particularly important for the physician to involve the child's teacher in monitoring any program of medication. Such an assessment should include some direct measure of the child's base-line status in the classroom, such as daily ten-minute samples of the child's attending behavior, before any drug is administered. Such data can be collected quite easily by a classroom aide or other paraprofessional. Medication should be initiated without the observer's knowledge so that any observed effect of the drug, such as an increase in attending behavior, is not an artifact of the observer's expectations. If the dosage is actually serving to increase the child's attention level and not just reducing hyperactivity, this should be reflected in the data. Continual monitoring in this fashion should not only assist the physician in titrating the dosage but also in deciding when to terminate a program of medication. While such direct monitoring may appear to require somewhat excessive effort by school staff, it is the author's contention, in the face of uncertainties regarding stimulant medication and possible side effects, that any evaluation procedures which are less systematic may not be as effective in helping the child to achieve independent classroom functioning in the quickest possible time.

In summary, the attention problems of the hyperactive child render it less likely that information acquisition will be complete and that effective learning will take place. Efforts at modifying a child's attending behavior through reducing distraction or through reducing his interfering motor behavior through medication have been successful with some hyperactive children but not all.

IMPULSE CONTROL

Another hypothesis concerning why hyperactive children have difficulty in learning is related to the dimension of impulse control. Keogh (1971) has suggested that hyperactive children may represent extreme examples of the impulsive children described by Kagan (1965, 1966). The hyperactive child, in other words, has an impaired decision-making process which causes him to make decisions too rapidly. He does not pause to consider possible alternatives before answering a question, does not reflect on the possible consequences of a decision, and tends to seize on the first response that comes to mind. Such impulsivity, as Kagan (1966) has illustrated, also causes a child to make many errors. A reflective child, on the other hand, takes longer to make a decision, pauses before he answers, and is generally able to consider alternatives more completely before responding. It is not difficult to see how school tasks, such as reading, tend to favor a reflective child. It has also been found that reflective children generally have higher rates of attending behavior than impulsive children (Lee et al., 1963; Zelniker et al., 1972) and that they tend to scan a greater portion of task material prior to responding (Drake, 1970).

As indicated earlier, it is not necessarily the hyperactive child's excessive motor activity which is at fault. Maccoby and her colleagues (1965) found that hyperactive kindergarten children were no more active than normal children during free play; however, when asked to play such games as "draw-a-line *slowly*" or "walk-a-pattern *slowly*" they could not as easily inhibit their motor activity. Additional evidence by Becker (1973) with high-risk children also supports this contention. Kagan and his colleagues (1966) have shown, on the other hand, that impulsive children can be trained to delay their responses and thus improve their performance in school-related tasks.

An example of such training is the study by Palkes and her colleagues (1968). In this study, hyperactive boys were trained to modu-

late their behavior during problem-solving. A set of rules was given ✗
to each child, with accompanying visual illustrations, which instructed the child to "stop," "listen," "look" and "think." Children
were made to verbalize these rules and go through the appropriate
motions prior to making a response. Palkes demonstrated that such
training made significant differences in learning performance and
attention of hyperactive children.

Training a hyperactive child to regulate his impulsivity, i.e., to
delay responding until he has sufficient information to make a correct
response, is a matter which can best be approached individually for
each child. The common problem of a child's guessing at a word
during oral reading is a case in point. With some children, practice
in looking at the configuration of a word is a good beginning point.
Such training may take the form of having the child match the visual
outline of common words to the word itself, thus sensitizing him to
form as a mediating variable to be considered before any response is
made. With other children a phonetic approach, in which sound and
sound-blending exercises are given, may be more appropriate. Phonetic training may begin to familiarize the child with a particular
regimen of word attack skills to be used prior to making a response.
With both types of children, the stop-listen-look-think approach
described above may need to be used either concurrently or as a
prerequisite to more specific training. Analytic observation of the
child's response pattern during common school tasks should provide
valuable clues regarding the type of training a teacher should initiate.
Once the child has begun to modify his conceptual tempo to suit the
task, systematic efforts should be made to help him generalize this
skill to other classroom situations.

In summary, some hyperactive children must be taught to mediate
their performance in a very basic way. Problems in impulsivity may
dictate that these children receive specific training in learning how to
learn before more academically demanding tasks are introduced.

MOTIVATION

The last area of concern, and one which is often neglected because
of the presumed organic basis of hyperactivity, is that of motivation.
A study which bears directly on this issue is that by Freibergs and
Douglas (1969) referred to earlier. In this study, hyperactive boys

who were given systematic social reinforcement for *each* correct answer (100 percent schedule of reinforcement) learned new concepts as well as normal children. However, their performance under a 50 percent schedule of reinforcement was markedly lower. As has been evident in previous sections of this paper, environmental manipulations alone could effect rather dramatic changes in the behavior of hyperactive children, who are often stereotypically regarded as "organically driven" and thus not apt to be responsive to such factors.

One of the first studies in which reinforcement principles were successfully applied to hyperactivity was that by Patterson (1965). In this study, the subject was a nine-year-old boy with a symptom pattern typical of children with minimal brain dysfunction, including prolonged anoxia at birth, hyperactivity, perceptual problems, aggressive behavior and reading difficulties. The study took place in a classroom situation and included two important variables. The first was a small black box containing a light and a response counter which was placed on the subject's desk and remotely controlled by the experimenter. During times in which the boy was sitting at his desk attending to his work, the light was on and the counter was operating. During periods of inattention, the light and counter were shut off. At the end of each period the boy received candy as reinforcement for the amount of time counted in on-task behavior. The second factor in this experiment may have been equally important to a successful outcome. The boy's classmates were told about the purpose of the "magic box" and that they would all share equally in the candy which the subject earned during each session.

The subject's hyperactive behavior decreased markedly during the first few sessions and remained at low levels throughout the study. It was not clear whether this change was due to the primary reinforcer of candy or to the so-called "bootleg" social reinforcement which the boy received from his classmates who would spontaneously drop by his desk at the end of each session to find out how he had done and praise him for his performance. Indeed, the secondary social reinforcement afforded the boy by his new status may have been the deciding factor in changing his behavior. Both factors have subsequently been shown to be effective. Doubros and Daniels (1966), for example, replicated the Patterson study but in a nonclassroom context to control for the effects of social reinforcement. They demonstrated that the work-box technique alone was sufficient to decrease hyperactive behaviors. Subsequent studies on the effects of social reinforcement alone have also been successful with overactive and disruptive children (Becker et al., 1967; Cobb et al., 1970; Patterson et al., 1969).

Indeed, the misuse of social reinforcement has been shown to be an important issue in the management of hyperactive children in the classroom. Becker and his colleagues (1967) have demonstrated that "sit-down" commands actually serve as unintended reinforcement which maintains out-of-seat behavior. They have further shown how a combination of ignoring disruptive behavior while praising on-task behavior is a more effective method of decreasing disruptive behavior in the classroom. A study by O'Leary and his colleagues (1970) suggests that the nature of the reprimand itself is an important variable. In this study, "soft" reprimands, i.e., those spoken softly and heard by the target child only, were more effective than loud reprimands, i.e., those which could be heard by other children in the class.

The practice of ignoring disruptive behavior may often be the critical first step in managing the hyperactive child in the classroom. It is not difficult to see how out-of-seat behavior operates as an attention-getting mechanism. Take as an example the hyperactive child who sits in his seat for the first half-hour of class and tries diligently to complete his work. As is normally the case in a large classroom, such a child at that point receives very little attention from his peers or his teacher. When, after a period of time, he finally does leave his seat to engage in some form of disruption, the teacher is then *forced* to attend to him, and he subsequently becomes an object of attention for his classmates as well. Such attention may unwittingly serve to reinforce disruptive behavior and ultimately becomes counterproductive. If, on the other hand, the teacher approaches the child's desk at more regular intervals and praises him when he is engaging in some on-task behavior, such reinforcement may prevent him from seeking attention through disruptive means. At the same time, the teacher must refrain from attending in any way to his disruptive behavior. The child must be ignored when he is out of his seat. This increases the probability that the child will seek and receive attention only for on-task activities.

In more extreme forms of classroom misbehavior, when ignoring is either insufficient or leads to further disruption, it is possible for the teacher to initiate some form of "time out" procedure. For example, a child can be placed for a brief period of time just outside the classroom door on a chair or bench and returned to class only after a specified time has elapsed. Such a procedure is effective only if accomplished with a minimum of verbalization and contact by the teacher and if immediately contingent on specified behaviors (Forness, 1970). While, to a teacher, such preventive approaches may appear to represent inordinate investments of time, it must be remembered that the same amount of time, or perhaps more, may currently be invested in dealing with the child's misbehavior after the fact.

The direct and systematic use of punishment has seldom been an issue with hyperactive children except for very severely disturbed subjects. Ethical concerns generally preclude the direct use of punishment and tend to cause teachers to favor some combination of ignoring disruptive behaviors and praising behaviors incompatible with disruption. Jones and Miller (1971) have demonstrated, however, that a mild reprimand contingent on the first sign of disruptive behavior was generally more effective than simply ignoring such behavior during class discussions. The use of punishment in the classroom remains a rather complex matter involving several factors such as timing, intensity and consistency of the aversive stimulus as well as the relationship between the punishing agent and the recipient. For a more complete review of these issues, the reader is referred to the paper by MacMillan, Forness and Trumbull (1973).

Another aspect of the behavior modification approach includes having the child chart his own behavior. In the Patterson study referred to earlier, a later phase of the experiment involved having the subject record, according to predetermined categories, his own disruptive behavior as well as that of some of his classmates. The effect was to make the child aware of certain behaviors which interfered with classroom learning. This heightened awareness, combined perhaps with the mildly aversive aspect of recording each behavior separately, led to a further reduction in inappropriate behavior.

As suggested earlier, teacher charting of a child's behavior is an important preliminary to any endeavor involving behavior change. Werry (1968) has suggested that serious consideration be given both to the antecedents of a hyperactive child's behavior and to its consequences. If the teacher charts the child's behavior systematically over a period of days, critical factors can be pinpointed. If, for example, disruptive behavior occurs with greater frequency at a particular time of day, the teacher can examine behavior during that period more critically for antecedent events which may be precipitating the disruption. For instance, the active physical movement occurring during recess may be related to disruptive outbursts in the math period which follows. Such precision allows the teacher not only to plan certain interventions with a hyperactive child more carefully but to carry them out at certain designated times when a particular investment is more likely to achieve measurable results.

In summary, while behavior modification has not been used extensively with hyperactive children, it is clear that such approaches to classroom management and motivation have demonstrated their usefulness. Teachers of hyperactive children may select from a variety of approaches under this rubric, ranging from traditional token economies to systematic social changes in the child's classroom environment.

CONCLUSION

Although only three areas of educational management have been discussed here, there are certainly other areas of difficulty which bear mentioning. Hyperactive children characteristically present with a wide range of specific learning problems, including perceptual motor difficulties, for which a variety of approaches have been suggested. Since these are not necessarily specific to the hyperactive child and largely beyond the scope of the present paper, the reader is referred to several recent textbooks in the area of learning disabilities, including those by Frostig and Maslow (1973), Johnson and Myklebust (1967), Kirk and Kirk (1971) and McCarthy and McCarthy (1969).

Another area of current concern is exactly where the hyperactive child will be taught and under what conditions. As mentioned earlier, there needs to be a range of possible placements available to each hyperactive child. At present, however, such a child usually receives adequate attention and management only within a special classroom. Indeed, the approaches discussed herein have been largely conceived and tested in a special class context, though most could be applied in the regular classroom with a minimum of adaptation.

There is, as we have seen, considerable heterogeneity within the group of children labeled "hyperactive," particularly with regard to their educational needs. It is satisfying to conclude this paper by reporting that several states have begun to adopt noncategorical approaches to these and other types of exceptional children (cf. California, 1973). Such approaches allow a range of different possibilities for educational management and, more importantly, provide for early identification and preventive education for all exceptional children, including the hyperactive child. It is conceivable within this framework that the term "hyperactive" will disappear from the educational lexicon to be replaced with terms which more adequately describe an individual child's educational needs.

REFERENCES

Becker, L. (1973). Modifiability of conceptual tempo in educationally "high risk" children. Unpublished doctoral dissertation, University of California at Los Angeles.

Becker, W. C., Madsen, C. H., Arnold, C., and Thomas, D. R. (1967). The contingent use of teacher attention and praise in reducing classroom behavior problems. *Journal of Special Education* 1:287–307.

California State Department of Education (1973). *A Master Plan for Special Education in California*. First draft, Sacramento.

Cobb, J., Ray, R., and Patterson, G. (1970). Direct intervention in the schools. Paper presented at the American Psychological Association, Miami (September).

Conners, C. K., and Rothschild, G. (1968). Drugs and learning in children. In J. Hellmuth, ed., *Learning Disorders*, Vol. 3. Seattle: Special Child Publications.

Cruickshank, W. M., Bentzen, F. A., Ratzeburg, F. H., and Tannhauser, M. T. (1961). *A Teaching Method for Brain-Injured and Hyperactive Children: A Demonstration Pilot Study*. Syracuse, N.Y.: Syracuse University Press.

Cruse, D. B. (1962). The effects of distraction upon the performance of brain-injured and familial retarded children. In E. Trapp and P. Himelstein, eds., *Readings on the Exceptional Child*. New York: Appleton-Century-Crofts, pp. 492–99.

Doubros, S. G., and Daniels, G. J. (1966). An experimental approach to the reduction of overactive behavior. *Behavior Research and Therapy*, 4:251–58.

Drake, D. M. (1970). Perceptual correlates of impulsive and reflective behavior. *Development Psychology* 2:202–14.

Forness, S. (1970) Behavioristic approach to classroom management and motivation. *Psychology in the Schools* 7:356–63.

_____ (in press). Implications of recent trends in educational labeling. *Journal of Learning Disabilities*.

_____ and Esveldt, K. (in press). Classroom observation of learning and behavior problem children. *Journal of Learning Disabilities.*

Freeman, R. D. (1969). Review of drug effects on learning in children. Paper presented at International Conference of the Association for Children with Learning Disabilities (Boston).

Freibergs, V., and Douglas, V. L. (1969). Concept learning in hyperactive and normal children. *Journal of Abnormal Psychology* 74:388–95.

Frostig, M., and Maslow, P. (1973). *Learning Problems in the Classroom.* New York: Grune and Stratton.

Grinsted, A. D. (1939). Studies in gross bodily movement. Unpublished doctoral dissertation, Louisiana State University.

Hewett, F. M. (1968) *The Emotionally Disturbed Child in the Classroom.* Boston: Allyn and Bacon, p. 239.

_____ with Forness, S. (1974). *Education of Exceptional Learners.* Boston: Allyn and Bacon.

Johnson, D. J., and Myklebust, H. R. (1967). *Learning Disabilities: Educational Principles and Practices.* New York: Grune and Stratton.

Jones, F., and Miller, W. H. (1971). The effective use of negative attention for reducing group disruption in special elementary classrooms. Unpublished manuscript, University of California at Los Angeles, Department of Psychiatry.

Kagan, J. (1965). Reflection-impulsivity and reading ability in primary grade children. *Child Development* 36:609–28.

_____ (1966). Reflection-impulsivity: the generality and dynamics of conceptual tempo. *Journal of Abnormal Psychology* 71:17–24.

_____, Pearson, L., and Welch, L. (1966). The modifiability of an impulsive tempo. *Journal of Educational Psychology* 57:359–65.

Keogh, B. K. (1971). Hyperactivity and learning disorders: review and speculation. *Exceptional Children* 38:101–09.

_____, Becker, L. D., Kukic, M., and Kukic, S. (1974). Programs for EH and EMR pupils: review and recommendations. *Academic Therapy* 3:187–98.

Kirk, S. A., and Kirk, W. D. (1971). *Psycholinguistic Learning Disabilities: Diagnosis and Remediation.* Urbana: University of Illinois Press.

Lee, L., Kagan, J., and Rabson, A. (1963). Influence of a preference for analytic categorization upon concept acquisition. *Child Development* 34:433–42.

McCarthy, J. J., and McCarthy, J. F. (1969). *Learning Disabilities.* Boston: Allyn and Bacon.

Maccoby, E. E., Dowley, E. M., Hagen, J. W., and Degerman, R. (1965). Activity level and intellectual functioning in normal preschool children. *Child Development* 36:-761–70.

MacMillan, D. L., Forness, S. R., and Trumbull, B. M. (1973). The role of punishment in the classroom. *Exceptional Children* 40:85–96.

O'Leary, K. D., Kaufman, K. F., Kass, R. E., and Drabman, R. S. (1970). Effects of loud and soft reprimands on the behavior of disruptive students. *Exceptional Children* 37: 145–55.

Palkes, H., Stewart, M., and Kahana, B. (1968). Porteus maze performance of hyperactive boys after training in self-directed verbal commands. *Child Development* 39: 817–36.

Patterson, G. R. (1965). An application of conditioning techniques to the control of a hyperactive child. In L. P. Ullman and L. Krasner, eds., *Case Studies in Behavior Modification.* New York: Holt, Rinehart and Winston, pp. 370–75.

_____, Shaw, D., and Ebner, M. (1969). Teachers, peers, and parents as agents of change in the classroom. In F. A. Benson, ed., *Modifying Deviant Social Behaviors in Various Classroom Settings,* Department of Special Education Monograph No. 1. Eugene, Ore.: University of Oregon Press.

Turnure, J. E. (1970). Children's reactions to distractors in a learning situation. *Developmental Psychology* 2(1):115–22.

Wedell, K. (1970). Early identification of children with potential learning problems: perceptuo-motor factors. In B. Keogh, ed., Early identification of children with potential learning problems. *Journal of Special Education* 4:323–31.

Werry, J. S. (1968). The diagnosis, etiology, and treatment of hyperactivity in children. In J. Hellmuth, ed., *Learning Disorders,* Vol. 3. Seattle: Special Child Publications.

Zelniker, T., Jeffrey, W., Ault, R., and Parsons, J. (1972). Analysis and modification of search strategies of impulsive and reflective children on the Matching Familiar Figures Test. *Child Development* 43:321–35.

Chapter Eleven

A Critical Review of Therapeutic Modalities with Hyperactive Children

DENNIS P. CANTWELL, M.D.

In the previous chapters on management of the hyperactive child, four experts have presented their personal views on a specific form of therapeutic intervention. This final chapter on management will attempt to critically review the evidence for the efficacy of each of these modalities of treatment, and of others, as they actually have been applied to behaviorally defined hyperactive children.

In beginning a discussion of treatment, it is well to emphasize that for management purposes the hyperactive child is best considered a multi-handicapped child requiring a multiple-modality treatment approach (Feighner and Feighner, 1973). Any or all of the intervention approaches discussed in previous chapters or below may be necessary for an individual child. Treatment must be individualized and based on a comprehensive assessment of each child and his family. The notion that there is only *one* hyperactive child who requires only *one* treatment is a "scientific myth" (Fish, 1971).

PHARMACOTHERAPY

Drug treatment is the easiest, least time-consuming and most frequently used intervention technique in the management of the hyperactive child. It is not surprising then that most of the literature on treatment of the syndrome consists of reports of drug treatment. Several critical reviews of the voluminous literature on this subject are available (Fish, 1968; Millichap and Fowler, 1967; Conners, 1970; Conners et al., 1972; Freeman, 1966; Werry and Sprague, 1972). Thus only selected aspects will be discussed here.

Several points made by Dr. Fish in her discussion of the use of stimulant drugs with hyperactive children are worth reemphasizing: (1)hyperactive children are a heterogeneous group and stimulants are effective for only some of them. Even the children in the "hyperactive behavior disorder" category of the American Psychiatric Association manual do not constitute a truly homogeneous group and it is likely that stimulants are effective for only some of this more selective group; (2)even in children for whom they are effective, stimulants may produce benefit in only some areas; (3)a comprehensive diagnostic evaluation is essential prior to starting any medication; (4)careful monitoring of the medication is necessary; (5)other interventions will be necessary with all children, particularly those with significant learning problems.

The literature on stimulant and other drug studies with behaviorally defined hyperactive children (corresponding to the APA "hyperactive behavior disorder" group) will be briefly reviewed here. Some recommendations for clinical use and future research studies will be considered.

The stimulants methylphenidate and dextroamphetamine have been shown to be effective in two-thirds to three-fourths of behaviorally defined hyperactive children (Millichap and Fowler, 1967; O'Malley and Eisenberg, 1973). They produce a decrease in hyperactivity and impulsivity and an increase in attention span. A number of studies have shown that the total amount of bodily activity is actually increased by the stimulant drugs and that the major change is an increase in directed or controlled motor activity (Witt et al.; Millichap and Boldrey, 1967). The stimulants have also been shown to produce small improvements in tests of general intelligence and visual-motor perception and to enhance performance in learning tasks (Knights and Hinton, 1969; Epstein et al., 1968; Werry et al., 1970; Conners et al., 1967). The improvement shown in learning tasks may be secondary to increased attention to the tasks, increased physiological arousal or increased motivation (Conners et al., 1967). Some investigators (Breitmeyer, 1969) have suggested that stimulants produce a state-dependent learning effect in hyperactive children; that is, the children do not retain material they learn while on medication after the medication is stopped. A series of studies from Sprague's laboratory (Sprague, 1972; Sprague and Werry, 1971), however, has failed to substantiate a state-dependency hypothesis.

Some investigators have found the two stimulants to be equally effective (Conners, 1971) while others have found that certain hyperactive children respond to one or the other but not to both (Bialer et al., 1972). The methodology of many of these drug studies has been severely criticized on a number of grounds (Werry and Sprague, 1972; Fish, 1971; Knights, 1972), but there is general agreement that some hyperactive children do have a dramatic short-term response to one or the other of these stimulants.

Little is known about predictors of treatment response or about the mechanism of action of the stimulant drugs. The presence of "organic factors" has been claimed by a number of authors (Pincus and Glaser, 1966; Zrull et al., 1966; Epstein et al., 1968; Conrad and Insel, 1967; Satterfield, 1973) to predict a good response to stimulant treatment, but the findings have not always been consistent (Burks, 1964; Werry, 1968). Moreover, the concept of organicity itself is so poorly defined and the indicators of organicity used in different studies vary greatly, making results difficult to compare.

In one of the few attempts to discover clinical predictors of response, Barcai (1971) found both the clinical interview and a "finger twitch test" to be useful in differentiating responders to amphetamine from non-responders. With the child sitting opposite the examiner, hands hung between his knees in a normal position with the fingers moderately flexed, the interval between the start of the test and the time of the first twitch of a hand or finger was recorded. The finger twitch appeared in all nine responders after twenty-five seconds and in eighteen of twenty-one positive or equivocal responders before twenty-five seconds had elapsed. The items from the clinical interview with the child found most helpful in differentiating responders from non-responders were the presence in the drug responders of excess body movements, poor language ability, lack of ability to abstract and use imagination constructively, lack of adjustment to the values of society and lack of planning ability.

Werry (1968) found that drug response was unrelated to family background, while Conrad and Insel (1967) found that children whose parents were rated as "grossly deviant" or "socially incompetent" were less likely to respond positively to medication, even in the face of other factors which tended to predict a good response. Other authors (Knobel, 1962; Kraft, 1968) have noted that the attitude of the family to the child's taking medication is likely to affect treatment response. However, few studies have attempted to look at family variables in a systematic way.

In a series of studies, Satterfield and his associates (Satterfield et al., 1974) found nine predictors of response to methylphenidate: low skin conductance level, high amplitude EEG, high energy in the low frequency band of the EEG, large amplitude evoked cortical response, slow recovery of the evoked response, an abnormal EEG, four or more "soft signs" on neurological exam, more behavioral abnormalities reported by the teacher, and age (older children had a better response). Six of these predictors were electrophysiological measures consistent with the hypothesis that the pathophysiology of the majority of children with the hyperactive child syndrome is low central nervous system arousal level. This theory has been reviewed by Dr. Satterfield in Chapter Four.

More systematic research in this area is sorely needed, with careful, comprehensive consideration of stimulus factors, response parameters and social, familial and organismic factors that might be related to treatment response (Conners et al., 1972).

The list of other drugs that have been tried with hyperactive children reads like the pharmacopeia. There is general agreement that the sedatives, such as phenobarbital, are usually contraindicated (Conners et al., 1972). The rather large literature on the use of major and minor tranquilizers consists of mostly uncontrolled studies and contradictory findings (Freeman, 1970; Sprague and Werry, 1971), although there is general agreement that the major tranquilizers produce deleterious effects on learning and cognitive functioning (Hartlage, 1965; Conners, 1971). Although the antihistamine diphenhydramine (Benadryl) has been advocated by some, as is pointed out in Chapter Seven, the efficacy of this medication has not as yet been proven in a controlled comparative trial using objective measures of evaluation. Lithium carbonate (Whitehead and Clark, 1970; Wender et al., 1973) and the anticonvulsants (Conners et al., 1972) have been used with varying success. There is no evidence that anticonvulsants are indicated for hyperactive children with abnormal EEG's in the absence of seizure activity.

Other stimulants have also been tried. Magnesium pemoline is a weak central nervous system stimulant which has the advantage of a long duration of action so that one daily dose is sufficient. Preliminary results indicate that it decreases hyperactivity and produces improvement on the Performance Scale of the WISC (Conners et al., 1972; Millichap, 1973). Deanol also acts as a central nervous system stimulant by being converted to acetylcholine within neurons. A recent review of the literature indicates that the better controlled studies with Deanol tended to show little or no drug effect (Conners, 1973). Coffee (with caffeine the presumed active ingredient) twice a day has been reported to be as effective as methylphenidate in one study (Schnackenberg, 1973), but preliminary results of a well-controlled study using caffeine tablets fail to substantiate this finding (Arnold, 1974).

The tricyclic antidepressants have been found to be very effective by some investigators (Huessy and Wright, 1970; Winsberg et al., 1972; Waizer et al., 1974) and not as effective as methylphenidate by other investigators (Rapoport et al., in press). In the later study the dosage of imipramine was lower than that used in some studies which found it effective. Huessy and Wright were able to employ a single bedtime dose with the therapeutic effect being evident the next day. Again this dosage schedule offers a distinct advantage if future studies support the efficacy of the antidepressants. In those children who respond positively to a stimulant but also become depressed, the author has personally found imipramine alone and imipramine in conjunction with a reduced dose of the stimulant to be effective in alleviating the depression and improving the hyperactivity.

More controlled studies are needed to evaluate the efficacy and safety of these various drugs with hyperactive children, but in general none have consistently been found to be as effective as the stimulants in the studies already published (Millichap and Fowler, 1967; Millichap, 1973).

Both Conners et al. (1972) and Sprague (1973) have recently made very important recommendations for all future drug studies with children. Fixed dosages of medication should not be employed; rather, a flexible titration of the medication should be carried out with each individual subject until clinical improvement is noted or until side effects necessitate discontinuation of the drug. If a placebo is being used, matched placebo capsules are required so that the "pill-taking set" is the same for both the drug and placebo conditions. The exact number of pills (drug and placebo) taken during the study should be recorded on a dosage record form.

The sample of children should be as homogeneous as possible with regard to reason for referral, behavioral picture, age, race, sex, socio-economic status and evidence of organicity. If the entire sample is large enough, stratified samples and statistical control for certain variables may be possible.

The patient population should be described in detail by the use of standardized ratings made by different observers in different settings: the parents in the home, the teacher in the school and the clinician in the office. These ratings must be shown to have reliability necessitating explicit criteria for making the ratings. The means, variances and frequency distributions for all data should be reported in summary form for the entire sample.

For a new drug, a double-blind comparison with placebo in a randomly assigned large sample is the first step. With smaller samples, and as a second step if the drug is shown to be more effective than a placebo, a double-blind crossover is recommended, with proper precautions such as adequate time for drug washout. Adequate dosage and an adequate length of time to show optimum therapeutic effect must be employed. Any other treatment used during the course of the study with one child must be used with all children.

In addition to the standardized rating scales noted above, objective performance measures should be employed to assess drug effect. Pre- and post-treatment measures of Intelligence, Academic Achievement, Motor Performance and Experimental Tasks should be carried out. Based on their demonstrated utility in drug studies with children, Sprague (1973) strongly recommends the Wechsler Intelligence Scale for Children, the Porteus Mazes and Reitan's Motor Steadiness Battery. He also suggests the use of the Wide Range Achievement Test, a Paired Associate Learning Task, a Continuous Performance Test, Seat Activity measurement and a Recognition Learning Task. The author feels the Peabody Individual Achievement Test is preferable to the WRAT because of its more in-depth assessment of reading ability. Post-treatment measures should ideally be at the point of maximum clinical benefit for each subject but should be at a point roughly comparable in time for all subjects. Side effects should also be systematically and specifically rated at fixed points in time.

Finally, the use of forms precoded for statistical analysis will facilitate analysis of the data and simplify record-keeping. It goes without saying that the data should be subjected to proper statistical analysis. It is preferable to have the statistical consultant help to design the study rather than wait until the study is partly completed to call him in. Very few of the published drug studies meet all of these requirements. In the future it is hoped that all investigators involved in psychopharmacological studies with children will follow these recommendations and use the same assessment tools to facilitate comparison between investigators (Department of HEW, 1973).

This discussion of pharmacotherapy of hyperactive children has concentrated on research issues but there are also clinical issues important to the practitioner.

The mechanics of stimulant drug treatment are not only of great practical importance to the clinician but are also of some theoretical importance. Dosages of 0.5 mg./Kg. of methylphenidate and 0.25 mg./Kg. of dextroamphetamine are often effective. However, an individual child may require a great deal more since there are large individual differences in blood levels in children of the same body weight for comparable doses of the same drug (Conners, 1970). Moreover, either drug may have a therapeutic effect for a particular child only at a particular blood level. From the clinical standpoint, then, the best procedure is to increase the dosage until the desired clinical effect is obtained or until side effects prohibit an increase. Children considered "non-responders" often have simply not been given an effective dose.

The latency of onset of action for both stimulants is approximately thirty minutes with a three- to six-hour duration of action. Methylphenidate must be given at least twice a day to ensure an effective dose throughout the school day. If dextroamphetamine is given in the long-acting spansule, it need be given only once a day. Response to treatment is probably singly best evaluated from behavior at school but, as in research studies, the more standardized ratings made by different observers in different settings, the greater the likelihood that one will attain the desired therapeutic effects. It is important to recognize that the optimal dose for improvement in learning may not coincide with doses that produce behavioral control. Sprague and Sleator (1973) have presented evidence that the effect of a drug on attention and learning may peak at a certain dose and then deteriorate at a higher dose, while increased improvement in classroom behavior as rated by the teacher continues to occur with the higher dose. Thus the importance of having some measure of learning to assess drug effect cannot be overemphasized.

If improvement occurs and then disappears, dosage should be increased since tolerance often develops. Parents should be forewarned about side effects to allay anxiety. Anorexia, insomnia, headache, stomach ache, nausea, tearfulness and pallor are common with both stimulants, but anorexia and insomnia seem more frequent and more severe with dextroamphetamine. Long-term use of stimulants is known to produce depression in adults. This side effect is rarely mentioned in the literature on stimulant drug treatment of hyperactive children (Ounsted, 1955). However, the author has had several children who developed mild to moderate depressive episodes in the course of treatment with both methylphenidate and amphetamine. These episodes required the cessation or reduction of dosage of the stimulant plus the use of imipramine following which the depression lifted. Since depression in children may be difficult to detect, particularly in a child who was previously hyperactive, it should be looked for systematically in children receiving stimulant medication. There does not seem to be a predilection for hyperactive children who have been medicated to become drug abusers (Freedman, 1971). There is some suggestion that suppression of weight and height may occur with prolonged use of dextroamphetamine and suppression of weight but not height with methylphenidate (Safer et al., 1972; Safer and Allen, 1973). However, the results are inconsistent. Clinical experience suggests that most side effects of medication usually subside with time (Eisenberg, 1972), but there has been next to nothing in the way of systematic investigation of long-term side effects.

The clinician who is faced with a child who has not responded or who has responded negatively to a therapeutic dose of the stimulants may want to try one of the other medications discussed above. However, he has little other than his clinical intuition to guide him. He must be prepared for a "trial and error" process as outlined in Chapter Seven and he must take great pains to prepare the parents for this process, which can be a long and frustrating one.

INDIVIDUAL PSYCHOTHERAPY WITH THE CHILD

As with the other psychiatric disorders of childhood (Levitt, 1957, 1963; Rachman, 1971), evidence for the efficacy of individual psychotherapy with children with the hyperactive child syndrome is lacking (Cytryn et al., 1960). However, psychotherapy may be indicated for the secondary emotional symptoms of depression, low self-esteem and poor peer relationships. And a good deal of psychotherapy, using the term in a broad sense, needs to be done with the child in conjunction with the use of medication. At the very least, the treating physician should help the hyperactive child understand the nature of his difficulties and how medication (and other therapeutic interventions) are intended to help the child help himself. The role and action of the medication in his life then can make more sense to the hyperactive child and he will hopefully see the medication as one of *his* tools, not something forced on him by his parents, his teachers or his doctor (Kehne, 1974; Wender, 1971, Chapter Seven).

BEHAVIOR MODIFICATION

A strong case for the use of behavioral approaches to the hyperactive child syndrome has been made by Dr. Simmons in Chapter Eight. However, until recently, actual studies of hyperactive children using operant conditioning techniques have been limited to single cases (Patterson et al., 1965; Ward, 1966) or to very small numbers of children (Doubros and Daniels, 1966; Sprague, 1973). Jacob (Jacob et al., 1974) has recently reported a study of eight hyperactive children treated in ordinary classroom settings using a program involving daily evaluations of problem behaviors by each child's teacher. He instituted a daily reward system in which the parents of each child gave preselected reinforcers to the child in the home setting if the child achieved certain predetermined goals in school. Each teacher sent home a note with the child each day the criterion reward was fulfilled and also delivered certain reinforcers herself in the classroom. The study was conducted over a three-month period and significant improvement occurred in all children as judged by a variety of rating and observational measures. Although there was no direct comparison made with drug treatment, the changes obtained on the Conner's Teacher Rating Scale (Conners, 1969) compared favorably with changes on the same scale obtained by treatment with stimulant medication in other studies.

In a direct comparison of behavioral and drug treatment, Christensen and Sprague (1973) compared six children receiving placebo and behavior modification with six children receiving methylphenidate and behavior modification using seat activity and daily quizzes as outcome measures. The drug plus behavior modification group had significantly lower seat activity than the placebo plus behavior modification group, but there were no significant differences between the groups on the number of correct answers on the daily quizzes. In a similar study, Christensen (1973) found a number of significant differences between groups on a variety of measures including Conner's Teacher Rating Scale, the Werry-Quay observational measures, productivity and accuracy of academic material, and seat activity. The behavior modification procedures alone accounted for most of the significant improvements over base-line recordings. Methylphenidate was not found to be consistently superior to behavior modification alone on any measure. This latter study, however, was conducted with institutionalized, mentally retarded, hyperactive children, and the results may not be generalized to other children with the syndrome.

These results of behavior therapy are promising; however, further research is needed with larger numbers of children, over longer periods of follow-up, and using multiple measures of outcome, particularly measures of academic performance.

SURGERY
There are reports of amygdalotomies (Naraghayshi et al., 1963) and stereotaxic hypothalamotomy (Balasubramaniam et al., 1970) to treat the hyperactive child syndrome, even in very young children. Seventy-five percent improvement has been reported with little in the way of side effects. However, this would appear to be a drastic therapeutic intervention reserved only for very severe, intractable cases, if it is to be used at all.

EDUCATIONAL MANAGEMENT
Each year a child spends about 1,400 hours out of 8,760 in the school setting (McCarthy, 1973). Most hyperactive children can tolerate a

regular classroom setting. And despite the advances made by some states described in Chapter Nine, most hyperactive children will need to remain in a regular classroom due to a shortage of specialized programs. Thus it is important that classroom teachers be as familiar with the syndrome as parents and there must be consistency of expectations and methods of behavioral reinforcement between the home and the school. In-service training programs can help the teacher learn to recognize the syndrome and learn methods of modifying the child's classroom behavior. Simple classroom measures such as placing the child close to the teacher and away from distractions, and giving one-to-one attention through the use of teachers' aides may be helpful. And the teacher plays an indispensable role with those children placed on medication. It is the author's contention that a child cannot be properly maintained on medication without regular, standardized reports from the school. The teacher is likely to be the only person to regularly see the child in a group setting where he is required to do the same tasks as a large number of peers of the same age. Thus, in a sense, the teacher is in a position to compare the performance of a hyperactive child with a non-hyperactive "control group" on a daily basis.

For those children with significant learning problems, specific remediation procedures based on a thorough psychoeducational assessment are a necessity. However, there is little hard evidence to support the efficacy of most special education programs for *any* type of child (Dunn, 1967; Haywood, 1966). Well-controlled studies of special education programs for hyperactive children are few in number and diappointing in results. The Conrad study (Conrad et al., 1971) reviewed in Chapter Three is a rare example of a well-controlled study comparing special education techniques with another intervention. The results are most disappointing not only because tutoring alone produced little improvement, but because those children who received stimulant medication *alone* did better than those who received *both* tutoring and stimulant medication. A harsh interpretation of these data would be that the tutoring somehow impeded rather than helped the children.

Although successful approaches for training *individual* hyperactive children have been described (Palkes et al., 1968; Santostefano and Stayton, 1967; Meichenbaum and Goodman, 1971), long-term follow-up studies are lacking and the availability of such individualized special training in the public school system is limited at best. Too often hyperactive children are relegated to "special" classes with euphemistic names which only become "baby-sitting" rooms for children who are found to be "unmanageable" in the regular classroom setting. If this situation is to change, a concerted effort will have to be made by those involved in the training of teachers, those involved in research in remedial educational techniques, those involved in everyday teaching and administration in the public schools, and most importantly those involved in setting funding priorities for the schools.

FAMILY INVOLVEMENT

Successful management of the hyperactive child syndrome requires involvement of the entire family. In the absence of severe psychopathology in the parents, the author has also found the use of parent groups as described in Chapter Ten to be an effective treatment modality. Parents are taught the nature and phenomenology of the syndrome, the basics of behavior modification and the principles of structuring the child's environment so that there are regular daily routines and firm limits on his behavior. The importance of avoiding situations known to cause difficulty, overstimulation and excessive fatigue are emphasized. Ms. Feighner has described how she has found it helpful to videotape segments of parent-child interaction and to play back maladaptive behaviors with explicit instructions to the parents on how to deal with them. The use of brothers and sisters to modify the behavior of their hyperactive siblings is a promising new technique (Brown and Guiliani, 1972). The presence of psychopathology in the parents may require individual treatment of the parent and/or a more dynamically oriented family therapy approach, particularly if the hyperactive child has been the "family scapegoat."

SUMMARY

Successful management of an individual child will involve the use of multiple treatment approaches. A critical review of the literature dealing with treatment of the hyperactive child reveals the following:
(1) Most of the literature consists of drug studies.
(2) These drug studies indicate that:
    (a) Central nervous system stimulants are effective for some symptoms with some children, over the short haul.

(b) Other drugs, in general, have not been found to be as effective as the stimulants, though the tricydic antidepressants show promise.

(c) Little is known about how to predict which child will respond to which drug.

(d) Next to nothing is known about the long-term effects, good or bad, of any of the medications.

(e) The methodology of a large number of these drug studies can be severely criticized.

(3) Studies of other treatment modalities are few in number. The criticisms made of the drug studies apply with equal or greater force to these investigations.

(4) Involvement of the family is critical to the success of any management program, but familial factors are rarely mentioned in studies of treatment.

REFERENCES

Arnold, L. (1974). Personal communication.
_____, Kirilcuk, V., Corson, S., and Corson, E. (1973). Levoamphetamine and dextroamphetamine: differential effect on aggression and hyperkinesis in children and dogs. *American Journal of Psychiatry* 130: 165–71.

Balasubramaniam, V., Kanaka, T., and Ramamurthi, B. (1970). Surgical treatment of hyperkinetic and behavior disorders. *International Surgery* 54: 18–23.

Barcai, A. (1971). Predicting the response of children with learning disabilities and behavior problems to dextroamphetamine sulfate: the clinical interview and the finger twitch test. *Pediatrics* 47: 73–80.

Bialer, I., Kupietz, S., and Winsberg, H. (1972). A behavior rating scale for assessing improvement in behaviorally deviant children: a preliminary investigation. *American Journal of Psychiatry* 128: 1432–36.

Breitmeyer, J. M. (1969). Effects of thioridazine and methylphenidate on learning retention in retardates. Unpublished master's thesis, University of Illinois.

Brown, N., and Guiliani, B. (1972). Siblings as behavior modifiers. Paper presented at 6th annual meeting, Association for the Advancement of Behavior Therapy.

Burks, H. F. (1964) Effects of amphetamine therapy on hyperkinetic children. *Archives of General Psychiatry* 11:604–09.

Christensen, D. (1973). The combined effects of methylphenidate (Ritalin) and a classroom behavior modification program in reducing the hyperkinetic behavior of institutionalized mental retardates. Unpublished doctoral dissertation, University of Illinois.

———— and Sprague, R. (1973). Reduction of hyperactive behaviors by conditioning procedures alone and combined with methylphenidate (Ritalin). *Behaviour Research and Therapy* 11:331–34

Conners, C. (1969). A teacher rating scale for use in drug studies with children. *American Journal of Psychiatry* 126: 152–56.

———— (1970). The use of stimulant drugs in enhancing performance learning. In W. L. Smith, ed., *Drugs and Cerebral Function*. Springfield, Ill: Charles C. Thomas.

———— (1971) Recent drug studies with hyperkinetic children. *Journal of Learning Disabilities* 4:476–484.

———— (1973). Deanol and behavior disorders in children: a critical review of the literature and recommended future studies for determining efficacy. *Psychopharmalogical Bulletin*, Department of Health, Education and Welfare, 188–95.

————, Eisenberg, L., and Barcai, A. (1967) Effect of dextroamphetamine in children. *Archives of General Psychiatry*. 17:478–485.

————, Taylor, E., Meo, G., Kurtz, M., and Fournier, M. (1972). Magnesium pemoline and dextroamphetamine: a controlled study in children with minimal brain dysfunction. *Psychopharmacologica* 26: 321–36.

Conrad, W., and Insel, J. (1967). Anticipating the response to amphetamine therapy in the treatment of hyperkinetic children. *Pediatrics* 40: 96–99.

————, Dorkin E., Shai, A., and Tobiessen, J. (1971). Effects of amphetamine therapy and prescriptive tutoring on the behavior and achievement of lower class hyperactive children. *Journal of Learning Disabilities* 4: 45–53.

Cytryn, L., Gilbert, A., and Eisenberg, L. (1960). The effectiveness of tranquilizing drugs plus supportive psychotherapy in treating behavior disorders of children. *American Journal of Orthopsychiatry* 30: 113–28.

Department of Health, Education and Welfare. Pharmacotherapy of Children. *Psychopharmacology Bulletin*.

Doubros, S., and Daniels, G. (1966). An experimental approach to the reduction of overactive behavior. *Behavior Research and Therapy* 4: 251–58.

Dunn, L. (1967). Special education for the mildly retarded—is much of it justifiable? Paper presented at the Illinois Council for Exceptional Children.

Eisenberg, L. (1972). The hyperkinetic child and stimulant drugs. *New England Journal of Medicine* 287:249–50.

Epstein, L., Lasagna, L., and Conners, C. (1968). Correlation of dextroamphetamine excretion and drug response in hyperkinetic children. *Journal of Nervous and Mental Disease* 146: 136–46.

Feighner, A., and Feighner, J. (1973). Multi-modality treatment of the hyperkinetic child. Presented at 126th annual meeting, American Psychiatric Association.

Fish, B. (1968) Methodology in child psychopharmacology. In D. H. Efron, et al., eds., *Psychopharmacology, Review of Progress, 1957–1967*. Public Health Service Publication No. 1836, 989–1001.

———— (1971). The "one child, one drug" myth of stimulants in hyperkinesis: importance of diagnostic categories in evaluating treatment. *Archives of General Psychiatry* 25:193–203.

Freedman, D. (1971). Report on the conference on the use of stimulant drugs in the treatment of behaviorally disturbed young school children. Washington, D.C., Department of Health, Education and Welfare.

Freeman, R. (1966). Drug effects on learning in children: a selective review of the past thirty years. *Journal of Special Education* 1: 17–44.

―――― (1970). Psychopharmacology and the retarded child. In R. Menolascino, ed., *Psychiatric Approaches to Mental Retardation.* New York: Basic Books.

Hartlage, L. (1965). Effects of chlorpromazine on learning. *Psychological Bulletin* 64: 235–45.

Haywood, H. (1966) Perceptual handicap: Fact or artifact? *Child Study* 28:2.

Huessy, H., and Wright, A. (1970). The use of imipramine in children's behavior disorders. *Acta Paedopsychiatrica* 37: 194–99.

Jacob, R., O'Leary, K., and Price, G. (1974). Behavioral treatment of hyperactive children: an alternative to medication. Submitted to *Archives of General Psychiatry.*

Jones, H., MacFarlane, J., Eichorn, D. (1960). A progress report on growth studies at the University of California. *Vita Humana* 3: 17–31.

Kehne, C. (1974). Social control of the hyperactive child via medication: at what cost to personality development: some psychological implications and clinical interventions. Read before annual meeting, Orthopsychiatric Association.

Knights, R. (1972). Psychometric assessment of stimulant-induced behavior change. Presented at Abbott Laboratory, "Symposium on the Clinical Use of Stimulant Drugs in Children" (Key Biscayne, Florida).

―――― and Hinton, G. (1969). The effects of methylphenidate (Ritalin) on the motor skills and behavior of children with learning problems. *Journal of Nervous and Mental Disease* 148: 643–53.

Knobel, M. (1962). Psychopharmacology for the hyperkinetic child—dynamic considerations. *Archives of General Psychiatry* 6: 198–202.

Kraft, I. (1968). The use of psychoactive drugs in the outpatient treatment of psychiatric disorders of children. *American Journal of Psychiatry* 124:1401–07.

Laufer, M. (1971). Long-term management and some follow-up findings on the use of drugs with minimal brain dysfunction. *Pediatrics* 39:55–58.

Levitt, E. (1957). The results of psychotherapy with children: an evaluation. *Journal of Consulting Psychology* 21:189–96.

―――― (1963) Psychotherapy with children: a further evaluation. *Behavior Research and Therapy* 1:45–51.

McCarthy, J. (1973). Education: the base of the triangle. *Annals of the New York Academy of Sciences* 205:362–69.

McCord, W., and McCord, J. (1960). *Origins of Alcoholism.* Stanford, Calif.: Stanford University Press.

Meichenbaum, D., and Goodman, J. (1971) Training impulsive children to talk to themselves: a means of developing self-control. *Journal of Abnormal Psychology* 77: 115–26.

Millichap, J. G. (1973). Drugs in management of minimal brain dysfunction. *Annals of the New York Academy of Sciences* 205:321–35.

―――― and Boldrey, E.E. (1967) Studies in hyperkinetic behavior. *Neurology* 17:467–517.

―――― and Fowler, G. (1967). Treatment of minimal brain dysfunction syndrome. In

J. Millichap, ed., *The Pediatric Clinics of North America. Pediatric Neurology*, Vol. 14. Philadelphia: W. B. Saunders Co.

Naraghayshi, I., Nagao, T., Yoshida, M., and Naghata, M. (1963). Stereotaxic amygalotomy for behavior disorders. *Archives of Neurology* 9:1–16.

O'Malley, J., and Eisenberg, L. (1973). The hyperkinetic syndrome. *Seminars in Psychiatry* 5:95–103.

Ounsted, C. (1955). The hyperkinetic syndrome in epileptic children. *Lancet* 269: 303–11.

Palkes, H., Stewart, M., and Kahana, B. (1968). Porteus maze performance of hyperactive boys after training in self-directed verbal commands. *Child Development* 39: 817–36.

Patterson, G., James, R., Whittier, J., and Wright, M. (1965). A behavior modification technique for the hyperactive child. *Behavior Research and Therapy* 2:217–26.

Pincus, J., and Glaser, G. (1966). The syndrome of minimal brain damage in childhood. *New England Journal of Medicine* 275:27–35.

Quitkin, F., and Klein, D. (1969). Two behavioral syndromes in young adults related to possible minimal brain dysfunction. *Journal of Psychiatric Research* 7:131–42.

Rachman, S. (1971). *The Effects of Psychotherapy*. Oxford, England: Pergamon Press.

Rapoport, J., Abramson, A., Alexander, D., and Lott, I. (1971). Urinary noradrenaline and playroom behavior in hyperactive boys. *Lancet* 2:1141.

———, Quinn, P., Bradbard, G., Riddle, D., and Brooks, E. (in press). Imipramine and methylphenidate treatments of hyperactive boys. *Archives of General Psychiatry*.

Safer, D., and Allen, R. (1973). Long-term side effects of stimulants in children. Presented at 126th annual meeting, American Psychiatric Association.

———, Allen, R., and Barr, E. Depression of growth in hyperactive children on stimulant drugs. *New England Journal of Medicine* 287:217–20.

Santostefano, S., and Stayton, S. (1967). Training the preschool retarded child in focusing attention: a program for parents. *American Journal of Orthopsychiatry* 37:732–43.

Satterfield, J.H. (1973) EEG issues in children with minimal brain dysfunction. *Seminars in Psychiatry* 5:35–46.

———, Cantwell, D., and Satterfield, B. (1974). Pathophysiology of the hyperactive child syndrome. *Archives of General Psychiatry* 31:839–44.

Schnackenberg, R.C. (1973) Caffeine as a substitute for Schedule II stimulants in hyperkinetic children. *The American Journal of Psychiatry* 130:796–98.

Shelley, E. (1970). Syndrome of minimal brain damage in young adults. Read before annual meeting, American Psychiatric Association, (San Francisco).

Sprague, R. (1972). Psychopharmacology and learning disabilities. *Journal of Operational Psychiatry* 3:56–67.

——— (1973a). Minimal brain dysfunction from a behavioral viewpoint. *Annals of the New York Academy of Sciences* 205:349–62.

——— (1973b). Recommended performance measures for psychotropic drug investigations. *Psychopharmacology Bulletin*, Department of Health, Education, and Welfare, 85–88.

——— and Sleator, E. (1973). Effect of pyschopharmacological agents in learning disorders. *Pediatric Clinics of North America* 20:719–35.

——— and Werry, J. (1971). Methodology of psychopharmacological studies with the retarded. In N. Ellis, ed., *International Review of Research in Mental Retardation,* Vol. 5. New York: Academic Press.

Waizer, J., Hoffman, S.P., Polizos, P., Engelhardt, D.M. (1974) Outpatient treatment of hyperactive school children with imipramine. *The American Journal of Psychiatry,* 131:587–91.

Ward, M. (1966) Experimental modification of "hyperactive" behavior. Unpublished B.S. thesis, University of Illinois.

Weiss, G., Minde, K., Werry, J., Douglas, V., and Nemeth, E. (1971). Studies on the hyperactive child. VIII. Five-year follow-up. *Archives of General Psychiatry* 24:409–14.

Wender, P. (1971). *Minimal Brain Dysfunction in Children.* New York: Wiley-Interscience.

———, Greenhill, L., Rieder, R., Buchsbaum, M., and Zahn, T. (1973) Lithium carbonate in the treatment of hyperactive children. *Archives of General Psychiatry* 28:636–46.

Werry, J. (1968). Studies on the hyperactive child. IV. An empirical analysis of the minimal brain dysfunction syndrome. *Archives of General Psychiatry* 19:9–16.

———, Sprague, R., Weiss, G., and Minde, K. (1970). Some clinical and laboratory studies of psychotropic drugs in children: an overview. In W. Smith ed., *Drugs and Cerebral Function.* Springfield, Ill.: Charles C. Thomas.

——— and Sprague, R. (1972). Psychopharmacology. In J. Wortis, ed., *Mental Retardation,* IV. New York: Grune and Stratton.

Whitehead, P.L. and Clark, L.D. (1970) Effect of lithium carbonate, placebo, and thioridazine on hyperactive children. *American Journal of Psychiatry* 127:824–825.

Winsberg, B., Bialer, I., Kupietz, S., and Tobias, J. (1972). Effects of imipramine and dextroamphetamine on behavior of neuropsychiatrically impaired children. *American Journal of Psychiatry* 128:1425–31.

Witt, P., Ellis, M., and Sprague, R. Methylphenidate and free range activity in hyperactive children. Unpublished paper written in support of NIMH grant #MH189–9, Children's Research Center, University of Illinois, Urbana.

Zrull, P., Patch, D. and Lehtinen, P. (1966). Hyperkinetic children who respond to d-amphetamine. Scientific proceedings summary, American Psychiatric Association (Atlantic City, N.J.).

PART IV

Epilogue

Chapter Twelve

A Medical Model for Research and Clinical Use with Hyperactive Children

DENNIS P. CANTWELL, M.D.

The preceding chapters of this volume have described the clinical picture of the hyperactive child syndrome, its natural history, current areas of research interest and various methods of treatment. This final chapter will describe a model developed by the author for research work with psychiatric disorders of childhood. The author has also found the model to be clinically useful as a framework for integrating the data obtained from the various parts of the evaluation outlined in Chapter Two. The use of the model will be illustrated by applying it to the hyperactive child syndrome.

The basic principles that underlie the model can be enunciated as follows (Guze, 1970, 1972; Robins and Guze, 1970):

(1) Child psychiatry is a branch of medicine and a "medical model is entirely appropriate for the investigation of the psychiatric disorders of childhood."

(2) The medical model requires a primary focus on the *condition* that a child presents with—whether this condition is called a "disease," "disorder," "illness," "sickness," or some other term.

(3) A corollary of this focus on a patient's disorder is the notion that patients may present with many types of disorders that differ in their pathogenesis, etiology, symptomatology, natural history and response to treatment.

(4) Precise definition and classification of the various psychiatric disorders of childhood are necessary and essential steps in the advancement of the field.

193

(5) It is precisely because psychologic processes and phenomena in children are more subjective, more difficult to measure and quantify, that we should adapt a "tough-minded" approach in psychiatric research. In clinical and research endeavors we must demand more, rather than less, in the way of systematically obtained data.

THE SIX-STAGE MODEL
In using this model an investigator begins with an index population of children and carries out studies that can be grouped under six "stages" of investigation. These six stages are as follows:

1. Clinical Description
A careful clinical description of the behavior problem the child presents with is the starting point for investigative work in this model. Obtaining this requires detailed, systematic, yet flexible questioning of the parents; obtaining reliable information from the school; and performing a reliable and valid diagnostic interview with the child. It also requires taking into account age appropriateness of behaviors, sex of the child, race, social class and other factors that may affect the clinical picture.

2. Physical and Neurologic Factors
A systematic physical and pediatric neurologic examination should be performed and the results recorded in a standardized fashion. Special attention should be given to the evaluation of neurodevelopmental abnormalities. It is important to inquire systematically about events in the history suggesting possible CNS involvement.

3. Laboratory Studies
Included here are the results of all types of laboratory investigations: blood, urine, spinal fluid, EEG, neurophysiological, etc. Valid, reliable psychometric studies can also be considered as laboratory investigations in this context.

4. Family Studies
Included in this stage are two different types of investigations: (a)studies of the prevalence and types of psychiatric disorders in the close relatives of a clinically defined index group of child patients, and

(b)studies of the relationships and interactions occurring between the members of a family.

5. Longitudinal Natural History Studies

Prospective and retrospective follow-up studies of an index population of children to trace the course and outcome of their disorder help determine whether the original group formed a homogeneous diagnostic category. They also provide a standard against which to judge the effectiveness of various forms of treatment.

6. Treatment Studies

At our present level of knowledge, marked differences in response to adequate trials of the same treatment, such as between complete recovery and marked deterioration, can be considered as evidence that the original group of children did not form a homogeneous group. Thus differential treatment response can also be used to subdivide the original index population of patients.

APPLICATION OF THE MODEL TO THE HYPERACTIVE CHILD SYNDROME

(1) Clinical Description

Chapter One outlined the clinical picture of the hyperactive child in some detail. The cardinal symptoms seem to be those of hyperactivity, impulsivity, distractibility and excitability. In selecting a population of children who chronically manifest this symptom pattern, in both the home and school settings, an investigator will surely begin with a heterogeneous group of children. Some attempts can be made at making the study population more homogeneous by such steps as limiting the index group to (a)white boys between six and nine years of age, (b)currently attending school, (c)with tested normal vision and hearing, (d)with no evidence of any gross neurologic disease, and (e)with a full-scale IQ of 85 or above on the Wechsler Intelligence Scale for Children. The population remaining after application of these inclusion and exclusion criteria will still be a rather heterogeneous one. Thus various subgroups of the original population should be formed when studies in the other five stages of the model are carried out with this index population. Some possible subgroups will be discussed below under each stage of the model.

(2) Physical and Neurologic Factors

Since several investigators have confirmed the presence of minor physical anomalies (stigmata) in some hyperactive children (Waldrop and Halverson, 1971; Rapoport et al., 1974; Quinn and Rapoport, 1974), an index population of hyperactive children can be divided into "high" and "low" stigmata subgroups. The next step is to see if these two subgroups also differ in other stages of this research model. When this is done it is found that as a group the high stigmata group is also characterized by differences in *clinical picture* (earlier onset of the disorder, greater severity of hyperactivity, and more aggressive behavior); other *physical factors* (history of obstetrical difficulties in the mother); *lab studies* (higher level of plasma dopamine-β-hydroxylase activity); *family studies* (history of hyperactivity in the father) (Rapoport et al., 1974; Quinn and Rapoport, 1974). It is also notable that within the high stigmata group there is little overlap between those with a history of hyperactivity in the father and those with a history of obstetrical difficulties in the mother. This suggests that there may be two distinct subgroups of high stigmata hyperactive children: a genetically determined one and one determined by adverse events occurring early in pregnancy. If so, comparing the "genetic stigmata" group with the "obstetrical stigmata" group should result in finding differences between the two groups in clinical picture, laboratory findings, natural history or response to treatment.

Based on the presence or absence of minor abnormalities on neurologic examination, an index population of hyperactive children can also be divided into "high soft sign" and "low soft sign" subgroups. The "high soft sign" subgroup has been found to have a significantly greater likelihood of response to stimulant drug treatment (Satterfield et al., 1973), suggesting that this may also be a meaningful subgroup.

Interestingly, no significant correlation has been found between the presence of soft neurologic signs and the presence of physical stigmata (Quinn and Rapoport, 1974). This suggests different etiological factors for the two types of abnormalities.

(3) Laboratory Studies

Hyperactive children can also be divided into subgroups using an *abnormal EEG* as the index. Those with an abnormal EEG have been found to differ from those with a normal EEG in: *clinical picture* (greater anxiety at home and school, greater motor restlessness in the classroom [Quinn and Rapoport, 1974; Satterfield et al., 1974]); *lab studies* (significantly higher WISC Full-Scale and Performance IQ, significantly lower Bender Perseveration Scores [Satterfield et al., 1974]); and *treatment* (greater likelihood of response to stimulant drug therapy).

Neurophysiologic studies have revealed a subgroup of hyperactive children who have lower levels of basal resting physiological activation than age-matched normals. This subgroup is also characterized by more restlessness, distractibility, impulsivity and attentional problems in the classroom, as well as greater likelihood of positive response to stimulants (Satterfield et al., 1972, 1974).

Thus hyperactive children, selected on the basis of certain laboratory parameters, have also been found to differ in other stages of this model. This suggests that these and possibly other laboratory indices can be used to differentiate a heterogeneous group of clinically defined hyperactive children.

(4) Family Studies

Chapter Six reviewed the evidence indicating that there is a subgroup of hyperactive children who have a history of hyperactivity in their family (FH$^+$). If the FH$^+$ group represents a genetically determined subgroup, then it is reasonable to assume that one should find clinical, laboratory, neurologic or other differences between the FH$^+$ and FH$-$ groups. Very little work has been done in this area to date. As noted previously, the FH$^+$ group does have a higher incidence of physical stigmata and there is preliminary evidence that, within a group of high stigmata hyperactive children, fathers who were hyperactive in childhood have high levels of plasma β-dopamine hydroxylase while fathers who were not hyperactive in childhood have low levels (Rapoport and Quinn, in press). These results are strongly suggestive that the FH$^+$ group is biochemically different from the FH$^-$ group.

As noted in Chapter Six, little has been done in the way of family interaction studies with hyperactive children. However, it does seem that the group of hyperactive children being reared in homes with a mentally ill parent are more likely to have an antisocial outcome, and a poorer response to stimulant drug therapy (Weiss et al., 1971; Conrad and Insel, 1967). These data suggest that differences in certain aspects of family interaction are associated with differences in other stages of this model, but more research is needed in this area.

(5) Longitudinal Natural History Studies

Data presented in Chapter Three indicate that the long-term outcome of hyperactive children is not a uniform one. The syndrome seems to predispose to the development of sociopathy, educational retardation, depression and possible psychosis. This model offers a research strategy for unraveling the various factors that lead to these various outcomes.

For example, since we know that antisocial behavior is prevalent in hyperactive children, we can test two hypotheses regarding the nature of the association between hyperactivity and sociopathy: (1)"antisocial hyperactive" children form an etiologically distinct subgroup of children with the syndrome; (2)the antisocial behavior develops secondarily to the cardinal symptoms which define the syndrome.

A plausible argument can certainly be made for the hypothesis that the antisocial behavior develops as a reaction to the primary symptoms of hyperactivity, distractibility, excitability and impulsivity. Children who repeatedly find themselves rejected at home and school, who cannot master the normal developmental tasks of childhood, might be expected to rebel against the values of the system in which they are unable to find success. If the antisocial behavior is a secondary problem and antisocial hyperactive children do not form an etiologically distinct subgroup, then at initial evaluation the two groups should be similar in all stages of the model. To support the hypothesis that the antisocial and non-antisocial hyperactive children are etiologically distinct, one should find significant differences between the groups in one or more stages. The only evidence currently available on this point reveals that antisocial hyperactive children differ from non-antisocial hyperactive children in being rated more aggressive at initial evaluation, in having more physical stigmata, and in coming from families characterized by mentally ill parents and negative parent-child interaction (Weiss et al., 1971; Mendelson et al., 1971; Quinn and Rapoport, 1974). These data do not conclusively support either hypothesis.

Rutter (Rutter et al., 1970) has suggested that one mechanism of the development of antisocial behavior in childhood is through educational failure. He has presented convincing evidence that children who are frustrated by inability to attain status and satisfaction in school work rebel and seek satisfaction in activities running counter to everything the school stands for. Alternatively, his data suggested that in some cases the temperamental characteristics of motor restlessness and poor concentration (both major symptoms of the hyperactive child syndrome) lead both to the antisocial behavior and to the educational failure. Longitudinal studies of hyperactive children through their formative school years, with careful monitoring of both behavior and academic performance, will allow one to determine if it is the hyperactive children with significant educational retardation who develop antisocial behavior. The strongest association between family influences and deviant behavior in childhood is that between family discord and antisocial behavior (Rutter, 1972). Family interaction studies combined with longitudinal studies should also be revealing regarding the genesis of antisocial behavior in hyperactive children.

However, there are several lines of evidence supporting the hypothesis that antisocial hyperactive children are an etiologically distinct subgroup. The family and adoption studies (Chapter Six) suggest a genetic relationship between hyperactivity in childhood and sociopathy in adulthood. Recent research on waking autonomic functions and EEG patterns in sociopathic adults and in hyperactive children suggest that both groups may have the same underlying neurophysical abnormality: lower levels of basal resting physiological activation than age-matched normals (Satterfield and Cantwell, in press). Were this "low arousal" group of hyperactive children found to be the group with antisocial fathers who were also hyperactive as children, this would be even stronger evidence that antisocial hyperactive children are a meaningful subgroup. It would also suggest that in this group there may be a genetically transmitted neurophysiological abnormality that leads to hyperactivity in childhood and sociopathy in adulthood. There is also indirect evidence that among hyperactive children, antisocial and aggressive behaviors may be mediated by dopamine while the symptoms of hyperactivity may be mediated by norepinephrine (Arnold et al., 1973). This tends to indicate a possible biochemical difference between antisocial and non-antisocial hyperactive children.

All of these findings are well worth pursuing in larger groups of hyperactive children over longer periods of time since many important questions remain to be answered regarding the mechanism of the association between hyperactivity and sociopathy: Is it the hyperactive child with evidence of low CNS arousal who is most likely to develop antisocial behavior? Is antisocial behavior in hyperactive children mediated through educational retardation? Are the hyperactive children with antisocial parents more likely to develop antisocial behavior themselves? Do adopted hyperactive children (whose biologic parents may have been antisocial) being reared by non-antisocial adopting parents have the same incidence of sociopathy as children being raised by antisocial biologic parents?

Likewise by selecting educationally retarded hyperactive children and comparing them with hyperactive children who are functioning academically at the expected level, one can look for differences in clinical picture, physical and neurological factors, laboratory studies, etc., that will explain the nature of the educational retardation. The same research strategy can be used to determine the relationship between hyperactivity and later life depression and psychosis.

(6) Treatment Studies

There are very few systematic studies of treatment modalities with hyperactive children other than drug treatment. What little is known about predictors of treatment response has been reviewed in previous chapters. In the future, "responders" to *all* types of treatment modalities should be compared to "non-responders" in an attempt to find clinical, laboratory, familial or other factors that predict which child will respond to which therapeutic intervention or combination of interventions. Moreover, at our present level of knowledge, it is reasonable to assume that a group of hyperactive children who respond dramatically to one form of treatment have an etiologically different condition than a group of children with the same clinical picture who do not respond to adequate trials of the same treatment. If this is so, one would expect to find differences between these groups in one or more of the other five stages of this investigative model.

It is apparent from the above discussion that the six stages of this model interact with one other. New findings in one stage may lead to changes in one or more of the other stages.

For example, beginning with a population of children with the clinical picture of the hyperactive child syndrome, we find that one group has a positive response to stimulant medication while another group has a negative response. When we compare these two groups —the "responders" and "non-responders"—we find they differ in a number of other parameters. The responders have laboratory evidence of low central nervous system arousal, more abnormal EEG's, and a greater number of minor abnormalities on neurologic exam. Thus this group begins to look like they have their disorder on a neurodevelopmental basis. One might then go back and take a closer look at the clinical picture of the two groups, using techniques such as cluster analysis to see if differences can be found in the behavioral picture. A family study of the two groups may yield different familial patterns of illness. Follow-up studies should reveal a different natural history for the two groups, if they do in fact have different disorders.

Or, beginning with the same population of children, we find one group with a positive family history and one with a negative family history, as in the studies described previously. We might then compare the behavioral picture of the two groups or look at a variety of laboratory measures. Since the family studies offer tentative evidence for a possible genetically determined subgroup of hyperactive children, it is reasonable to assume that one might find metabolic, biochemical or chromosomal differences between the FH^+ and $FH-$ groups.

Thus the continued application of this model to the same index population leads to increasingly refined diagnostic criteria, and ultimately to more homogeneous subgroups of the original index patient population. These homogeneous populations provide the best starting point for studies of etiology and treatment. The role of dynamic factors, family relationships, sociological factors, genetic factors, etc., in the etiology of any condition is more easily elucidated when the patient population under study is as diagnostically "pure" as possible. Likewise, response to any treatment modality, be it psychotherapy, pharmacotherapy, behavior therapy or some other modality, is best evaluated in a homogeneous patient population.

MISCONCEPTIONS ABOUT THE MEDICAL MODEL
There are certain misconceptions that arise when one mentions the term "medical model" in a child psychiatric setting. I would like to

outline and briefly comment on some of these misconceptions (Guze, 1970, 1972).

Misconception #1 "The medical model implies the existence of 'organic disease entities' and therefore organic modes of treatment." This model does not assume that childhood psychiatric disorders are disease entities, nor does it a priori assume any etiology or that any one type of therapeutic intervention is better than another. It only assumes that a patient who presents with *disorder A* may have a different condition than a patient who presents with *disorder B.* Furthermore, if disorder A is truly different from disorder B, then the two conditions should be able to be characterized and differentiated from each other as outlined in this six-stage model.

Misconception #2 "The focus on the patient's disorder minimizes the importance of the patient as an individual." The medical model does imply that the focus of scientific inquiry is *disorder A* or *disorder B* rather than the *patient* with disorder A or B. Important questions that need to be answered include: What factors do cases of disorder A have in common? What factors do cases of disorder B have in common? What factors are present in disorder A that are not present in disorder B and vice versa? However, this focus of inquiry in no way diminishes the importance of the patient as an individual. Every patient is a unique human being, and this uniqueness must be taken into account in any doctor-patient relationship. This is part of the art of medicine. Nevertheless, excess emphasis on the unique aspects of each patient and lack of recognition of the common factors shared by patients who present with a particular disorder will impede scientific study. For if patients share no common factors, then training and experience are valueless, and dealing with each new patient becomes a research project in itself.

Misconception #3: "The process of diagnosis is merely a form of labeling a child and is a meaningless exercise for clinical purposes." Making a diagnosis does result in applying a label to the *psychiatric disorder* a child presents with. It does not result in applying a label to a *child.* Just as a child may have measles at one age and pneumonia at another age, he may present with one psychiatric disorder at one age and with another psychiatric disorder at a different age. For clinical purposes, no one would state that it is a meaningless exercise to distinguish between measles and pneumonia. Therefore, it is difficult to fathom why it should be a meaningless exercise to similarly distinguish between two psychiatric disorders.

For research purposes, a valid diagnostic classification scheme is a vital necessity (Rutter, 1965). If findings from various centers are to be compared, investigators with different theoretical backgrounds must have a "common language" with which they can communicate. A proper classification system will serve this purpose. It should be recognized that a classification system emphasizes what a particular patient has in common with other patients. It is not to be confused with a diagnostic formulation—which emphasizes what a particular patient has that is different from other patients. Both are necessary and one cannot do the work of the other.

Misconception #4: "A disorder oriented approach in investigative work is incompatible with a humanitarian approach in therapeutic work." A tough-minded scientific approach in the study of psychiatric disorders is far from being incompatible with a warm, compassionate, humanitarian approach in therapeutic work. From my own personal standpoint, I feel that the techniques of evaluating children and their families that I learned in my investigative work have made me a better clinician. From a more general standpoint, it is difficult to see how *more* knowledge about a patient's *disorder* makes one *less* effective in dealing with the *patient* as an individual.

The effective use of knowledge about a child's psychiatric disorder to relieve the suffering to the child and his family caused by that disorder is humanitarian in the highest sense of the word. The psychiatrist who uses this knowledge can do so in a warm, compassionate way, or in a cold, unsympathetic way—quite independently of the model he uses in his investigative work (Guze, 1972).

DIRECTIONS FOR FUTURE RESEARCH

The hyperactive child syndrome should merit serious consideration, for research purposes, as one of the more important psychiatric disorders of childhood. The reasons for doing so include its high prevalence in child guidance clinic populations and its likely role as a precursor to the development of serious social and psychiatric pathology in adulthood. A great deal of the past research has been limited to studies of drug treatment, though new areas of investigation have recently opened up that look promising. However, there are a large number of important, unanswered questions that future investigations should focus on. Among these are the following:

How can children with the syndrome be divided into meaningful subgroups, whose conditions differ in etiology, prognosis and re-sponse to treatment? The work of the Washington University Psy-chiatry Department in using family and follow-up studies to define psychiatric disorders in adults offers an excellent example to follow in this regard (Woodruff et al., 1974).

What percentage of children with the syndrome recover com-pletely, and at what age do they do so?

Do hyperactive children contribute more than their fair share to the pool of psychiatrically ill and maladjusted adults? If so, what specific types of adult problems does the syndrome predispose to?

What are the factors within the child, within his family or within his social milieu that predict which hyperactive child will develop into a healthy adult and which child in later life will manifest social and psychiatric pathology?

What treatment modalities influence the later life development of the hyperactive child and how do they do so?

These questions can only be answered by careful, long-term, an-terospective studies of large groups of hyperactive children, viewed from several different theoretical vantage points, at several different points in time. For hyperactive children, their families and society, the rewards from such investigative efforts should be great. The model proposed in this chapter is offered as a unifying framework for such studies.

REFERENCES

Arnold, L., Kirilcuk, V., Corson, S., and Corson, E. (1973). Levoamphetamine and dextroamphetamine: differential effect on aggression and hyperkinesis in children and dogs. *The American Journal of Psychiatry* 130:165–71.

Conrad, W., and Insel, J. (1967). Anticipating the response to amphetamine therapy in the treatment of hyperkinetic children. *Pediatrics* 40:96–99.

Guze, S. (1970). The need for tough-mindedness in psychiatric thinking. *Southern Medical Journal* 63:662–71.

——— (1972). Psychiatric disorders and the medical model. *Biological Psychiatry* 3: 221–24.

Meichenbaum, D., and Goodman, J. (1971). Training impulsive children to talk to themselves: a means of developing self-control. *Journal of Abnormal Psychology* 77: 115–26.

Mendelson, W., Johnson, J., & Stewart, M.A. (1971) Hyperactive children as teenagers: A follow-up study. *Journal of Nervous Mental Disorders* 153:273–79.

Quinn, P., and Rapoport, J. (1974). Minor physical anomalies and neurologic status in hyperactive boys. *Pediatrics* 53:742–47.

Rapoport, J., and Quinn, P. (in press). Multiple minor physical anomalies (stigmata) and elevated plasma DBH: a major biologic subgroup of hyperactive children. *International Journal of Mental Health.*

———, Quinn, P., and Lamprecht, F. (1974). Minor physical anomalies and plasma dopamine-beta-hydroxylase activity in hyperactive boys. *American Journal of Psychiatry* 131:386–90.

Robins, E., and Guze, S. (1970). Establishment of diagnositc validity and psychiatric illness: its application to schizophrenia. *American Journal of Psychiatry* 126:983–87.

Rutter, M. (1965). Classification and categorization in child psychiatry. *Journal of Child Psychology and Psychiatry* 6:71–83.

——— (1972). Relationship between the psychiatric disorders of childhood and adulthood. *Acta Psychiatrica Scandinavia* 48:3–21

———, Graham P. & Yule, W. (1970) *A Neuropsychiatric Study in Childhood.* Lavenham, Suffolk: The Lavenham Press, Ltd.

Satterfield, J., and Cantwell, D., (in press). Psychopharmacology in the prevention of antisocial and delinquent behavior. *International Journal of Mental Health.*

———, Cantwell, D., Lesser, L., and Podosin, R. (1972). Physiological studies of the hyperactive child. I.*American Journal of Psychiatry* 128:1418–24.

———, Cantwell, D., Saul, S., Lesser, L., and Podosin, R. (1973). Response to stimulant drug treatment in hyperactive children: prediction from EEG and neurological findings. *Journal of Autism and Childhood Schizophrenia* 3:36–48.

———, Cantwell, D., Saul, R., and Yusin, A. (1974). Intelligence, academic achievement and EEG abnormalities in hyperactive children. *American Journal of Psychiatry* 131:391–95.

Waldrop, M., and Halverson, C. (1971). Minor physical anomalies and hyperactive behavior in young children. In J. Hellmuth, *The Exceptional Infant,* Vol. 2. New York: Brunner-Mazel.

Weiss, G., Minde, K., Werry, J., Douglas, V., and Nemeth, E. (1971). Studies on the hyperactive child. VIII. Five-year follow-up. *Archives of General Psychiatry* 24:409–14.

Woodruff, R., Goodwin, D., and Guze, S. (1974). *Psychiatric Diagnosis.* New York: Oxford University Press.

Index